Field Book of
THE SHORE FISHES
OF BERMUDA
AND THE WEST INDIES

By

WILLIAM BEEBE, Sc.D.

and

JOHN TEE-VAN

Dover Publications, Inc., New York

Published in Canada by General Publishing Company, Ltd., 30 Lesmill Road, Don Mills, Toronto,
Ontario.
Published in the United Kingdom by Constable
and Company, Ltd., 10 Orange Street, London WC 2.

This Dover edition, first published in 1970, is a
republication of the work originally published in
1933 by G. P. Putnam's Sons under the title *Field
Book of the Shore Fishes of Bermuda*. The text is
unabridged, and the color illustrations which formerly appeared within the book are here reproduced on the book covers.

International Standard Book Number: 0-486-22148-2
Library of Congress Catalog Card Number: 75-116824

Manufactured in the United States of America
Dover Publications, Inc.
180 Varick Street
New York, N.Y. 10014

Dedicated
to the Entire Population
of Bermuda
all of whom have had a kindly hand
in this Work

PREFACE

The first reference to the fishes of Bermuda is that of the distinguished Oviedo whose vessel touched at the Islands in 1515, four hundred and eighteen years ago. The passage is transcribed in Governor Lefroy's "Memorials," I, 1877, p. 3. His account embodies both natural, historical, moral and religious values.

"While I remayned here, I saw a strife and combat betweene these flying fishes, and the fishes named giltheads, and the fowles called sea mewes, and cormorants, which surely seemed vnto me a thing of as great pleasure and solace as could be deuised. While the giltheads swam on the brim of the water, and sometimes lifted their shoulders above the same, to raise the flying fishes out of the water to drive them to flight, and follow them swimming to the place where they fall, to take and eate them suddenly. Againe on the other side, the sea mewes and cormorants, take many of these flying fishes, so that by this meanes they are neither safe in the Aire, nor in the water. In the selfe same perill and danger doe man liue in this mortal life, wherein is no certaine securitie, neither in high estate, nor in lowe. Which thing surely ought to put vs in remembrance of the blessed and safe resting place which God hath prepared for such as loue him who shall acquiet and finish the trauailes of this troublesome world, wherein are so many dangers, and bring them to that Eternall life where they shall find eternal security and rest."

As far as we know this is the first mention of Bermuda fish.

The last summary of the ichthyologic fauna is that of Dr. Tarleton H. Bean, published twenty-seven years ago. This is chiefly a catalogue of names and localities, and numbers seventy-four families and two hundred and sixty-one species, including about a dozen accidental records of deep-sea fish. The present list is confined strictly to shore fishes and numbers ninety-two families and three hundred and thirty-five species, of which we have described seven as new.

Our intention in publishing this brochure is to clear the field for the more detailed work on complete life histories of Bermuda shore fish; also to invite the supplying of records of rare or additional species, unusual sizes, abundance, and other facts of interest, and at the same time to make available for tourists, for fishermen and others, a means of identification of the fishes of Bermuda.

Keys to the groups and to the species have been prepared and will be found on the later pages of this volume. The treatment of each species is reduced to the simplest outline consistent with the accomplishment of the purposes intended. Under each species will be found, Bermuda and Technical Names, Field Characters, Color and Size, Diagnosis and Distribution.

This leaves for future treatment all detailed descriptions, both external and internal, scalation, sense-organs, color-changes, osteology, digestive tract, otoliths and general variation, relative abundance, exact distribution among the Bermuda Islands, method of capture, migration, food, enemies, proportions of sexes, size at maturity, spawning season, eggs, young, general habits, and value to man from the points of view both of sport and food, on all of which we are now at work.

Four Bermuda Oceanographic Expeditions have been undertaken by the Department of Tropical Research of the New York Zoological Society, with the ambitious object of the study of the life histories and general ecology of all shore, pelagic and deep-sea fish in Bermuda waters. In this work, Dr. William Beebe, Director, has been ably assisted by his staff, Mr. John Tee-Van, General Associate; Miss Gloria Hollister, Technical Associate, and Miss Joce-

lyn Crane, Laboratory Associate. The undertaking has been
made possible by the generosity of Mr. Harrison Williams,
the late Mr. Mortimer Schiff and the Trustees of the New
York Zoological Society.

The present volume represents the second installment of
results, and the information has been obtained chiefly by
the intensive study and collection of shore fishes about
Nonsuch Island, Castle Harbor and the reefs off Gurnet
Rock during the years 1929, 1930, 1931 and 1932.

In addition to this we have thoroughly searched the literature relating to the fishes of Bermuda, and have examined
the types and collections of Bermuda fish in the Field Museum of Chicago, the Museum of Comparative Zoology in
Cambridge, the United States National Museum in Washington, and the American Museum of Natural History in New
York. We are grateful to the Directors and other officials
of these institutions for allowing us to study and borrow
specimens.

From every Bermudian who has heard of our work on
Nonsuch we have had unfailing courtesy and encouragement,
and from the fishermen and especially from Mr. Louis L.
Mowbray information of great value.

CONTENTS

CONTENTS

ILLUSTRATIONS

IN BLACK AND WHITE

ACKNOWLEDGEMENT OF ILLUSTRATIONS

All photographs not otherwise credited were made by members of the staff of the Department of Tropical Research of the New York Zoological Society. The majority of the photographs credited to Mr. Elwin R. Sanborn were made at the New York Aquarium and have been used at various times in the publications of the Zoological Society. We wish to express our appreciation to Mr. Sanborn and Dr. C. H. Townsend for allowing us to use them.

One hundred and twelve new line cuts, maps and diagrams have been made for this work, eighty-four of these having been drawn by Helen D. Tee-Van. The remaining line cuts have been used previously in the following publications, to the authors of which we express our gratitude: "The Marine Fishes of New York and Southern New England" by J. T. Nichols and C. M. Breder, Jr., "The Fishes of Port-au-Prince Bay, Haiti" by W. Beebe and J. Tee-Van and "Field Book of Marine Fishes of the Atlantic Coast" by C. M. Breder, Jr.

Field Book of
THE SHORE FISHES
OF BERMUDA
AND THE WEST INDIES

BERMUDA

· SCALE · 5 MILES ·

ATLANTIC OCEAN

CORAL.

IRELAND ISLAND

GREAT SOUND

LITTLE SOUND

REEFS

BIOLOGICAL
STATION

ST. GEORGE'S

ST. DAVID'S ISLAND

CASTLE
HARBOUR

COOPER'S ISLAND

AQUARIUM

HARRINGTON
SOUND

NONSUCH
ISLAND

HAMILTON

AREA
DEVOTED TO
DEEP-SEA
TRAWLING AND DIVING
BY THE
OCEANOGRAPHIC EXPEDITIONS
OF THE
NEW YORK ZOOLOGICAL SOCIETY

T-V

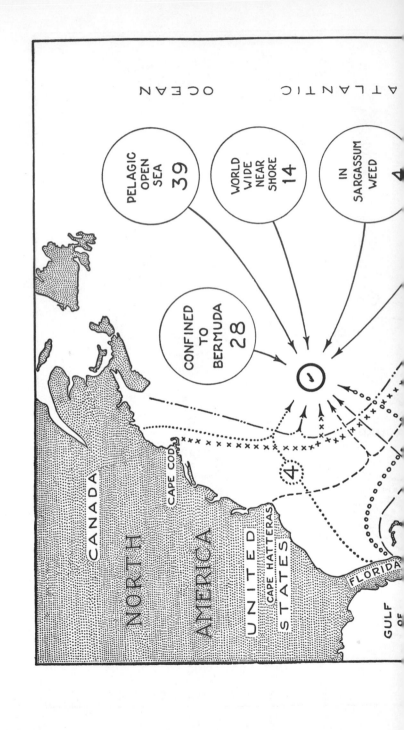

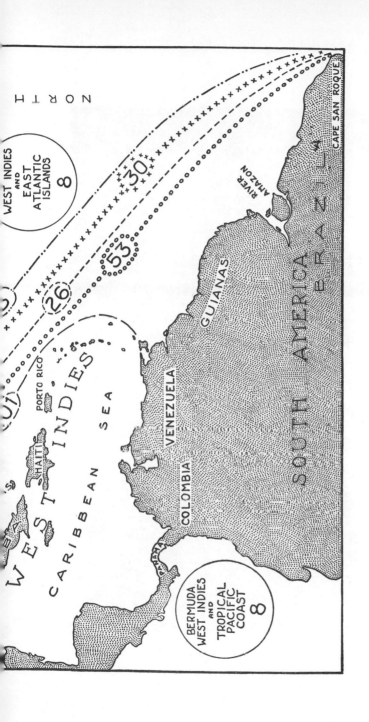

NORTH

WEST INDIES AND EAST ATLANTIC ISLANDS
8

30
53
26

PORTO RICO

WEST INDIES

HAITI

CARIBBEAN SEA

VENEZUELA

COLOMBIA

GUIANAS

AMAZON RIVER

BRAZIL

SOUTH AMERICA

CAPE SAN ROQUE

BERMUDA WEST INDIES AND TROPICAL PACIFIC COAST
8

Photo by P. Dowle

THE SHALLOW WATERS AND REEFS OF BERMUDA FROM THE AIR

INTRODUCTION

A BRIEF STORY OF FISHES

What is a Fish?—There is probably no one who does not recognize a typical fish when he sees one, but nevertheless it is not easy to

Define a Fish.—It is a Back-boned Aquatic Animal—but so is a penguin or whale.

It has Scales—but so have sea-snakes.

It breathes with Gills—but so do tadpoles and newts.

It has FINS, and this is the key word of definition: The typical Fin of a fish consists of thin skin stretched between numerous soft or bony rods. It is neither fleshy nor supported by the bones of erstwhile fingers and toes.

Number of Fish.—In NUMBER OF SPECIES fish excel any other group of vertebrates, about forty thousand already being known.

In Bermuda, the number of back-boned animals is about as follows:

Mammals	12
Birds	250
Reptiles	10
Amphibia	4
Shore Fishes	335

In actual NUMBER OF INDIVIDUALS fish surpass all the other groups of back-boned animals put together. Two facts will illustrate this: The number of herring caught every year in the Atlantic is three billion, and a single female Ling has been known to develop twenty-eight million eggs.

Among Bermuda fish the Porcupinefish may be mentioned in this respect, for we have dissected one with an

5

ovary which, at a conservative estimate, contained 280,000 eggs.

Distribution of Fish.—Fish are to be found in every watery quarter of the globe: in icy Arctic as well as in warm Tropical seas, on the surface and, for a few seconds at a time, in the air; at depths down to three miles or more; in fresh-water lakes and rivers, buried in the mud of swamps, in hot springs, and in the cold, rushing torrents of lofty mountain streams.

In the waters about Bermuda, fish are to be found in all places from half-dried tide-pools down to a depth of two miles.

Origin of Bermuda Fish Fauna.—To get a true perspective of the origin of this great world of Bermuda fish we must think back to a time before the volcano existed, on the summit of which Bermuda rests today.

At this period, deep-sea fish swam in the black, icy depths, and oceanic surface fish drifted over what is now Hamilton and St. Georges. Later when the volcanic peak reached the surface, and sand and shells began to collect, shallow water fish appeared, never voluntarily, but blown by currents and wind-driven waters, and carried by the Gulf Stream far from their own homes.

A less usual method is the transportation of fish in water-spouts and hurricanes. Many cases are known of large numbers of fish drawn up into watery columns, carried considerable distances and redistributed over land and sea, the so-called "rains of fishes."

Singly and in pairs, fish reached the newly raised Bermuda, found shelter and food, and when mates were available established themselves. In very recent years a few species have been introduced by man, but none of these have become abundant, and the Bermuda fish fauna as we find it today represents the gradual, natural stocking.

So we may resolve the total of 602 species of Bermuda fish into the following divisions:

Deep Sea and Oceanic Surface Fish—267

Shore Fish—335 $\begin{cases} \text{Indigenous—323} \\ \text{Introduced—12} \end{cases}$

We will treat of the deep sea fish in other volumes. Here we are concerned only with the surface fish and those of shallow waters. These latter inhabit the tidepools and outer reefs down to a depth of five hundred feet, as well as the island bays and the few marshes and land-locked, brackish ponds. Goldfish, guppys and other small fish have been introduced into fresh water pools and water-tanks for the purposes of devouring mosquito larvæ, but these are only artificially sustained and do not come within the scope of this work.

It is interesting to trace the ORIGIN OF BERMUDA FISH to see from what countries they have come to this isolated speck of shallow water in mid-ocean. The GEOGRAPHICAL DISTRIBUTION of the species of shore fish is as follows:

Bermuda only—28
Bermuda, Florida and the West Indies—101
Bermuda, West Indies, south to Brazil—53
Bermuda, West Indies, Hatteras to Brazil—26
Bermuda, West Indies, Cape Cod to Brazil—30
Bermuda, West Indies, Maine to Brazil—3
Bermuda, West Indies, East Atlantic Islands, a few from
    the coast of Europe—8
Bermuda, West Indies, Atlantic and Pacific Coasts—8
Bermuda and the United States Coast—4
Among Sargassum weed—4
Pelagic (surface of the open sea)—39
World-wide near shore—14

This shows that by far the dominant source of Bermuda fish life is the West Indies, comprising about 75% of the whole. In addition to this only 1½% have come direct from the coast of the United States, another 1½% from the shallow waters of Europe and the Eastern Atlantic, while

13% may be accounted inhabitants of the surface of the high seas, occurring only accidentally near Bermuda. Finally, 9% are peculiar to Bermuda, having lived there so long that they have changed in one or more characters.

Migration of Fish.—Fish migrate like birds, and the regularity of their arrival and departure is often very definite. This shifting is caused by a search for food or a suitable place to deposit their eggs. Salmon are hatched far inland, swim out to sea, and later return to lay their eggs in the fresh water; the common eel is hatched in mid-ocean off the West Indies, then makes its way back to the river from which its parents came, and there lives its life until maturity recalls it to the far-distant waters of its birth.

In Bermuda the Mackerel is a good example of a migrant, and in October and November fishermen may be seen perched upon high, outjutting cliffs watching for the arrival of great schools of these fish, exactly as sportsmen in their blinds, await the coming of migrating ducks and geese.

The most marked migration of fishes about Bermuda is a general outward shift into deep water of many species at the approach of cold weather. In the Bathysphere, when thirty feet down, I once saw a migration of thousands of giant blue parrotfish. There is also a Bermudian night and day migration, illustrated by the Puppy Sharks, which pour by the score into Castle Harbour every evening and return to deeper waters at dawn.

The Shape of Fishes.—A typical fish, such as the Mackerel, has a spindle-shaped body, with fins for balancing and propulsion. When a group of mammals, like the dolphins, take to a water life, they find that this fish shape is the very best for swift swimming.

Fish vary greatly in SHAPE. Here are the extremes among Bermuda fish:

> Long and snake-like—Moray Eel.
> Round—Puffer.

Triangular—Trunkfish.
Thin—Triggerfish.
Flat—Flounder.

Size and Weight of Fishes.—This is a subject of especial interest to big game fishermen, but it is also of value as showing the extremes between which fish find life possible on the earth. The LARGEST recorded fish is the Whale Shark, which reaches a length of over fifty feet and a weight of many tons. The SMALLEST fish is a Philippine Goby, which is no more than a half inch in length.

In Bermuda the two extremes are the Devilfish, of which I have taken a specimen twenty-two feet across the wings and weighing a full ton, and the Bronze-headed Goby, which measures about one inch.

Scales of Fishes.—The skin of sharks is covered with DENTICLES, forming the familiar shagreen. They cover the whole body and in the young even the lips, where, becoming larger, they are continued into the mouth as teeth.

Typical fish have SCALES, overlapping like tiles on a roof. They vary in size in Bermuda species from the TWO-INCH silvery scales of the Tarpon, to the MINUTE embedded scales of the Eel.

Bermuda fish show great variation in body covering, from the normal scalation of a Bream, to the SPINES of the Porcupinefish, and, in another direction, from the HARD FLEXIBLE COAT of the Filefish, to the more IMMOBILE ARMOR of the Trunkfish, Seahorse and Pipefish.

Mouths of Fishes.—Fishes use their mouths for BREATHING and for PROCURING their FOOD. In typical fish such as a Snapper, the jaws are equal, and the mouth is close to the front of the head. In Bermuda fish, mouths and their uses may be classified as follows:

Long, toothed jaws for seizing active prey—Gars.
Short under jaw, and long upper jaw used as a weapon—
Spearfish and Sawfish.

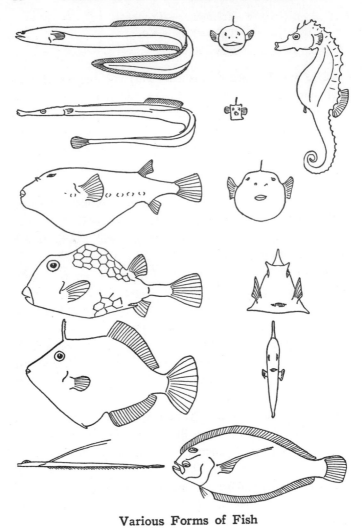

Various Forms of Fish
Eel, Pipefish, Puffer, Trunkfish, Triggerfish, Flounder and
Seahorse.

Short upper jaw, and long under one for scooping up bits
of seaweed—Halfbeaks.

Long tubular snout, with terminal mouth for sucking in
food—Trumpetfish and Pipefish.

Lips almost absent, exposing teeth for grazing—Parrotfish.

Many fish use the mouth and the breathing apparatus as
a SUCTION PUMP. A Flounder or a Grouper can draw in
living fish from a distance of several inches with such
rapidity as to make the operation invisible.

Teeth of Fishes.—Teeth are intimately concerned with
FOOD.

Sharks have teeth in several rows, the outermost of which
are erect and ready for use, while the RESERVE TEETH spring
up and advance whenever a gap occurs. In the Bermuda
Puppy Shark the teeth are sharp, for SEIZING AND HOLDING
PREY; in the Spotted Eagle Ray they are flat like a pavement
for CRUSHING shellfish.

The common Bream has SHARP teeth when young and
feeds on living shrimps; as it grows older FLAT MOLAR
teeth appear, reflecting the change to a vegetable diet.

Blue and Yellow Demoiselles have normal teeth, while
the closely related Yellow-tailed Demoiselles have long,
slender, movable teeth, like the close-set palings of a fence.
Why this is, we do not know.

Parrotfish have the teeth solidified into a solid plate, giving
a strong chisel-edge for GNAWING hard coral and PRYING
off seaweed. These, as well as many other fish, have a
SECOND SET of teeth in the back of the throat, serving to cut
up the food (like the grit in a chicken's gizzard), which
the real teeth have procured.

Coloration.—In COLORATION fishes are supreme among all
creatures of the earth, not only for the bewildering variety
of pattern and range of pigment, but for the ability to
change both pattern and color under stress of emotion. In

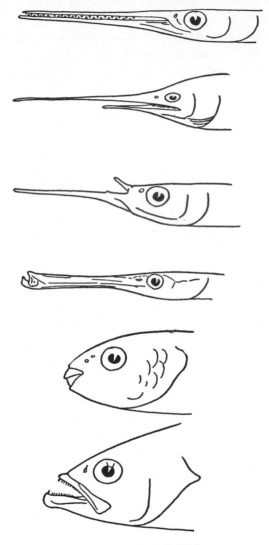

The Mouths of Fish
Gar, Spearfish, Halfbeak, Trumpetfish, Parrotfish and
Snapper.

the course of these studies of Bermuda fishes we have had occasion to do away with seven species which had been based on color phases alone. Unlike the colors of butterflies and birds, those of fish fade at death.

The study of the meaning of color in fish is difficult. There is no doubt that in many cases it serves for concealment, as in the Bermuda Lizardfish and Flounders which are exactly the hue of the sand on which they rest, or the Flyingfish of the open ocean, which is a mixture of ultramarine water and white foam; or the Sargassum or Frogfish, which is indistinguishable from its floating seaweed home.

On the other hand, the great blue and red Parrotfish and the gorgeous Angelfish seem to have few enemies. I have seen them undisturbed in the presence of sharks and barracudas, and their conspicuous coloring may be of a warning nature, signaling some method of defense of which we are ignorant.

The pattern and color of any one species of fish is usually quite regular, but now and then, as in the Sea Perch (*Hypoplectrus*), these characters seem to run riot and a score of different variations are known, recalling the display feathers of male Ruffs.

Some of the Bermuda fish, such as the Hind, have shallow and deep water color forms, those from deeper water being redder. Color in fish is a thing which for real appreciation requires a painting rather than description, or observation in an aquarium, or, best of all, a walk under sea in a diving helmet.

How Do Fishes Move?—A fish Swims, usually by strong lateral movements of the tail fin, but if you wish to see the extremes in swimming, go to the Aquarium and watch a Moray Eel UNDULATE through the water, then look at a Trunkfish progress by STIFFLY WRIGGLING its fins through small loop-holes cut through its rigid body armor, holes like the oar-holes in an ancient galley.

A Parrotfish FLIES through the water, and a Devilfish FLAPS like a bird in the air. A Flyingfish does not actually fly, but GLIDES. It has no muscles for flapping, and simply holds its large fins outstretched and rigid. The Banded Moray, usually to be seen in the Aquarium, is of great interest as having lost all trace of fins, and hence sinks helpless through open water and can only WRIGGLE in and out of the reefs. Mackerel and Mullets and even little schools of Fry can LEAP high out of the water, and our Molly Millers HITCH themselves overland from one tidepool to another.

Fish differ greatly in regard to SPEED. One of the swiftest of Bermuda fishes is the Bonito, and one of the most leisurely is the Seahorse, whose hard, protecting coat of mail discourages attack from enemies.

Respiration.—Although fish breathe in a manner so unlike ourselves yet the accomplished result is the same, to procure oxygen and to get rid of the poisons in the blood. In spite of the great activity shown by both fish and ourselves, yet a human being uses up about 50,000 times as much oxygen as a fish of medium size.

While gills thus seem a rather imperfect means of oxygenating the blood, yet we should not look askance at them, for at one period in our own embryonic life we possess as many gills as a fish, and all the blood in our body flows to them.

In the tropics there are fish with damp reservoir chambers in their head, and these fish are able to pass overland for long distances. I have seen Catfish wriggling through the dead leaves of the jungle, headed for the nearest water, though how they knew the direction we have no idea.

In Bermuda the little Molly Millers show the nearest approach to this ability to live out of water, for they can exist in half dried tidepools by using the upper part of the pectoral fins as additional gills.

THE CLIFFS OF NONSUCH WITH TIDEPOOLS AND GURNET'S ROCK IN THE DISTANCE

Strange Characteristics.—Fish inflict severe wounds with teeth and spines, but some have true POISON GLANDS or MUCUS. The Sting Ray is an example.

Grunts, Triggerfish, Surgeons, Seahorses and other fish can make loud SOUNDS under water, in several ways, by gritting the teeth, by means of the air in the swim bladder, or the friction of movable bones.

Several unrelated fish—rays, catfish and eels—can produce strong ELECTRIC SHOCKS for defense. No Bermuda fish is included in this list.

Many deep sea fish have the ability to ILLUMINATE themselves and the water around them. Rarely a small luminous fish is cast up dead on a Bermuda beach, but no shore fish possesses this property.

Food of Fishes.—Every group of plant and animal life within reach of the water is used by fishes for food. The tiny Fry feed upon the smallest eggs, worms and seaweed spores, while from the stomach of an Anglerfish seven wild ducks have been taken.

The habits and activity of a fish usually reflect the character of its food—the slow, bovine grazing of the vegetarian Parrotfish, as compared with the swift, nervous, feline searching of a Yellowtail on its lone hunt for food. On the other hand, the little Sargassumfish is slow and quiet in its movements and yet will swallow one after another of its own brethren if confined with them in a small aquarium.

Here is an estimate of one minute fraction of fish eating fish in the open ocean, figures almost astronomical in their immensity: About a thousand million Bluefish spend four months each year on the Atlantic coast of the United States; each Bluefish eats on an average ten fish a day. Which means that ten billion fish are killed every day, or 1,200,000,000,000 fish during the four months.

Courtship and Nests.—In the great majority of fishes the eggs are sent out into the open water and there fertilized by the male, there being no more need for courtship, mating or care of the eggs and young than in wind pollination of the flowers of plants. This may partly be the result of environment, for in fishes which inhabit streams and ponds, and other restricted localities such as the weeds along the shore, there are many which build nests and go through an elaborate courtship.

I chose three homes from among the many of Bermuda fishes. Flyingfish in some clever, unknown way bind a mass of sargassum weed into a round ball with many yards of tough, silken thread, and deposit hundreds of eggs within the weed. The ball drifts along on the surface and the eggs finally hatch, and in a week the young fish begin to spread their tiny wings and to glide through the air (see "Nonsuch," Chapter IV).

Near shore, a pair of Demoiselles select some crevice or hollow in the coral reef, lay their eggs in it and defend it fearlessly against all comers. The male Seahorse, among the weeds of the shallows, collects the eggs of his mate into a fleshy pouch on the front of his body, like a diminutive kangaroo, and guards them until they hatch, several hundred sea colts or ponies emerging within a few hours, to take up their lives along the shore of the great ocean (see "Nonsuch," Chapter XIV).

Eggs of Fishes.—Some fishes bring forth their young alive, but most of them lay eggs and these are of great diversity in size and shape. Those of Sharks and Rays are horny, oblong, and usually have a tendril at each corner. The eggs of Flyingfish and Gars are surrounded by many short hairs which hold the eggs fast in seaweed. The fish of the open sea lay transparent, round or spindle-shaped eggs which float at the surface until hatched. The eggs of some of the fish nearer shore sink to the bottom. Others, like those of Gobies, are glued to coral and shells.

Development.—In the great majority of fishes the young hatch from the egg in a shape not greatly unlike that of the parents. A good example is the exquisite Blue and Yellow Demoiselles which, a short time after hatching, in August and September, are common in Bermuda tidepools—diminutive replicas of the old fish.

If we draw a net at night behind a boat across a bay or harbor, or let it float out with the tide from a bridge or wharf, we will sometimes catch a transparent ribbon of a creature, with large, iridescent eyes and long sharp fangs. This is the young of some species of Eel, and it passes through this and other larval forms before it attains the shape of the adult Eel.

Still another type of development is the Flounder. When it comes from the egg it swims upright like all fish. Then it begins to sag to one side, until finally it settles to a flat, flounder position. Meanwhile the mouth twists, and all the bones of the body become somewhat bent in striving to adapt themselves to this new shift in space. The lower eye actually twists around or even partly through the head, until it too looks upward, alongside of its fellow on the exposed side of the head.

Psychology.—Fishes have more sense than we would imagine from watching them swim around and around an aquarium. We have just begun to learn something about this, but we can observe many new facts for ourselves by watching fish in their natural haunts from a small, glass-bottomed boat or a diving helmet.

The relative SOCIABILITY of Bermuda fish is very marked. Here are four examples:

> Large schools—Blue Fry.
> Small schools—Doctorfish.
> Pairs—Butterflyfish.
> Solitary—Sharks.

As extremes of FEAR and CURIOSITY we may take Rockfish, which vanish at once when we dive, and Sergeant Majors, which crowd about and even nibble at our shoulders.

Fishes SLEEP, although they have no eyelids. I have a list of thirteen different ways in which I have found fish asleep. They can be picked up and put down again without waking.

Two examples of mutual ASSISTANCE are common. When the large blue Parrotfish get their mouth and head covered with grit from gnawing at the coral, they stand on their tail in mid-water, while small Wrasse in crowds swarm around and thoroughly clean them, the benefit to the Wrasse being the tiny bits of food they find.

Snappers will often remain stationary with their mouths wide open, while Butterflyfish probe about far inside, pulling off and eating the parasites which cling to the throats of the big fish.

Relation to Mankind.—In Bermuda, fish are an important item of food. Every day in the year when storms are not raging, many fishing boats put to sea and bring back hundreds of fish, large and small, which are distributed to the hotels and to private buyers or are salted for future use. The principal methods of fishing are by hook and line, especially in the deeper, outer waters, fish-traps and seines.

Game fishing is furnished by Sharks, Barracudas, Yellow-tails and Rockfish.

As to the age-old yarns about all sharks being man-eaters, mankind is gradually relegating them to the limbo of fairy tales and Munchausen. There are authentic cases of a swimming man being bitten and killed by a shark. But these are exceedingly rare, and confined altogether to men who were swimming or stirring up the water at the surface. In Bermuda, in the West Indies and in the Pacific we have dived for years in bathing suit and helmet with sharks and barracudas often in sight, and have never given them a thought. The best place to get shark panic is when sitting by a cozy, open fire, surrounded by files of old newspapers

and the type of volume which has an exciting adventure
on every page.

Things We Do Not Know About Fish.—Not one complete life history of a Bermuda fish is known.

In making this list we have discovered and named seven
new species of Bermuda fish, and have added to the fauna
forty-four not hitherto recorded. So there are undoubtedly
many more species to be found.

Careful comparisons of the fish taken by hook, seine and
trap in mid-summer and in mid-winter, would yield valuable
scientific data as to seasonal migration.

The scales of fishes have been only superficially studied.
Thorough work on even the commonest species is needed.

We know only a few facts about the teeth of fish, both
in the adult, and in the change from young to full-grown.

Color changes should be studied by selecting some par-
ticular pattern and color as the focus for each species, and
recording all variations from this. Also the exact shift due
to changing emotions and the immediate change after death.

A valuable piece of research work would be the recording
of food in some abundant fish, day by day, throughout a
whole year.

Courtship, nests, eggs and larval fish offer a field of
which only the edges have been so far investigated.

Of the mental side of fishes it would be interesting to
know how tame they can become, and how they react (always
in their natural haunts) to sound and light. Also how they
are affected by normal possible changes in their surroundings.

W. B.

HOW TO FIND YOUR UNKNOWN FISH

Every one wants to have a handle attached to the fish that he has caught or seen,—some name to which the animal can be referred. This volume attempts to supply that need for those who may want to know something about the fishes that live near Bermuda.

If you have an idea as to which group your fish belongs, the problem is simple, and the table of contents and index will indicate the page where the fish can be found.

If, however, the fish is totally unknown to you, it will be necessary to proceed to the identification keys on pages 263 to 316. By following the directions given, the key will eventually send you to some species in the body of the book. Under any circumstances it is necessary to compare your fish with the illustrations, field characters and diagnoses, to make certain of the identification.

As far as color is concerned, fish are the most unstable of creatures, and some latitude must be allowed in comparing them with the colors given in the Field Characters. An attempt has been made here, to state as briefly and clearly as possible the color variation found within the species.

Common names of fishes in Bermuda, as in every part of the world, are a source of uncertainty for the student, and often are extremely confusing. One species may have several names, and several species may have the same name. This is especially true of some of the snappers and rockfish. At times two fishermen debate the name of a fish that is before them. Fortunately most of the commoner fish have been well christened, and their names have become standardized.

THE SHORE FISHES OF BERMUDA

LANCELETS

These small creatures are among the most interesting of living beings, as they probably closely resemble the ancestors of all fishes. They are the lowest and most simply made of all backboned animals on the earth today. Two forms are found in Bermuda.

Family BRANCHIOSTOMIDÆ
Bermuda Amphioxus
Branchiostoma bermudæ Hubbs

Field Characters.—Small, elongate, colourless and worm-like. Amphioxus has no scales, paired fins or distinct head. A median black dot represents the one eye, the gills are numerous and the twenty-two to twenty-eight square reproductive pouches are developed on both sides of the body. It grows to about two inches in length.

Diagnosis.—Ray-chambers relatively few, averaging 208 in the dorsal and 21 in the pre-anal fin; origin of the caudal lobe as near tip of tail as atriopore; myotome formula 34 to 36 + 12 to 14 + 6 to 9 = 54 to 57; gonad pouches 22 to 28, averaging 26.6.

Distribution.—This species is confined to Bermuda, where it lives in coarse sand from one to six fathoms down. It is much less common than the Lancelet.

Family EPIGONICHTHYIDÆ
Lancelet
Asymmetron lucayanum Andrews

Field Characters.—Similar to Amphioxus, except that the reproductive pouches number twenty-six to thirty-one, and are developed only on the right side of the body. Grows to a little over an inch in length.

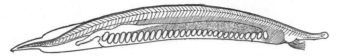

Diagnosis.—A long urostyloid process; pre-oral hood extensive, the cirri united by membrane for most of their length; myotome formula 50 to 55 to the anus, and 11 to 15 postanal, a total of 62 to 68 with an average of 66.

Distribution.—Bermuda and the West Indies south to Brazil. In Bermuda it is found buried in sand under open tidal waters, and is especially abundant in parts of Castle Harbour near Nonsuch.

SHARKS AND RAYS
See Key, p. 273

The skeletons of sharks and rays are soft and cartilaginous, and this separates them widely from the true fishes with bony skeletons. Sharks have changed little for three million years; in general they are of large size, covered with very small denticles or shagreen, and with five gill-openings instead of one. They are carnivorous and some have the reputation, usually undeserved, of being man-eaters.

Ten species of sharks and three rays occur in Bermuda, these being divisible into seven families. One species of Nurse Shark (*Ginglymostomidæ*) represents a low, generalized group of bottom-feeders. Eight species of typical Grey or Requiem Sharks (*Carchariidæ*) are present, varying from the small Dogfish to the great Tiger Shark. The strange, weirdly-shaped Hammerhead (*Sphyrnidæ*), and the swift, strong Mackerel Shark (*Lamnidæ*), are the only members of their respective families. The Sawfish (*Pristidæ*) is a remarkable creature intermediate in many ways between sharks and rays. The absence of extensive sandy-bottomed shallows has restricted the large group of typical rays to two, the Eagle Ray (*Ætobatidæ*) and the Manta or Devilfish (*Mobulidæ*), which are pelagic in habit.

Family GINGLYMOSTOMIDÆ
Sand or Nurse Shark
Ginglymostoma cirratum (Gmelin)

Field Characters.—A sluggish, blunt-headed shark with small eyes; mouth near the tip of the snout and furnished with a pair of barbels; two large dorsal fins placed far back, the first over the pelvics. Olive brown above, paler below. Reaches a length of ten feet.

Diagnosis.—Gill-slits five, the last two very close together; very small spiracle back of eye; pelvic fins larger than the anal; pectorals nearly as broad as long, nearer snout than pelvics.

Distribution.—Bermuda and the West Indies, extending from the Carolinas to Panama and Brazil and also on the western coast of Mexico. In Bermuda small and medium sized individuals are taken occasionally by fishermen on sandy shallows, and the Aquarium almost always has specimens on exhibition.

Discussion.—The Bermuda fishermen apply the name Nurse Shark to *Cynias canis,* which is more properly a dogfish.

Family LAMNIDÆ
Mackerel Shark
Isurus tigris (Atwood)

Field Characters.—A large-sized, swift shark with a large lunate tail and with well-developed keels on the sides of the caudal peduncle; snout more or less conical, elongate, sharp; teeth long, narrow, pointed and with smooth edges. Brown above, white below. Reaches a length of ten feet.

Distribution.—Bermuda, the West Indies and Gulf of Mexico, north to Cape Cod. This is a pelagic species, rare in Bermuda, occasionally taken in the harbours while pursuing mackerel.

Family CARCHARIIDÆ
Dogfish or Nurse Shark (Bermuda)
Cynias canis   (Mitchill)

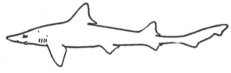

Field Characters.—Small sharks, with elongate, flattened head; two large dorsal fins, widely separated, but of almost equal size; ventral surface flat; teeth small, blunt, pavement-like, with one or more accessory points; origin of dorsal above posterior border of pectoral; eye contained three times in snout. Colour grey above, white below. Reaches three to five feet.

Diagnosis.—Compared with the following species, the dermal denticles have the lateral edges straight, the points broader; ridges not prominent.

Distribution.—Bermuda, West Indies, Cape Cod to Argentina; Southern Europe. Not seen by us in Bermuda.

European Dogfish; Smooth Hound
Mustelus mustelus   (Linnaeus)
Field Characters.—Small sharks with elongate, flattened head; two large dorsal fins, widely separated, but of almost

equal size; ventral surface flat; teeth small, blunt, pave-ment-like, with entire free border, rounded, lacking acces-sory points; origin of first dorsal well in front of posterior border of pectoral; eye two and a half in snout. Grey above and white below. Reaches a length of six feet.

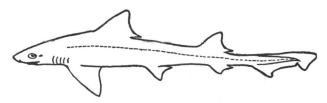

Diagnosis.—Dorsal denticles with the lateral edges no-ticeably concave, making the points narrow, more acute; ridges well developed.

Distribution.—Bermuda, occasional on North American coast as in New Jersey; its center of distribution the coasts of Southern Europe. In Bermuda, two specimens taken by us on hook and line.

Tiger or Spotted Shark
Galeocerdo arcticus (Faber)

Field Characters.—A large, heavy shark with blunt head; caudal fin large with very long upper lobe; teeth alike in both jaws, semicircular, with serrated edges, the tips turned obliquely outward, with a deep notch. Brownish-grey with numerous black spots on the body, fins and tail, especially in young individuals. Reaches a length of fifteen to thirty feet.

Diagnosis.—Spiracles, labial folds, nictitating membranes and caudal pits present; caudal long, slender, pointed and with a double notch; caudal 3 to 4 in total length.

Distribution.—Bermuda and West Indies; tropical and temperate seas in general, north in the Atlantic to Cape Cod and Iceland. A fifty-inch specimen taken on hook and line in Murray's Anchorage, and other smaller ones seen or taken from time to time.

Great Blue Shark
Prionace glauca (Linnaeus)

Field Characters.—Large, elongate, tapering sharks, with short head, long, tapering, pointed snout; first dorsal fin nearer pelvic than pectoral fins; pectoral fins very long and narrow; teeth in 29 to 31 rows, the upper triangular, the lower narrower and erect, all strongly serrated; mouth with a small, short labial fold. Colour above deep rich blue. Reaches twelve feet and more in length. A ten-foot specimen weighed 225 pounds.

Diagnosis.—Head less than one-fourth total length; nostrils nearer mouth than snout; anal fin base extending slightly in front of that of the second dorsal; tail slender.

Distribution.—Warm seas generally. Taken by us off the shore of Bermuda.

Puppy or Cub Shark; Shovel-Nosed Shark
Carcharias platyodon (Poey)

Field Characters.—A moderate sized shark, with short, broadly rounded snout, its length equal to width of mouth; nostrils about midway between snout and mouth; 28 teeth in the front row, the upper ones broad and triangular, the lower ones narrower; pectorals two-thirds as broad as long, reaching beyond the origin of first dorsal; internarial space greater than length of mouth; two rear gill openings above

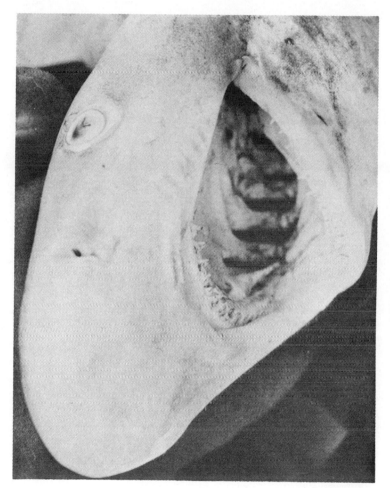

BERMUDA PUPPY SHARK
Carcharias platyodon

the pectoral; dorsal denticles small with three to five keels; caudal long, one-fourth of the total length. Colour grey above, pale below. Said to reach an extreme length of fifteen feet. Three to four feet is the average of Bermuda specimens with a maximum of eight feet.

Distribution.—Bermuda, West Indies, Gulf of Mexico and the Caribbean Sea. Commonest Bermuda Shark.

Scythe-Finned Shark
Carcharias falciformis Bibron

Field Characters.—Large, slender sharks, with moderate, deeply concave pectorals; 30 rows of teeth, upper ones much broader than lower and deeply notched on the outer margins; second dorsal and anal fins equal in size and at the same vertical. Reaches a length of ten feet.

Diagnosis.—Differs from *platyodon*, its nearest Bermuda relative, in the following particulars: length of snout not equaling width of mouth; nostrils nearer mouth and eye than tip of snout; internarial space not greater than length of mouth; teeth in 30, not 28 rows; three, not two gills above pectorals; gill opening wider than eye; inner angle of pectoral not reaching beyond origin of dorsal; anal is not behind second dorsal; subcaudal lobe not rounded.

Distribution.—Bermuda and West Indies. Uncommon at Bermuda, taken off shore and on Challenger Banks.

Dusky Ground Shark
Carcharias obscurus   (Le Sueur)

Field Characters.—Moderate to large sized shark, with broadly rounded snout; second dorsal smaller than the anal and placed slightly behind it; upper teeth triangular, much broader than the lower; pectoral fins nearly twice as long as wide.   Greyish brown above, whitish below.   Rarely reaches a length of fourteen feet.

Diagnosis.—Head depressed, much broader than deep; outer angle of nostril nearer to eye than to snout; mouth large, its length one-half of its width; teeth $\frac{30}{29}$ rows, median upper two very small; eyes small, one-half length of gill opening; caudal fin more than one-fourth of total length.

Distribution.—Bermuda, West Indies, and generally over the North and Middle Atlantic.   Uncommon at Bermuda, taken well off shore.

Grey or Requiem Shark; Southern Ground Shark
Carcharias commersonii   (Blainville)

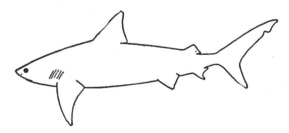

Field Characters.—A large, sluggish, blunt-headed, heavy bodied shark, the upper teeth triangular, much broader than the lower; second dorsal well in advance of the anal.   Colour above dark grey, lower parts sometimes with dark blotches; fins tipped with black. Reaches a length of ten feet and a weight of 400 pounds.

Diagnosis.—Snout one and a half in base of first dorsal; eye small, slightly larger than nostril; mouth once and a half as broad as long; 30 or 31 teeth in outer row of jaws; lateral skin denticles five-keeled and scalloped; pectorals long and falcate, reaching beyond base of first dorsal.

Distribution.—Bermuda, West Indies and the tropical Atlantic in general, straying northwards to Massachusetts; also found in the Mediterranean and the Pacific. Near Bermuda it rarely occurs near shore, but is the commonest surface shark off shore, taking the hook readily.

Family SPHYRNIDÆ
Hammerhead Shark or Strizzle-Nose
Sphyrna zygæna   (Linnaeus)

Field Characters.—A large shark with the head expanded from side to side into the shape of the head of a hammer, the eyes placed on the forward part of the lateral expansions. Lead grey above, lower parts greyish white; tips of pectoral fins black; tips of other fins dark. Reaches a length of seventeen feet and a weight of 1500 pounds.

Distribution.—Bermuda and West Indies, extending throughout most tropical waters and as far north as Maine and Japan. A nine-foot specimen taken on hook and line off Gurnet's Rock, and smaller ones are seen now and then in Bermuda waters.

Family PRISTIDÆ
Sawfish
Pristis pectinatus Latham

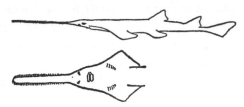

Field Characters.—Shark-like rays with a long, flattened extension of the upper jaw resembling a double-edged saw. Reaches a length of eighteen feet.

Distribution.—Bermuda and West Indies, straggling north to New Jersey. Tropical Atlantic in general. An eighteen-inch saw taken from a fish several years ago by a St. David's fisherman, a large individual seen off Gurnet's Rock in January, 1931, and we also have a young individual taken from the stomach of a dolphin.

Family ÆTOBATIDÆ
Whip or Eagle Ray
Stoasodon narinari (Euphrasen)

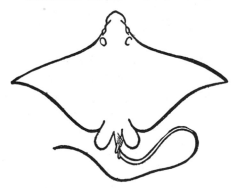

Field Characters.—Flattened rays with pointed wings; tail long and lash-like with two serrated spines at the base. Upper surface greyish brown with numerous round, white spots. Reaches a length of twelve feet and a weight of 450 pounds.

Distribution.—Bermuda and West Indies north to Virginia. Tropical seas in general. We have occasionally seen them in Castle Harbour and off shore.

Family MOBULIDÆ
Giant Devilfish or Manta; Blanketfish
Manta birostris (Walbaum)

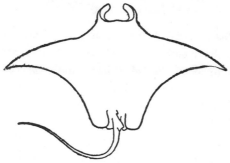

Field Characters.—A flattened ray growing to great size; wings pointed and curved; two large, fleshy, cephalic flaps; a short, whip-like tail. Black above, often marked with white. Reaches a width of 22 feet and a weight of over 3000 pounds.

Distribution.—Bermuda and West Indies, rarely north to New York. Tropical seas in general. Small ones seen occasionally in and near Bermuda waters, and individuals up to twelve feet across off shore.

STURGEONS

The sturgeons represent the remnant of a low and generalized type of fish and only about twenty species still remain alive on the earth. They are large, bottom feeding, toothless fish, with the skin characterized by five series of large, bony plates. The eggs are of considerable economic importance as forming the basis of caviar.

Most sturgeons are migratory, living in the sea but ascending rivers to spawn. The chance of one occurring near Bermuda, except by the merest accident, is very slight.

Family ACIPENSERIDÆ

Sea Sturgeon

Acipenser sturio   Linnaeus

Field Characters.—A large fish with pointed, overhanging snout, the mouth well underneath; body armed with five series of bony, keeled shields, the skin between the shields usually covered with minute plates; small barbels placed on the lower surface of the snout well in front of the mouth. Reaches a length of eighteen feet.

Distribution.—Both sides of the North Atlantic from Scandinavia to the Mediterranean, and from the St. Lawrence River to the Gulf of Mexico. Included in the Bermuda list on two records, Jones in 1876, and Hurdis in 1887.

HERRING-LIKE FISHES

See Key, page 275

This important order of fishes (*Isospondyli*) is the most primitive among the bony forms and extends farthest back in geological time. It includes salmon, trout, smelt and herrings, all of which are essentially inhabitants of cold waters, and all of which are of great economic importance to man. Only eight species reach Bermuda, three of which, tarpon, ten-pounders and bonefish, are solitary in habit, while the others live in large schools often numbering many thousands. The tarpon, which are very rare, reach a large size while the anchovies and round herrings are among the smallest of Bermuda fish. All show a great deal of shining silver on the scales, and all are carnivorous.

The larger forms pass through an eel-like, transparent larval stage. The smaller species are of great importance as food for many kinds of fish and furnish the best bait for fishermen.

Family ELOPIDÆ
Ten-Pounder
Elops saurus   Linnaeus

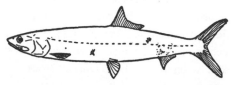

Field Characters.—A slender, elongate fish with a normally shaped mouth, between the arches of which, ventrally, is a bony plate; a single, small, soft-rayed dorsal fin on the middle of the back; adipose eyelid very large; scales small and absent on the head. Uniform bluish above, silvery on sides and below. Reaches a length of three feet.

Diagnosis.—Dorsal 22 to 24; anal 15 or 16; depth 5.34 to 5.7; head 4.15 to 4.35; snout 3.7 to 3.95; eye 5.2 to 5.75, with a well-developed adipose eyelid in the adult; interorbital space 5; gill-rakers about 14; scales 114 to 116.

Distribution.—Known from all warm seas. Included in the Bermuda list on the basis of a single record, that of Linton in 1908.

Family MEGALOPIDÆ
Tarpon
Tarpon atlanticus   (Cuvier and Valenciennes)

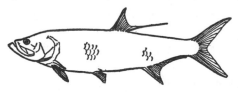

Field Characters.—Large, silvery, compressed fish with a large mouth, and an undershot, projecting lower jaw, between the branches of which is a bony plate; a single, soft-rayed dorsal fin in the middle of the back, the last ray of which is long and filamentous; scales very large and heavy. Uniform bluish silvery above, sides and lower parts bright silvery, pectoral and pelvic fins pale. Grows to eight feet.

Diagnosis.—Dorsal 12 to 15; anal 19 to 23; depth 3.4 to 3.85; head 4 to 4.3; eye 3.9 to 4.65; snout 4.8 to 5.1; maxillary 1.5 to 1.7; gill-rakers slender, 32 to 36 on lower limb of first arch; scales very large, 42 to 47.

Distribution.—Bermuda, West Indies; Long Island to Brazil. Uncommon in Bermuda; several four-foot fish have been seen when diving near Gurnet Rock.

Family ALBULIDÆ
Grubber; Ladyfish; Bonefish; Banana Fish
Albula vulpes   (Linnaeus)

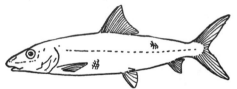

Field Characters.—Cylindrical, somewhat spindle-shaped fish with small mouth placed well back of the projecting, pig-like snout; a single, soft-rayed dorsal fin in the middle of the back; scales rather small. Brilliant silver, the scales, especially above, with a greenish tinge; top of head greenish; tips of dorsal and caudal rays, anterior portion of the anal and the pelvic rays spotted with dusky. Grows to thirty inches and a weight of fourteen pounds.

Diagnosis.—Dorsal 16 to 18; anal 8; depth 4.15 to 4.9; head 3.4 to 3.7; eye 4 to 6.1, with a very large adipose eyelid in the adult; snout 2.4 to 2.5; maxillary 2.7 to 3; scales 65 to 75.

Distribution.—Known from all tropical seas. In Bermuda, found commonly, but in small numbers over sandy areas.

Family CLUPEIDÆ
Anchovy; False Sardine
Sardinella anchovia Cuvier and Valenciennes

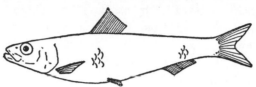

Field Characters.—Small, compressed, rather elongate fish; a single, soft-rayed dorsal fin in the middle of the back; sharp scutes along the ventral surface; mouth small, jaws weak; gill-rakers numerous. Silvery. Grows to 6 or 7 inches.

Diagnosis.—Dorsal 16 to 18; anal 16 to 18, last two enlarged; depth 3.85 to 5.3; head 3.5 to 4.5; eye 3.5 to 4.5; snout as long as, or longer than eye, 3 to 3.8; maxillary extends to below anterior third of eye, 2.5 to 2.85; gill-rakers 45 (young) to 160 (adult); scales 42 to 48, 12 to 14 in transverse series. Ventral scutes 18 to 20, plus 13 to 16.

Distribution.—Bermuda, West Indies; Cape Cod to Brazil. Uncommon close in shore but very abundant in mid-water in greater depths.

Pilchard
Harengula sardina Poey

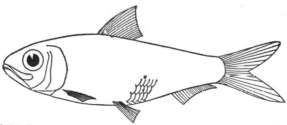

Field Characters.—Small, bright silvery fishes with a single small dorsal fin composed of rays only; a series of 15 to 17 plus 10 to 12 bony scutes along the ventral surface of the body; scales easily lost, those on the sides with vertical striæ. Bright silver becoming whitish below; upper surfaces greenish blue-grey. Colour of the upper surface often sharply marked off by a silvery line slightly different in texture and color from the silver of the rest of the body. Small yellow-bronze patch at top of opercular margin; traces of yellow bronze lines along the sides. Grows to about 8 inches.

Diagnosis.—Dorsal 17 or 18; anal 17 or 19; depth 3 to 3.4; head 3 to 3.55; eye 2.6 to 3.05; adipose eyelid well developed; maxillary 2 to 2.2; snout 3.4 to 4; gill-rakers 25 to 30 on the lower limb of the first gill-arch; scales 37 to 40; scutes on ventral surface 15 to 17 anterior to the pelvic fin base, 10 to 12 posterior to the pelvic base.

Distribution.—Bermuda, Florida and West Indies. Abundant in Bermuda, widely used for bait.

Hard-Scaled Pilchard
Harengula macrophthalmus (Ranzani)

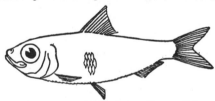

Field Characters.—Small, bright silvery fishes with a single small dorsal fin composed of rays only; a series of 15 to 18 plus 12 to 13 bony scutes along the ventral surface of the body; scales firm, without vertical striæ. Bluish black above, sides silvery; a humeral spot usually present; sides with a dark streak, bounding the dark of the back; a paler streak above this; these streaks most evident in the young. Grows to about six inches.

Diagnosis.—Dorsal 16 or 17; anal 16 to 18; depth 2.7 to 3.8; head 3.3 to 3.9; eye 2.6 to 3; snout 3.35 to 4.5; maxillary reaching from anterior margin of pupil to middle of eye; gill-rakers about 32; scutes on ventral surface,

15 to 18 before the pelvic fins, plus 12 or 13 posterior to the pelvic fins; scales 38 to 40.

Distribution.—Bermuda, West Indies, Florida to Brazil. In Bermuda, less abundant than the preceding species.

Bermuda Herring or Thread-Herring
Opisthonema oglinum (Le Sueur)

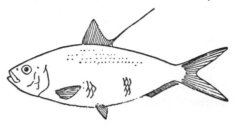

Field Characters.—Small, compressed, silvery-scaled fishes with toothless mouths; ventral surface with sharp keels; pectoral and pelvic fins small; a soft-rayed dorsal fin in middle of back, the last ray of which is produced into a long filament. Reaches 12 inches.

Diagnosis.—Dorsal 17 to 20; anal 22 to 25; depth 2.7 to 3.8; head 3.5 to 4.7; eye 3.1 to 3.9, adipose eyelids well developed; snout 3.4 to 4.1; maxillary reaches anterior margin of pupil; gill-rakers long and slender, numerous; scales 47 to 50; ventral scutes 17 to 19 plus 12 to 15.

Distribution.—Bermuda and West Indies; north to the Carolinas, occasionally to Massachusetts, south to Brazil. Seined occasionally in Bermuda.

Family DUSSUMIERIIDÆ
Green Fry or Dwarf Herring
Jenkinsia lamprotænia (Goose)

Field Characters.—Small, elongate, moderately compressed herrings with rounded bellies and terminal mouths; a single dorsal composed of rays only. Greenish, silvery; sides with a silvery band; rows of dots along the dorsal surface. Grows to 2½ inches.

Diagnosis.—Dorsal 11 to 14; anal 14 to 17; depth 5.5 to 6.1; head 3.7 to 3.8; eye 2.8 to 3.2; maxillary reaches to front of pupil; scales about 36.

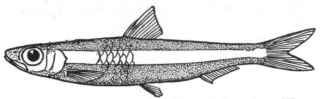

Distribution.—Bermuda and West Indies; Key West to Yucatan. An abundant species about the island.

Family ENGRAULIDÆ
Hog-Mouth Fry
Anchoviella chœrostoma   (Goode)

Field Characters.—Small, elongate, compressed fish with a single soft-rayed dorsal fin; short pectoral fins; snout projecting far beyond the lower jaw; maxillary long. Brownish or greyish with a silvery lateral stripe about as wide as eye from' shoulder to caudal fin. Grows to about 2½ to 3 inches.

Diagnosis.—Dorsal 13; anal 23 to 24; depth 5.25 to 5.7; head 3.2; eye 4 to 4.4; snout long, projecting; maxillary very long, projecting backward far beyond the eye; gill-rakers 24 on lower limb of the first arch, as long as eye; scales about 38.

Distribution.—Bermuda and West Indies. A fairly common species• about Bermuda.

EELS
See Key, p. 276
Marine eels are easily recognized by their elongate, snake-like form, the single pair of gill-openings, the absence of

scales or with these structures minute and embedded in the skin, the lack of pelvic fins and sometimes of pectorals, and the long dorsal and anal fins.

They are chiefly nocturnal, and spend the day buried in sand or mud, hidden in crevices of reefs or of rocks along the shore. They are carnivorous, quick-tempered, and dangerous to handle, but pay no attention to divers. The young pass through a strange metamorphosis, the larvæ being leaf-like, transparent, and known as Leptocephali. In Bermuda there are twenty-four species of eels, distributed through six families.

Moray eels in Bermuda are spoken of always with fear, but there is no instance of an unprovoked attack upon human beings. They are most vicious, however, when caught. Thirteen species of this family are known from Bermuda, and owing to their nocturnal life and their habit of living in deep crevices, others will doubtless be discovered. In size they range from two inches to over eight feet.

Family ANGUILLIDÆ
Common Eel
Anguilla rostrata (Le Sueur)

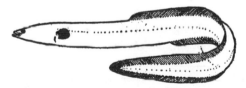

Field Characters.—Elongate eels with rather large mouth, the lower jaw projecting; skin covered with rudimentary embedded scales, placed at right angles to each other (difficult to see without a magnifying glass); dorsal fin continuous with the anal around the tail; teeth small, in bands on jaws and vomer; dorsal fin beginning two-thirds of the distance from snout to anal fin; anterior nostril tubular, situated on the upper lip. Colour varies from

olive brown to bluish grey, uniform, almost whitish below.
Grows to 4 or 5 feet.

Distribution.—Bermuda and West Indies; Atlantic coast
from Southern Canada to Brazil. In Bermuda recorded from
brackish ponds.

Family ECHELIDÆ
Worm-Eel
Myrophis punctatus Lütken

Field Characters.—Small, very elongate, worm-like eels,
similar in shape to the following species; anterior nostrils
in a tube placed on upper lip; posterior nostrils without
tube and placed in upper lip, difficult to see; dorsal fin beginning much nearer the vent than the snout; pectorals
very short, 7 to 8 in head. Dull olive greenish, paler below;
upper body and head covered with small blackish chromato-
phores; dorsal and anal fins posteriorly with black dots
basally. Grows to about 13 inches.

Diagnosis.—Depth 40 to 45; head 11; eye 13 or 14;
gape about 3.5; snout moderate, 5.5 to 6; pectorals very
short, 6.8 to 8.3 in the head; tail 1.7.

Distribution.—Bermuda and West Indies. In Bermuda
caught in seines and by digging in sand.

Long-Snouted Worm-Eel
Myrophis dolichorhynchus Parr

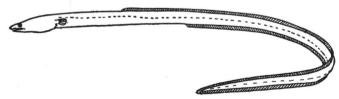

Field Characters.—Small, very elongate, worm-like eels;
anterior nostrils in a tube placed on upper lip; posterior
nostrils without tube and in the upper lip; dorsal fin beginning much nearer the vent than the snout; pectorals well

developed, 4.1 to 4.5 in head. Yellowish grey, the upper surface heavily dotted with small blackish spots. Grows to 11 inches.

Diagnosis.—Head 9.5 to 10.5; snout 4.4 to 5; eye 10 in head, 2.1 to 2.3 in snout; cleft of mouth from snout 2.5 to 2.9 in head; pectoral fins 4.1 to 4.5 in head.

Distribution.—Bermuda and the Bahamas. A single specimen taken swimming near the surface near Smith's Island, Bermuda.

Broad-Snouted Worm Eel
Myrophis platyrhynchus Breder

Field Characters.—Small, very elongate, worm-like eels, similar in shape to the preceding species; anterior nostrils in a tube placed on the upper lip; posterior nostrils without tube and in the upper lip; dorsal fin beginning approximately midway between snout and vent. Pale brownish, lower parts lighter; body thickly covered with many small, dark brown spots, especially marked on the upper surface of the head. Iris greenish silvery, very brilliant. Grows to about 8 inches.

Diagnosis.—Head 3.14 to 3.5 in head and trunk; head and trunk 2.7 to 2.8 in total length; tail 1.6 in length; depth 2.3 to 3.5 in head; eye 1.2 to 1.7 in snout, 6.5 to 7.5 in head.

Distribution.—Bermuda, Glover Reef and the Bahamas. Known from Bermuda from a single specimen caught with a hand net as it swam near the dock at Nonsuch.

Short-Bodied Worm Eel
Chilorhinus suensonii Lütken

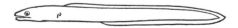

Field Characters.—Small, rather robust, considerably compressed eels with anterior nostrils in a short tube, posterior nostrils in the upper lip; pectoral fins minute; vertical fins well developed, becoming higher posteriorly, the dorsal beginning behind the gill opening. Sandy brown, the colour made up of innumerable small dots; belly silvery anteriorly. Grows to a little over 7 inches.

Diagnosis.—Depth 12 in total; head 1.5 in trunk, depressed; head and trunk 1.2 to 1.3 in rest of body; snout 6 in head; interorbital space equal to eye; mouth cleft, 4 in head, reaching posterior border of eye; vomerine teeth absent.

Distribution.—Bermuda and West Indies. A single specimen taken by us in Bermuda.

Family OPHICHTHYIDÆ
Finless Snake Eel
Sphagebranchus ophioneus   Evermann and Marsh

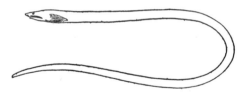

Field Characters.—Small, very elongate, worm-like eels with no trace of fins anywhere; snout projecting beyond the small mouth, giving a shark-like profile. Pinkish flesh colour with smooth metallic iridescence and pearly crackle. Head and under jaw paler than body, pinkish white. Gills red. Iris bluish silvery white beneath skin. Grows to over 11 inches long.

Diagnosis.—Depth 48 to 50; head 12.5 to 13.2; snout to vent 2.8 to 3.2 in length; snout 5.4 to 6 in head; gill-slits inferior, converging anteriorly, where they are very narrowly separated; nostrils not tubular.

Distribution.—Bermuda and Porto Rico. In Bermuda known from only two specimens, one of which was taken by us in sand in 36 feet of water near Gurnet Rock, Bermuda.

Dark-Spotted Snake Eel
Myrichthys oculatus (Kaup)

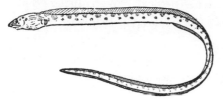

Field Characters.—Medium sized, elongate, more or less cylindrical eels with sharp-pointed finless tail, and with molar teeth; dorsal fin beginning on the head before the gill-opening. Brownish, with darker spots on a paler background. Grows to about 3 feet.

Diagnosis.—Dorsal about 492; anal about 354; depth 37.6; head 13.3; eye 14.4 in head, 2.6 in snout; snout 5.4; trunk 2.44 in length; tail 1.7 in length.

Distribution.—Bermuda and West Indies to Brazil; Cape Verde and Canary Islands. Rare in Bermuda.

Yellow-Spotted Snake Eel
Myrichthys acuminatus (Gronow)

Field Characters.—Medium sized, elongate, cylindrical eels with sharp-pointed finless tail. Teeth molar-like and blunt. Dorsal fin beginning on head before gill-openings. Body with series of round, whitish blotches on each side; head with small whitish blotches. Grows to 30 inches.

Diagnosis.—Dorsal about 480; anal about 310; depth about 3 in head, 37.5 in length; tail 1.66 in length; head 4 in trunk; snout 5.6 in head; eye 2 in snout; cleft of mouth 3 in head; pectorals very small, their bases as broad as gill-openings.

Distribution.—Bermuda, West Indies, and the Florida Keys. Recorded twice from Bermuda.

Gosling's Eel
Quassiremus goslingi Beebe and Tee-Van

Field Characters.—Medium sized, elongate, cylindrical, firmly-built eels with tip of tail forming a hard point, the dorsal and anal fins ending before the tail-tip; pectoral fins rudimentary, visible as a minute flap immediately back of the gill-opening. Brownish with conspicuous dark brown, orange and red spots, pale below. Grows to 28 inches.

Diagnosis.—Head and trunk 1.8; tail 2.2; depth 27; snout to dorsal fin 8.7 in length; head 11.4; eye 10; interorbital space 7.3; snout 4.5; length of gill-opening 9.5 in head.

Distribution.—Known only from Bermuda, where the three type specimens were captured in Castle Roads.

Spotted Sand Eel
Ophichthus ophis (Linnaeus)

Field Characters.—Medium to large sized, robust, cylindrical eels with sharp-pointed finless tail; teeth more or less equal in size, conical; dorsal and anal fins well developed, the former beginning behind the gill-opening; pectoral fins well developed. Body brown or buffy with black spots on the sides and upper surfaces. Grows to 56 inches.

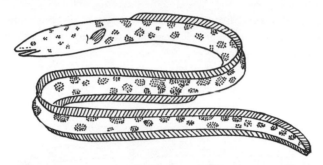

Diagnosis.—Head and trunk 2.4; tail 1.7; head 9.7 in length, 4 in head and trunk; eye 9.5; snout 4.7; snout to gape 2.7; pectoral length 4.5 in head; teeth biserial in upper jaw; lower jaw with a single row of teeth except for a slight overlapping of rows anteriorly; vomerine teeth in a single row, the anterior teeth slightly longer than the others.

Distribution.—Bermuda and West Indies. One published record from Bermuda.

Family MORINGUIDÆ
Golden Eel
Aphthalmichthys mayeri (Silvester)

Field Characters.—Small, elongate, worm-like eels with anterior nostrils in a short tube situated well above the upper lip; posterior nostrils rather large, without tube and placed just before the eye; dorsal and anal fins rudimentary, developed slightly on the tail, these fins present in a small groove. Golden yellow above; ventral surface pale blue or white. Reaches 12 inches in length.

Diagnosis.—Depth 54 to 65; head 13.4 to 13.9; tail 3.1 in length; lower jaw projecting; eye small, but not rudimentary; lateral line present, prominent; pectoral fin present, minute.

Distribution.—Bermuda and Porto Rico. Rare, known from Bermuda by a single specimen taken by us along the shore of Nonsuch.

Family CONGRIDÆ
Bermuda Conger Eel
Conger harringtonensis (Mowbray)

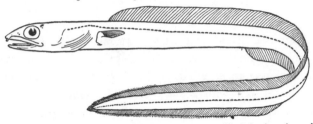

Field Characters.—Small, elongate, cylindrical eels with conspicuous lateral line, very large eye, the diameter of which equals the length of the snout; tongue large, conspicuous and free anteriorly; dorsal fin beginning over the middle of the rather large pectoral fin. In life almost transparent; silvery grey above, pale below, the viscera visible through the body wall. Fins pale, transparent. Grows at least to 15½ inches.

Diagnosis.—Dorsal about 238; anal about 171; depth 20; head and trunk 2.2; tail 1.82; head 5.85; eye 5.3; snout 5.1; snout to dorsal 5.2.

Distribution.—Known only from Bermuda, the single specimen having been taken in Harrington Sound.

Family MURÆNIDÆ
Mottled Conger Moray
Enchelycore nigricans (Bonnaterre)

Field Characters.—Medium sized eels without pectoral fins but with well developed dorsal and anal fins; anterior nostril in a long tube; posterior nostril a lengthwise, oblong slit; jaws meeting anteriorly only; teeth large, pointed. Deep brown changing to pale grey with dark mottlings. Reaches 2 feet in length.

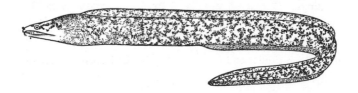

Diagnosis.—Depth about 19; head about 8; eye 12.5 in head, 2 in snout; snout 5 to 6; gape 2; teeth of upper jaw biserial, inner series of very long and depressible canines; lateral teeth of lower jaw slender, subequal, sharp and recurved; vomerine teeth with two very large, spike-like teeth anteriorly, posteriorly a row of very short, strong teeth.

Distribution.—Bermuda and West Indies. Rare in Bermuda.

Brown Conger Moray
Enchelycore brunneus (Nichols)

Field Characters.—Small, sharp-toothed eels without pectoral fins, similar in form to the preceding species; posterior nostril a long slit on top of head in front of eye; dorsal fin beginning over anterior portion of gill-opening. Colour uniform dark chestnut brown, including the fins which are unmarked. Grows to about 13 inches.

Diagnosis.—Depth 10 in head and trunk; head 3.1 in trunk; tail 1.9 in total length; gape 2.2 in head; snout 5.5 in head; eye 1.8 in snout, equal to interorbital; jaws curved, not quite closing.

Distribution.—Known only from Bermuda, where a single specimen, the type, was taken in Castle Harbour.

Dusky-Mouthed Moray Eel
Gymnothorax vicinus (Castelnau)

Field Characters.—Medium to large sized eels without pectoral fins. Greenish brown, with minute yellowish and brownish dots, the fins similarly coloured but with darker mottlings. Dorsal fin usually with a wide conspicuous black border; posteriorly this fin often has a narrow whitish border which continues as a broader band around the outer edge of the caudal end of the anal fin. Gill opening and gape dusky. Grows to 4 feet.

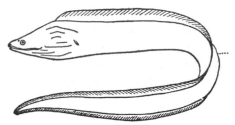

Diagnosis.—Body moderately slender; tail longer than the rest of the body; head long, about 2 in trunk; snout long and narrow; eye large, 2 in snout; mouth large, the gape reaching far beyond eye; jaws straight, the mouth capable of being completely closed; teeth entire, uniserial; lower jaw with about 22 teeth on each side.

Distribution.—Bermuda and West Indies to Brazil. Uncommon. A few specimens of this species have been taken by us in Bermuda.

Speckled Moray or Bird's-Eye Conger
Gymnothorax sanctæ-helenæ (Günther)

Field Characters.—Elongate eels lacking pectoral fins; teeth on sides of the jaws in two rows, the outer row of teeth considerably smaller than the inner; dark brown, with numerous small irregular greyish or yellowish spots, the largest about the size of the eye, the smallest mere dots. Grows to at least 3 feet.

Diagnosis.—Cleft of mouth less than half the head length; teeth of the jaws irregularly biserial; vomerine teeth biserial; snout rather produced and narrow; eye situated above the middle of the gape, 2.5 in the snout; cleft of mouth 2.25 in the head; head 2.5 in the distance from gill opening to anus; tail longer than rest of body.

Distribution.—Bermuda, St. Helena and east coast of South America. Rare in Bermuda, if not wholly absent, being confused with *G. moringa.*

Reticulated Moray Eel
Gymnothorax polygonius Poey

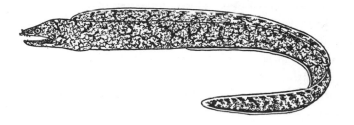

Field Characters.—Medium sized eels without pectoral fins and with anterior nostrils only in a tube. Yellowish white to pale brown, the entire body covered with dark brown or lilac reticulations, some of the reticulations wider and more prominent than the others and enclosing irregular-shaped figures within which the brown colour is found as smaller, less prominent reticulations; margin of anal fin broadly, and dorsal fin narrowly, tipped with yellowish or bright yellow. Angle of mouth dusky. Grows to 3 feet.

Diagnosis.—Teeth uniserial, stout and strong, not close set; eye 2.1 to 2.3 in snout; cleft of mouth 2 to 2.5 in head; head 2.3 to 2.8 in trunk.

Distribution.—Bermuda and Cuba. Not uncommon in deep water off shore.

Common Spotted Moray or Speckled Moray
Gymnothorax moringa   (Cuvier)

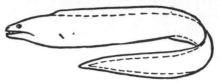

Field Characters.—Medium sized eels without pectoral fins, anterior nostrils only in a tube. Ground colour yellowish grey or cream colour, thickly covered with small dark brown spots; usually so thickly that the fish would be called a brown fish with yellowish reticulations. Fins coloured like rest of body; occasionally the dorsal has a black margin. Reaches a length of about 3 feet.

Diagnosis.—Tail usually a little longer than head and trunk; head 2 to 3.2 in trunk; snout 6 in head; eye large, 1.5 to 2 in snout; cleft of mouth 2.2 to 2.5 in head; teeth uniserial in jaws and on vomer.

Distribution.—Bermuda and West Indies; Florida to Brazil; also recorded from St. Helena. Common in Bermuda.

White-Jawed Moray Eel
Gymnothorax albimentis   (Evermann and Marsh)

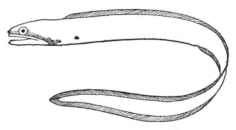

Field Characters.—Small eels without pectoral fins. Body dark brown, freckled with numerous, minute, irregular golden spots; entire lower jaw and lips of upper jaw white; fins narrowly pale-edged posteriorly. Known from three specimens, 2 to 2½ inches long.

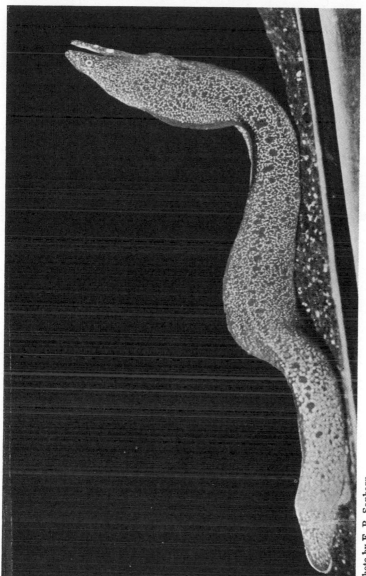

COMMON SPOTTED MORAY
Gymnothorax moringa

Photo by E. R. Sanborn

Diagnosis.—Head 6.4 to 7.2; snout 7 to 9; mandible 1.8 to 2; eye 9; teeth strong, in one rather irregular row in upper jaw, strongest in front; in lower jaw one row of similar teeth becoming smaller posteriorly, those in front stronger than in upper jaw.

Distribution.—Bermuda and Porto Rico. Rare in Bermuda, known from a single specimen taken by us in a small tide pool on Nonsuch.

Green Moray
Gymnothorax funebris Ranzani

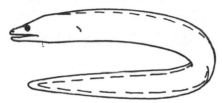

Field Characters.—Large eels without pectoral fins and with large pointed teeth, the posterior vomerine teeth in a double row. Colour usually bright green, sometimes brownish or slaty grey, sometimes slightly mottled, fins rather darker than the body, but never with a marked black edge as in *vicinus;* posterior edges of dorsal and anal fins often slightly edged with white; dorsal and anal usually with more or less distinct, dark, longitudinal stripes. Grows to six feet in length.

Diagnosis.—Head and trunk shorter than tail, 2.1 to 2.3 in total length; tail 1.75 to 1.9 in total length; head 2.9 to 3.5 in head and trunk; snout long, pointed, only slightly projecting, 5 to 6 in head; eye 9 to 12; mouth large, gape reaching far beyond eye, 2.1 to 2.5 in head, when measured from tip of lower jaw to angle of mouth; teeth uniserial in jaws in the adults; teeth on vomer uniserial or biserial.

Distribution.—Bermuda and West Indies; Florida to Brazil. Also recorded from the Cape Verde Islands. A fairly common Bermuda eel in the outer reefs.

Spotted Moray
Gymnothorax ocellatus Agassiz

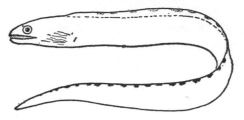

Field Characters.—Medium sized eels without pectoral fins and with the posterior edge of the larger teeth serrate. Brown or occasionally yellow above, and lighter below, with irregular light yellowish spots, variable in size, sometimes thickly placed, making the ground work appear as brown reticulations; dorsal fin with large black spots on the edge, these often running together and forming a black band; anal fin with a dark edge. Reaches a length of 2 feet.

Diagnosis.—Head 2 to 2.25 in trunk, 3.5 to 4.5 in tail; snout rather short and thick; eye rather small, 1.25 to 1.75 in snout; mouth large, capable of being closed, the gape 2.5 to 3 in the head; teeth all uniserial in the jaws, rather large and strong; vomer with a few small teeth or none; gill-opening narrow.

Distribution.—Bermuda and West Indies; Florida to Uruguay. Uncommon in Bermuda.

Conger Moray
Muræna miliaris (Kaup)

Field Characters.—Medium sized eels without pectoral fins, with pointed teeth, and with the posterior nostrils as well as anterior in a small tube. Body deep brown, covered with very small irregularly shaped pale white or yellow spots, these spots much closer together and smaller on the head and anterior body than on the tail region. Grows to a little over 20 inches.

Diagnosis.—Head 7.5 to 8; depth 14 to 16.5; eye about 2 in snout, 9.5 to 10 in head; snout 5.2 to 6.1 in head; mouth 2.2 to 2.5 in head; teeth biserial in upper and lower jaw, the posterior teeth of lower jaw uniserial.

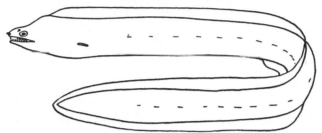

Distribution.—Bermuda and West Indies. Not uncommon in Bermuda.

Golden Moray Eel
Muræna aurea Mowbray

Field Characters.—Small eels without pectoral fins and with posterior nostrils as well as the anterior in a tube. Golden yellow in life, upper parts spotted, blotched and lined with dark brown markings; several, larger, asymmetrically placed blackish dots on the sides. Grows to 16 inches.

Diagnosis.—Head 3.5 in trunk, 7.4 in total; head and trunk 2.7 in length; gape 1.2 in head; eye 9, midway between snout and gape; snout 6.5 in head; teeth in a single series in both jaws posteriorly, 2 or 3 rows at the anterior portion of each jaw; two depressible, stout, rather blunt teeth on vomer anteriorly, behind these a single row of 13 or 14 blunt molar teeth; 9 slender, rather sharp teeth on the palatines; all teeth somewhat recurved.

Distribution.—Known only from Bermuda, where 3 specimens have been taken.

Chained Moray
Echidna catenata (Bloch)

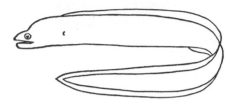

Field Characters.—Medium sized eels without pectoral fins and with the teeth obtuse and molar-like. Colour brownish black, marbled or reticulated with light yellow or white, the light markings sometimes forming narrow irregular cross-bars; under the jaw and on the belly the light yellow often predominates, enclosing dark spots. Grows to less than 3 feet in length.

Diagnosis.—Head 3 to 3.25 in trunk, 3.5 in tail; eye 1.5 to 2 in snout; cleft of mouth 3 to 3.5 in head; teeth of upper jaw more or less biserial.

Distribution.—Bermuda and West Indies to Surinam. Rare in Bermuda.

Banded Creeping Eel
Channomuræna vittata (Richardson)

Field Characters.—Medium to large sized eels without fins of any kind, or with very short fins confined to the extreme end of tail; tail short, considerably shorter than head and trunk. Yellowish brown, with about 17 irregular, broad, chocolate-coloured cross-bands varying in width, sometimes interrupted, sometimes bifurcated, some of them forming complete rings, the pale interspaces usually edged with lighter yellowish. Grows to 4 feet.

Diagnosis.—Lower jaw projecting; teeth slender, subequal, directed backward; teeth in lower jaw in two series, pointed backward, the inner teeth largest and movable; teeth in upper jaw in three series, the two inner series larger and more or less movable; vomerine teeth in a band, thick set anteriorly, posteriorly biserial; eye 1.5 in snout; snout 4.5 in gape; gape 2 in head; head about 4 in trunk, 2.66 in tail.

Distribution.—Bermuda and Cuba. Rare. Living specimens are usually on view in the Aquarium.

THE LIZARD FISHES
See Key, p. 280

This small group is well-named, for the scaly head, large eyes and mouth, conspicuous teeth and the habit of sitting upright on the tips of the pelvic fins, all combine to give a strikingly lizard-like aspect.

They spend their lives on sandy bottoms, alert, and creeping along in a truly reptilian fashion, pursuing and killing any fish which they desire for food. Their method of attack is by a sudden dash, either after a passing fish or the angler's spoon at the surface. They are solitary in habit and they seldom reach a greater size than eighteen inches. Three species have been recorded from Bermuda.

Family SYNODONTIDÆ
Lizard-Fish
Synodus intermedius (Agassiz)

Field Characters.—Small to medium sized elongate fish with single soft-rayed dorsal fin, small adipose fin, and with

flattened, scaled, lizard-like head. Brownish above, paler below; back and sides with about 8 cross bands, these occasionally alternating with indistinct ones; a jet-black blotch
on the shoulder girdle, just back of upper anterior angle
of the opercle; pelvic and anal fins pale, other fins dusky;
dorsal and caudal with evident bars. Grows to 18 inches.

Diagnosis.—Dorsal 11 or 12; anal 10 to 12; depth 7.6 to
8.7; head 3.6 to 4.2; eye 4.5 to 5.6; interorbital notably
concave, 5.4 to 9 in head; snout 4 to 4.5; maxillary 1.6;
gill-rakers, minute, bristle-like; scales 48 to 52.

Distribution.—Bermuda and West Indies; North Carolina
to Brazil. A common species in Bermuda.

Lizard-Fish
Synodus fœtens   (Linnaeus)

Field Characters.—Small, elongate, more or less cylindrical fish with flattened, lizard-like head; a single soft-
rayed dorsal fin followed by a small adipose fin. Greyish,
pale brown or more or less greenish, mottled above; pale
below; cross bars on sides in some specimens. No spot on
the shoulder girdle. Grows to about 12 inches.

Diagnosis.—Dorsal 10 to 12; anal 10 to 12; depth 6.8 to
8.7; head 4 to 4.3; eye 4.7 to 7.7; interorbital slightly concave, 5.2 to 9.2 in head; snout 3.25 to 3.8; maxillary 1.5 to
1.7; gill-rakers undeveloped; scales 58 to 63.

Distribution.—Bermuda and West Indies; Cape Cod to Brazil. Commonly taken over sand in Bermuda.

Snake-Fish
Trachinocephalus myops (Forster)

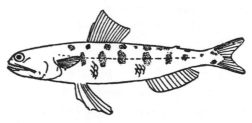

Field Characters.—Small, elongate fishes with a single dorsal fin composed of soft rays only, followed by an adipose fin; head short, blunt, compressed, the snout shorter than the eye. Brownish above, pale below, sides with yellowish and brown stripes, the upper ones more or less wavy; shoulder girdle with a large black blotch at upper anterior angle of opercle; a dark band from eyes across lower jaw; fins mostly plain, the dorsal with more or less distinct spots at the base. Grows to about 9 inches.

Diagnosis.—Dorsal 11 to 14; anal, 14 or 15; eye 4.35 to 6.5; interorbital space narrow, deeply concave, 8.9 to 11 in head; snout shorter than eye, 7 to 11 in head; maxillary 1.6 to 1.8; gill-rakers minute, spine-like; scales 51 to 56.

Distribution.—Widely distributed in warm seas. Uncommon.

MINNOWS

The total absence of rivers and lakes in Bermuda results in a complete lack of true fresh-water fish, but a single species of Minnow has established itself wherever there is a supply of brackish water or a zone of mangroves and mud. During its existence in this island this Minnow has developed an increased number of rays in the vertical fins, sufficient to set it apart from its nearest relatives.

Family CYPRINODONTIDÆ
Mangrove Mullet; Mangrove Minnow
Fundulus bermudæ Günther

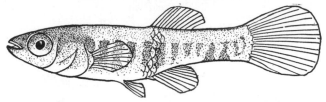

Field Characters.—Very small fishes, considerably compressed posteriorly; dorsal and anal fins almost equal in size, composed of soft rays only, situated on the posterior half of the body; tail rounded. Color light tawny yellow or greenish yellow with vertical, greenish-brown bands, the bands about equal to the interspaces in width. Found in brackish water. Grows to about two and one-half inches.

Diagnosis.—Dorsal 12 to 14; anal 11 to 12; depth 4; head 2.8 to 3.1; interorbital 2.33; snout short, about as long as eye; scales 35.

Distribution.—Bermuda. Abundant in brackish pools and ponds.

GARS, SKIPPERS AND HALFBEAKS
See Key, p. 280

These are all elongate fish, small in diameter and with the lower lobe of the tail longer than the upper. The Gars and Skippers have the jaws produced into a toothed beak, while in the Halfbeaks the lower jaw only is prolonged. The Gars are carnivorous but the Halfbeaks feed only on algæ and other vegetable matter floating at the surface of the water. The eggs of all have tufts of long, slender, floating threads, which serve to entangle masses of them together as well as to anchor them to grass and seaweed.

Six Gar-like fish and three Halfbeaks are found in Bermuda waters.

Family BELONIDÆ
Red-Finned Needlefish
Strongylura notata   (Poey)

Field Characters.—Small to medium sized, very elongate fishes with dorsal and anal fins on posterior portion of body; both jaws produced into a long beak. Clear hyaline green overshot with silvery; greenish about edge of opercle; a narrow greenish line from above origin of pectoral to base of caudal; vertical fins pale greenish brown, tinted with brick red. Grows to about 20 inches.

Diagnosis.—Dorsal 13 to 14; anal 13 to 14; depth 13 to 18 in length, about 5 in head; head 3 to 3.4; eye 10 in entire head, 2 in postorbital part of head; snout 3.4 in length; interorbital equal to eye; gill-rakers absent; scales in lateral line 150, about 80 to 85 before the dorsal.

Distribution.—Bermuda and West Indies; Florida. Rare, one record from Bermuda.

Slender Needlefish
Strongylura ardeola   (Cuvier and Valenciennes)

Field Characters.—Small to medium sized, elongate fishes with dorsal and anal fins on posterior portion of body; both jaws produced into a long beak; caudal peduncle depressed, with a wide lateral keel; dorsal fin originating behind origin of anal; jaws sometimes not quite closing at base. Greenish blue; brilliant silvery below. Grows to a foot or more.

Diagnosis.—Dorsal 12 to 15; anal 16 to 19; depth about 19 to 22; head 2.7 to 3.2 in body; eye 1.8 to 2.2 in postorbital part of head; snout 1.4 in head; scales 110 to 115 before the dorsal in a median series.

Distribution.—Bermuda and West Indies. A common species in Bermuda.

Hound
Tylosurus raphidoma   (Ranzani)

Field Characters.—Medium to large sized elongate fishes with dorsal and anal fins situated on posterior part of body; both jaws produced into a sharp beak. Dark green above, sides and below silvery; sides with an indistinct dark silvery band; middle of back with a darker band; dermal keel on caudal peduncle black; fins all more or less dusky; dorsal fin usually mostly black; distal third of pectorals black. Grows occasionally to 5 feet.

Diagnosis.—Dorsal 22 to 24; anal 20 to 22; depth 13.3 to 18 in length, or 4.35 to 5.8 in head; head 2.8 to 3.5; eye 8 to 9.3 in head; interorbital 1.4 to 1.6 in postorbital part of head; scales about 350.

Distribution.—Bermuda and West Indies, North Carolina, occasionally to New Jersey, south to Brazil. Not uncommon in Bermuda.

Hound-Fish
Tylosurus acus   (Lacepede)

Field Characters.—Medium to large sized elongate fishes with dorsal and anal fins on the posterior portion of the body; both jaws produced into long beaks. Above deep green, sides and below silvery white; anterior rays of dorsal and pectoral fins blackish; no definite silvery lateral band; a conspicuous black lateral keel on the caudal peduncle. Grows to 4½ feet.

Diagnosis.—Dorsal 23; anal 21 to 22; depth 18.5 to 20; head 2.6 to 3.25; eye about 2.5 in postorbital part of head; snout 5 in total length; scales 380 to 400.

Distribution.—Bermuda and West Indies; straying northward to Cape Cod. A common Bermuda gar.

Snook
Ablennes hians (Cuvier and Valenciennes)

Field Characters.—Large, elongate, slender fishes with both jaws produced into long beaks; body greatly compressed; dorsal and anal fins on posterior portion of body; lateral line low on body. Grassy-green above; sides and below clear silvery; snout dark green; about 15 black vertical bars on side, these most distinct in young; dorsal fin anteriorly green in young, becoming wholly black with age; caudal fin mostly green in young, largely black in adult. Grows to about 3 feet.

Diagnosis.—Dorsal 23 to 25; anal 25 to 27; depth 13 to 19.7; head 2.9 to 3.6, much deeper than wide; eye 8.8 to 12.3; snout 1.3 to 1.5 in head; interorbital 1.9 to 2.5 in postorbital part of head; scales about 420 in lateral series.

Distribution.—Widely distributed in warm seas. Found in the Indian, Pacific and Atlantic Oceans. On our shores it is known from Bermuda and West Indies, and from Carolina to Brazil. Fairly common in Bermuda.

Family SCOMBERESOCIDÆ
Needlefish or Skipjack
Scomberesox saurus (Walbaum)

Field Characters.—Small to moderate sized somewhat elongate fish with both jaws produced into a slender beak, the lower slightly longer; the jaws short in the young; 5

to 7 small finlets behind the dorsal and anal fins. Olive green to dark blue above with a silver band on each side at the level of the eye and about as broad as the latter; a dark green spot above the base of the pectoral; dorsal fin greenish; lower parts silvery with a golden gloss. Grows to 18 inches.

Diagnosis.—Dorsal 9 to 11, V to VII; anal 12 to 13, VI or VII; depth 9; head 3.5; scales 110.

Distribution.—Temperate parts of the Atlantic, Pacific and Indian Oceans. Uncommon in Bermuda.

Family HEMIRAMPHIDÆ
Gar
Hemiramphus brasiliensis (Linnaeus)

Field Characters.—Small to medium sized, elongate, vertical sided fishes with the lower jaw prolonged into a long beak; ventral fins inserted nearer the base of the caudal fin than gill-openings. Dusky greenish brown above, brilliant silvery on the sides and below; a dark streak along the sides from the upper angle of the gill-opening to the base of the caudal, wider and more diffuse posteriorly; in small specimens narrow dark lines on the back; upper lobe of caudal fin orange, lower dusky. Grows to about 17 inches.

Diagnosis.—Dorsal 13 to 14; anal 11 to 13; depth 5.45 to 9.8; head 4.35 to 6.35; eye 3.4 to 4.4; mandible 3.65 to 4.15 in length; snout 2.8 to 3.5; gill-rakers 21 to 24 including rudiments; scales 53 to 57.

Distribution.—Bermuda and West Indies; Chesapeake Bay to Bahia, occasionally straying north to Massachusetts. A common form in Bermuda.

Scissors; Pajarito
Hyporhamphus hildebrandi Jordan and Evermann

Field Characters.—Small to medium sized, elongate fishes
with the lower jaw prolonged into a long beak; small dorsal and anal fins placed far backward; about 29 gill-rakers
on the lower half of the first gill arch. Silvery, dark above,
sides with a bluish-silvery band, margined above with black;
tip of mandible red. Grows to about a foot in length.

Diagnosis.—Dorsal 14 to 16; anal 15 to 17; depth 9.7
to 10.5; head 4.6 to 5; snout 2.7 to 3 in head; eye 3.55 to
4 in head; scales 52 to 56.

Distribution.—Known from both coasts of tropical
America, West Indies and Bermuda. In Bermuda it is
rare, and if seen at all, it is likely to be confused with the
following species.

Scissors
Hyporhamphus unifasciatus   (Ranzani)

Field Characters.—Small, elongate fishes with slightly
convex sides and with the lower jaw prolonged into a long
beak; ventral fins inserted about midway between base of
caudal and gill-openings, considerably in front of origin
of dorsal fin; 19 to 21 gill-rakers. Pale green above,
silvery below and on the sides; upper surface of head and
mandible blackish, the tip of the latter red; sides with a
brilliant silvery stripe, widest posteriorly, bordered above
in black. Grows to about a foot.

Diagnosis.—Dorsal 13 to 16; anal 15 to 17; depth 6.3
to 9.8; head 4.4 to 5; eye 3.6 to 4.4; snout 2.5 to 3.1;
gill-rakers 19 to 21; scales 52 to 59.

Distribution.—Known from the Indian and Pacific Oceans and from Bermuda and West Indies; Rhode Island to Brazil. Very common over the beaches in Bermuda.

FLYINGFISH

See Key, p. 281

Ten species have been recorded from Bermuda, the presence of all being rather a matter of accident, for these fish of the open sea have no relation with islands or continental shores.

One or two pairs of wings are enlarged and fitted for gliding, but there are no flapping muscles, so the speed and duration of flight are due solely to initial velocity and sustaining wind. Like birds, flyingfish build nests, binding heads of sargassum weed tightly together with strong, silken strands and depositing their eggs in the mass. Two interesting methods of collecting these fish are, first, by scooping up the young from masses of weed, and second, by shooting the full-grown ones with a shotgun from the bow of a launch, as they rise in flight.

Family EXOCŒTIDÆ
Two-Winged Flyingfish
Halocypselus evolans (Linnaeus)

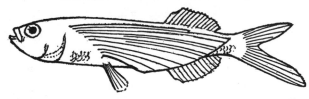

Field Characters.—Small flyingfish with very small pelvic fins. Olivaceous above, dotted with dark blue or silvery on sides and below; pectoral fins dark with a pale margin and no light central area through life. Grows to about ten inches.

Diagnosis.—Dorsal 13; anal 13; depth 5.33; head 4; eye 3.6 to 4.25; snout 4.5; interorbital 3; gill-rakers long and slender; scales 42.

Distribution.—Bermuda; warm seas generally. One record from Bermuda.

Two-Winged Flyingfish
Halocypselus obtusirostris (Günther)

Field Characters.—Small flyingfish with very small pelvic fins. Dark blue above, changing abruptly on sides to brilliant silver; lower lobe of caudal as well as posterior portion of anal fin dusky; dorsal fin with anterior margin, a spot at base of posterior middle rays, and a spot at tip of posterior rays black; pectoral pale with dark margin in young changing to a light margin and a light center separated by a dark band with age. Grows to over 6 inches.

Diagnosis.—Dorsal 13; anal 13; depth 5; head 4; eye 3; snout ⅔ diameter of eye; scales 40.

Distribution.—Bermuda and West Indies; Pacific coast. Uncommon. Four specimens taken by us off shore.

Butterflyingfish
Exonautes exsiliens (P. L. S. Müller)
Field Characters.—Small, four-winged flyingfish, with second ray of pectoral, as well as first, simple, not divided. Coloration of fins mottled, marbled, somewhat variable as to pattern; in specimens of 40 to 60 mm. the pelvics have a dark basal spot, a median and a terminal cross-band; lower caudal lobe with a black spot about one-third the distance

from its base. Known from specimens up to six inches long.

Diagnosis.—Dorsal 11; anal 11; depth 5.5; head 4; eye 2.33; snout 4.66; interorbital 2.25; scales 48 to 52.

Distribution.—Bermuda; open seas. Taken in Bermuda in weed off shore.

Black-Winged Flyingfish
Exonautes rondeletii (Cuvier and Valenciennes)

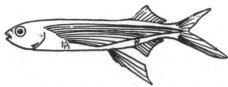

Field Characters.—Four-winged flyingfish with anal fin of 11 or 12 rays; second ray of pectoral fin simple, not divided. Pectoral fins more or less uniform, dusky, except for a scarcely evident distal transparent edge; pelvics darkest medially, with a light axil and a light tip; no black markings on dorsal or anal fins. Grows to 11 inches or more.

Diagnosis.—Dorsal 11; anal 11 or 12; depth 5.5; head 4.5; eye 3.2; interorbital 2.5; snout 4; scales 50.

Distribution.—Bermuda; cosmopolitan in warm seas. A few small specimens from Bermuda.

Brown-Winged Flyingfish
Exonautes rufipinnis (Cuvier and Valenciennes)

Field Characters.—Four-winged flyingfish with anal fin of 12 rays, second ray of the pectoral fin divided. Uniform brownish above, silvery below; pectorals colored like upper part of body, shading into darker toward their extremities; caudal uniform brownish; no dark markings on dorsal or anal fins. Grows to 9½ inches.

Diagnosis.—Dorsal 11; anal 12; depth 5.75; head 4.16; eye 3.5; snout equal to diameter of eye; interorbital 3; maxillary 4.25; scales 58.

Distribution.—Bermuda; tropical America, known from both coasts. One Bermuda record.

Nonsuch Flyingfish
Exonautes nonsuchæ Beebe and Tee-Van

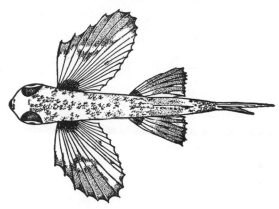

Field Characters.—Very small, four-winged flyingfish with 13 anal rays and without jaw barbels; 6th and 7th rays of the pectoral fins longest. Pinkish above with vertical orange crossbars on the sides; tips of pectorals and pelvic fins bright orange, the base of each of these fins with a dark blue or black spot. Tips of dorsal and anal fins orange. Grows to an inch in length.

Diagnosis.—Dorsal fin 12; anal 13; depth 6.4; head 4.9; snout 4.8; eye 2.4; interorbital 2.4; 49 scales in a lateral series.

Distribution.—This species is known only from the single young specimen collected in Sargassum weed near the shore of St. David's Island.

Atlantic Flyingfish
Cypselurus heterurus (Rafinesque)
Field Characters.—Large, four-winged flyingfish, with small anal fin composed of 9 rays. Dark blue above, silvery on sides and below; dorsal, anal and membranes of

pelvics pale, pelvic rays somewhat dusky; membrane of pectoral fins dusky or almost entirely clear; pigmentation of fins when developed, arranged around a clear, somewhat triangular, cross bar which does not reach the anterior edge of the fin. Grows to 15 inches.

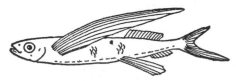

Diagnosis.—Dorsal 13 to 14; anal 9; depth 5.33; head 4.66; eye 3.2; snout 3.75; gill-rakers 15 plus 2 rudiments; scales 56 to 60, about 26 to .33 before the dorsal.

Distribution.—Bermuda; warm parts of Atlantic. A common species off shore in Bermuda.

Double-Bearded Flyingfish
Cypselurus furcatus (Mitchill)

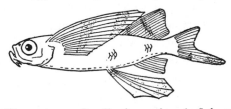

Field Characters.—Small, four-winged flying fish with short dark barbels on lower jaw. Body in small examples with five or six reddish or orange vertical bands; pectoral and pelvic fins mottled; the pectorals developing, with growth, an irregular band paralleling the outer border of the rays. In still larger fish the pigmented areas have enlarged until the wing is dark with a narrow, clear, median region extending from the inner border of the wing in a gentle curve toward the tip. Grows to about 6 inches

Diagnosis —Dorsal 13 to 14; anal 9 to 10; depth 5.2; head 4.5; eye 3; interorbital 3; snout pointed, compressed,

4.2; maxillary 4.75; scales about 46, 28 on median line before the dorsal.

Distribution.—Bermuda; warm seas, north to Cape Cod; Mediterranean. A common species, small specimens being taken constantly in Sargassum weed off Bermuda.

Dark-Winged Flyingfish
Cypselurus bahiensis (Ranzani)

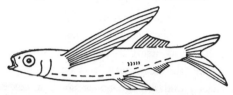

Field Characters.—Small, four-winged flyingfish. Dorsal fin with a large, rounded, black, distal spot; anal pale; pelvics with or without black spots on their membranes; dark pigmentation, when present on the pectoral fins, covering almost the entire fin, leaving only a very short and narrow posterior clear margin. Grows to about 12 inches.

Diagnosis.—Dorsal 13; anal 9 to 11; depth 5 to 6.5; head 4 to 5.33; eye 3 to 3.3; snout shorter than eye; scales 52 to 58, about 36 to 37 before the dorsal fin.

Distribution.—Bermuda; cosmopolitan in warm seas. Uncommon off Bermuda.

Spotted Flyingfish
Cypselurus lineatus (Cuvier and Valenciennes)

Field Characters.—Four-winged flyingfish with short anal fin of 10 rays. Pectoral with a narrow oblique white band across its lower half and with a whitish edge; pelvics white, the middle rays grayish; frequently a series of small brownish spots along each series of scales on lower half of body. Grows to sixteen inches.

Diagnosis.—Dorsal 13; anal 10; depth 6.5; head 4.8 to 5; eye 3 to 3.3; snout 4, or equal to eye; interorbital wider than eye; scales 60 to 63, 38 to 43 in advance of dorsal fin.

Distribution.—Bermuda; tropical Atlantic. Rare,—one Bermuda record.

FLOUNDERS
See Key, p. 282

This is one of the strangest of all groups of fish. The young look like ordinary fish, swimming in a vertical position, symmetrical in every way. Soon they show a tendency to rest on the bottom and to lean over to the right or left, and gradually they assume a flattened, horizontal plane. The entire fish adapts itself to this new position, the lower eye passes around the head until it is on the upper surface, the mouth twists, and all the bones show a corresponding distortion. Finally, the pigment disappears from the under side and becomes concentrated on the upper.

The pattern and coloring of flounders are under the control of the fish to a surprising extent and when an individual is changed from dark mud to light sand there is an almost instantaneous corresponding shift of color.

In northern waters all the general groups—flounders, soles, halibuts—are found in great abundance and are of great economic value to man as food. In Bermuda the extent of shallow, sandy bottom is so limited that only four small species of flatfish occur, plus one that has been introduced.

Family BOTHIDÆ
Eyed Plate-Fish
Platophrys ocellatus (Agassiz)

Field Characters.—Small sized flounders with eyes and color on the left side; both pectoral fins present; lateral line with a distinct arch in front. Light grayish with a reddish tinge, covered with small round spots of darker gray and with lighter rings enclosing spaces of the ground color; vertical fins similarly colored; 2 black spots on median line of the body divide the length into nearly equal thirds; other small black spots on the colored side. Grows to about 8 inches.

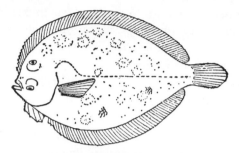

Diagnosis.—Dorsal 80 to 85; anal 59 to 67; depth 1.5 to 1.8; head 3.7 to 4.1; eye (lower) 3 to 3.4; interorbital 4.8 to 7.5; maxillary 3.3 to 3.6; snout 4 to 4.8; scales 65 to 75; gill-rakers very short, blunt, about 7 rudiments on lower limb of 1st arch.

Distribution.—Bermuda and West Indies; Long Island to Rio de Janeiro. We have had a number of specimens from dredgings in Castle Harbor, Bermuda. Uncommon.

Plate-Fish or Peacock Flounder
Platophrys lunatus (Linnaeus)

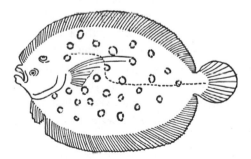

Field Characters.—Medium sized flounders with eyes and color on the left side; both pectoral fins present, that of the left side usually filamentous in the male; vomer toothless; lateral line with a strong arch in front; interorbital space very broad; snout projecting, prominent. Dark olive, variegated, with many rings, curved spots and small round dots of sky blue. Grows to 18 inches.

Diagnosis.—Dorsal 92 to 93; anal 70 to 74; depth 2; head 3.4 to 3.8; eye 6' to 6.3 (lower eye); interorbital 2.4; maxillary 2.66 to 3; gill-rakers short and thick, 9 developed on lower part of gill-arch.

Distribution.—Bermuda and West Indies to Florida. Uncommon in Bermuda.

Small-Scaled Flounder
Syacium micrurum   Ranzani

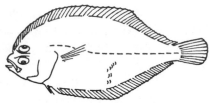

Field Characters.—Small, elliptically-shaped flounders with eyes and color on the left side; lateral line without an arch in front; interorbital space narrower in the female than in the male. Pale smoke gray, with scattered ocellations of grayish-olive, the latter circular with a strongly marked central spot. Grows to six or seven inches.

Diagnosis.—Dorsal 86 to 92; anal 54 to 70; depth 2.25 to 2.5; head 3.6 to 4; eye 4; interorbital about ⅔ the vertical depth of the eye; maxillary 2.5 to 3; gill-rakers about 7; scales 60 to 70.

Distribution.—Bermuda and West Indies; Florida to Rio de Janeiro. Uncommon in Bermuda.

Large-Scaled Flounder
Syacium papillosum   (Linnaeus)

Field Characters.—Small, elliptically-shaped flounders with eyes and color on the left side; lateral line without an arch in front. Color nearly plain brown, with darker dots or mottlings, no ring-like spots or ocelli; fins mottled; left pectoral barred; blind side sometimes wholly or partly dusky. Grows to about a foot.

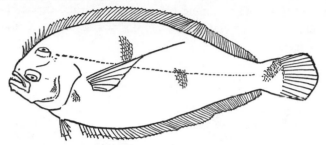

Diagnosis.—Dorsal 82; anal 63 to 70; depth 2.33; head 3.66; eye 4 to 5; interorbital greater than long diameter of eye in males, equal to vertical diameter in females; maxillary 2.66; gill-rakers about 8; scales 50 to 57.

Distribution.—Bermuda and West Indies; South Carolina to Brazil. Rare in Bermuda.

SQUIRRELFISH
See Key, p. 283

The soldierfish or squirrelfish are tropical forms of medium size and usually colored some shade of red or scarlet. The scales and opercles are rough or spiny and the eyes are unusually large, indicating a tendency toward nocturnal habits. Around every Bermuda coral reef squirrelfish can be seen timidly poking their heads out of shadowy crevices, but in the late afternoon they appear in numbers and contribute much to the bright coloration of the reef life. Five species have been recorded.

Family HOLOCENTRIDÆ
Bermuda Squirrelfish
Holocentrus meeki Bean

Field Characters.—Small, elongate soldierfish; soft dorsal and anal fins low, not produced; tail short, and with upper and lower lobes equal in length. Body above lateral line pale brown with a silvery sheen; below lateral line shining silver with a rosy tinge; membranes of spinous dorsal greenish or blackish, the space on the membrane immediately behind the spine pale; other fins pale, except the caudal which shows traces of dusky on the lobes. Grows to 3 inches.

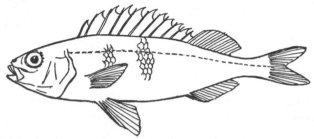

Diagnosis.—Dorsal XII, 14 or 15; anal IV, 10; depth 4 to 4.2; head 3.5 to 3.6; eye 3.4 to 3.5; snout 4.1; maxillary extending to anterior portion of eye or pupil; scales 54 to 55; gill-rakers 16.

Distribution.—Known only from Bermuda, where it is an uncommon species.

Squirrel; Common Squirrelfish
Holocentrus ascensionis (Osbeck)

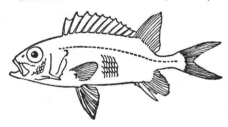

Field Characters.—Small to medium sized, oblong, compressed fishes with very large eyes; a long spine on the preopercle; scales strongly serrate; upper lobe of the caudal fin longer than the lower; anterior rays of the soft dorsal elevated. Color variable, occasionally so pale as to be almost white, often blotched with pink and white, but usually red or orange red above with bluish reflections and

brownish stripes between the rows of scales; head bright
red; spinous dorsal yellowish along the spines, the membrane
orange toward the tips; all other fins usually pinkish.
Grows to 2 feet but usually found less than a foot in
length.

Diagnosis.—Dorsal XI, 14 to 15; anal IV, 10; depth 2.8
to 3.2; head 3 to 3.55; eye 2.55 to 3.2; snout 3.9 to 4.4;
maxillary 2.15 to 2.3; gill-rakers 13 to 16; scales 47 to 51.

Distribution.—Bermuda, Florida and West Indies to
Brazil. In Bermuda found everywhere along shore and on
the reefs in rocky situations where they can easily swim to
shelter.

West Indian Squirrelfish
Holocentrus tortugæ   Jordan and Thompson

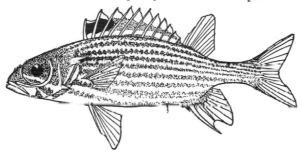

Field Characters.—Small, elongate, large-eyed, compressed, reddish fishes with long spine at the angle of the
preopercle; length of head greater than depth of body;
rosy red with about nine horizontal series of fine black and
darker brown dots, growing fainter ventrally; in specimens
somewhat paler these stripes appear as alternate bands of
silver and pinkish; maxillary and lower part of head whitish with a broad scarlet stripe from the lower edge of the
eye toward the center of the gill-covers; upper ⅔ of membrane between 1st to 3rd or 4th dorsal spines black; no
scarlet stripe along anterior edge of ventral, soft dorsal
and anal fins, nor along the upper and lower margins of
the caudal fin. No specimens longer than 4 inches were

seen and it is doubtful if the species grows larger than this.

Diagnosis.—Dorsal XI, 13; anal IV, 8; depth 3.4 to 3.5; head 2.7 to 3; eye 2.5 to 3; maxillary 2.2 to 2.4; gill-rakers 8 plus 3 rudiments; scales 42 to 46 in the lateral line; opercle with one or two, usually two, enlarged spines, of which the upper one is conspicuously longer than the lower.

Distribution.—Bermuda and West Indies. Common in Bermuda.

Black-Barred Squirrelfish
Holocentrus vexillarius (Poey)

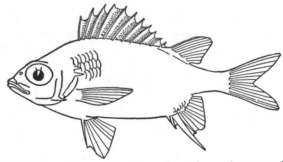

Field Characters.—Small, rather deep, large-eyed fish with a conspicuous spine on the preopercle. Usually rather dark in coloration, but color of body variable, often greenish, silvery or pink, with dark bands between the rows of scales; membrane of spinous dorsal dark red in front of each spine, a pale area in back of each spine, this pale area often not extending to the tip of the fin; membrane between the 1st and 3rd spine darker red than the remainder or black; anterior edge of soft dorsal, anal and the upper and lower margins of the caudal fin scarlet. Grows to about 4 inches.

Diagnosis.—Dorsal XI, 13; anal IV, 9; depth 2.6 to 2.84; head 2.8 to 3.1; eye 2.4 to 2.7; snout 4.15 to 4.4; maxillary 2.65 to 3.1; gill-rakers 8 to 10 plus 1 or 2 rudiments; scales 39 to 43.

Distribution.—Bermuda and West Indies. Quite common in Bermuda.

Goggle-Eyed Squirrelfish
Plectrypops retrospinus   (Guichenot)

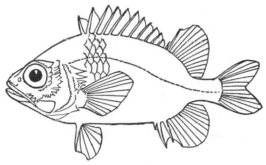

Field Characters.—Small, scarlet, robust, short fishes; suborbital bone with large recurved spines; eyes large, with anterior as well as lateral vision. Entire body and fins red, tips of membranes of the spinous dorsal fin translucent whitish. Grows to a little more than four inches.

Diagnosis.—Dorsal XI or XII, 14; anal IV, 11; depth 2.15 to 2.4; head 2.4 to 2.5; eye 3.4 to 3.9; interorbital 7.4; snout 4.9 to 5.8; maxillary 1.75 to 1.85; gill-rakers 14 or 15; scales 35 to 36; no preopercular spines; scales with enlarged median serræ.

Distribution.—Bermuda and West Indies. Taken in traps at night in 20 to 30 feet of water in Castle Roads, Bermuda. Uncommon.

PIPEFISH AND SEAHORSES
See Key, p. 284

These groups of fish combine a most quaint appearance with amazing life habits. All are small, slender and covered with a bony armor. The pipefish are straight and swim horizontally, the seahorses have the head bent sharply downward, a forward-curling, prehensile tail, and by means of tiny pectorals and a dorsal fin swim upright slowly through the water. The resemblance to a diminutive horse's head or to a knight chessman is striking.

Although their mouths are very small, all subsist on animal food, and they usually live in shallow water in close association with eelgrass and seaweeds.

The mother simply deposits the eggs and swims off, while the male parent receives them and carries them in a special pouch during the period of development. After hatching and when able to care for themselves the young seahorses emerge from the pouch, in the case of the Bermuda seahorse several hundred at a time. (For details of the breeding of the Bermuda seahorse see "Nonsuch: Land of Water," Chapter XIV, page 224.)

Family SYNGNATHIDÆ
Seahorse
Hippocampus punctulatus   Guichenot

Field Characters.—Small, rather robust fishes with head shaped somewhat like a horse and at right angles to the body; tail prehensile. Grows to 6 or 8 inches in length.

Diagnosis.—Dorsal 17 to 22 on 2½ plus 1 or 2 segments; body segments 11 or 12; tail segments 33 to 35.

Distribution.—Bermuda and West Indies; occasionally

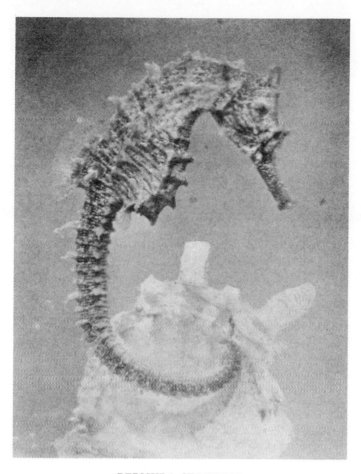

BERMUDA SEAHORSE
Hippocampus punctulatus

north to Carolina and New Jersey. Taken on weed-covered banks in Bermuda, fairly common.

Prehensile-Tailed Pipefish
Amphelikturus dendriticus   (Barbour)

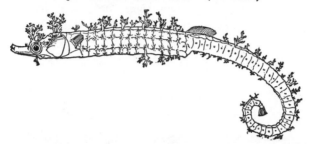

Field Characters.—Short-snouted, rather deep, long-tailed pipefish, the tail prehensile; dorsal fin short, of 16 rays on 1 body and 4 tail segments; many conspicuous, branching filaments on the body and head, especially conspicuous on the latter. Pale greenish gray, somewhat mottled; a small brown spot at junction of the segments on median lateral and inferior lateral keels, the ones on the median lateral keel most prominent; opercles and skin about eyes with small bluish spots. Grows to about 3 inches.

Diagnosis.—Dorsal 16 rays on 1 body and 4 tail segments; anal 2; depth 13; 14 body segments plus 39 to 40 tail segments; head 7; snout 2.7 to 2.8; eye 4.85.

Distribution.—Known only from Bermuda. Uncommon.

Jones's Pipefish
Micrognathus jonesi   (Günther)

Field Characters.—Small pipefish with short snout somewhat bent upward; short dorsal fin of 18 to 25 rays; the median lateral trunk ridge bent downward near the vent and continuous with the inferior caudal ridge. Variable, orange to blackish brown; upper surface often much lighter;

body and tail with darker irregular vertical bars, every third or fourth more conspicuous than others so that the fish has about three paler areas on the trunk and seven on the tail. Grows to about 4½ inches.

Diagnosis.—Dorsal 18 to 25 on 1 plus 3 to 5 rings; 15 to 17 body and 32 to 34 body rings; head and snout short, the latter bent upward, tail twice as long as trunk without head.

Distribution.—Bermuda and West Indies. Rare.

Harlequin Pipefish
Corythoichthys ensenadæ Silvester

Field Characters.—Small, elongate pipefish with short upturned snout; median lateral ridge of body continuous with lower tail ridge. Body with about 22 bright yellow and 22 darker cross-bands, each covering from one to two rings; some of these bands divide into two on the ventral surface. Grows to over four inches.

Diagnosis.—Dorsal fin with 19 rays on 0 to 1 trunk and 4 to 6 caudal rings; 17 to 18 body and 33 to 34 tail rings; head 9 to 10.5; body 1.5 in the tail.

Distribution.—Known only from Porto Rico and Bermuda, at the latter from one record.

Bermuda Pipefish
Corythoichthys bermudensis Beebe and Tee-Van

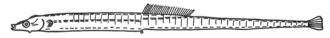

Field Characters.—Small, rather short and robust pipefish with upturned snout; dorsal fin of 23 rays on 0 body and 7 caudal segments; 17 body and 26 caudal segments; greenish brown, somewhat mottled and with vertical, irregular lighter patches. Grows to 2½ inches.

Diagnosis.—Dorsal 23 on 0 body and 7 caudal segments; head and trunk 2.3 in length; tail 1.77 in length; depth 16 in length; head 9.4 in length; snout 3.1 in head; eye 5.4 in head.

Distribution.—Known only from Bermuda, and only from the type specimen.

Louisiana Pipefish
Syngnathus louisianæ Günther

Field Characters.—Elongate pipefish with 20 to 23 body segments plus 35 to 38 tail segments. Brownish, lighter on lower part of trunk and below; sides with a distinct band of brown which extends through the eye to middle of snout. Grows to about 6 inches in length.

Diagnosis.—Dorsal 32 to 37 on 3 to 4 plus 4 to 6 segments; 20 to 23 body and 35 to 38 tail segments; tail 1.8 in length; head 7 to 7.6; eye 8.8; snout 1.6 to 1.7 in head.

Distribution.—Bermuda; Virginia to Texas. Recorded once from Bermuda.

Little Pipefish
Syngnathus pipulus Beebe and Tee-Van

Field Characters.—Small pipefish with a short tail of 26 segments; dorsal fin of 22 rays on 1 body and 4½ caudal rings; yellowish buff mottled with greenish.

Diagnosis.—Dorsal 22 on 1 plus 4½; head and trunk 2.15 in length; tail 1.87 in length; depth 20.5 in length; head 7.4 in length; snout 2.05 in head; eye 6.6 in head; body segments 18; caudal segments 26.

Distribution.—Known only from Bermuda.

Duck-Fish
Syngnathus elucens Poey

Field Characters.—Elongate pipefish with short dorsal fin of 18 to 25 rays on 1 plus 4 or 5 body segments. Greenish or brownish with lighter and darker mottlings on sides and upper parts; under surface of body light grass green, each segment (in males, possibly also in females) with a narrow, pale, yellowish transverse band.

Diagnosis.—Dorsal 18 to 25 on 1 plus 4 or 5 segments; 17 to 18 body and 31 to 34 tail segments; depth 19 to 22; head 7½; eye 5.3 to 6; snout 2 to 2.1 in head.

Distribution.—Bermuda and West Indies. A fairly common species about Bermuda.

Ocean Pipefish
Syngnathus pelagicus Linnaeus

Field Characters.—Elongate pipefish with tail of 31 to 33 segments, and dorsal fin of 28 to 33 rays. Coloration variable; usually pale brownish olive, with pale bands present across the back; vertical white bands present on the sides, sometimes alternating with whitish dots, the bands more marked ventrally, these bands faded and broadened posteriorly, equaling the brown interspaces in width; upper portion of gill cover dark, lower white with yellow or bronze spots; keels of body often dark at junction of segments; a brown band from eye toward tip of snout; dorsal fin mottled, dusky with yellow spots. Grows to 7 inches.

Diagnosis.—Dorsal 28 to 33 on 2 to 4 plus 4 to 7 segments; 16 or 17 body and 31 to 33 tail segments; depth 22 to 25; head 5.8 to 7; eye 6 to 8.3; snout 1.9 to 2.

Distribution.—Known from the Mediterranean and the North Atlantic, widely distributed in floating Sargassum weed. Common off shore at Bermuda.

Mackay's Pipefish
Syngnathus mackayi (Swain and Meek)

Field Characters.—Pipefishes with 28 or more rays in dorsal fin and with 35 to 39 segments in the tail. General color yellow, greenish, or buff, darker above, the center of each segment slightly darker, body usually more or less spotted with white or blue; snout mottled. Reaches a length of 8 inches.

Diagnosis.—Dorsal 28 to 32 on 1 to 3 plus 5 to 7 segments; 16 to 18 body and 35 to 39 tail segments; tail 1.7 to 1.8 in length; head 6.5 to 7.8; eye 7 to 9; snout 1.8 to 1.9.

Distribution.—Bermuda; Gulf of Mexico from Yucatan to Florida. A common species about Bermuda.

TRUMPETFISH
See Key, p. 285

The trumpetfish and the cornetfish are as bizarre looking as their names indicate. Around the outer Bermuda reefs can be seen, now and then, an elongate form, quite stiff from the bony plates in the skin, with a long tubular or trumpet-shaped mouth, and swimming quite as often head downward or upward as straight ahead. It winds in and out of the reefs, backing with as equal facility as it progresses. This will be a trumpetfish.

Family AULOSTOMIDÆ
Trumpetfish or Duck-Fish
Aulostomus maculatus Valenciennes

Field Characters.—Elongate, compressed fishes with small mouth at tip end of long head and snout; scales present, small; soft dorsal fin over the anal and of the same size; preceded by 8 to 11 spinous finlets. Olivaceous or pinkish red, with blue or brown dots along each side of back; longitudinal, silvery lines along lower sides; anterior part of dorsal and anal with a horizontal black band, parallel with base of fin, but remote from it. Grows 'to 3 feet, and possibly more.

Diagnosis.—Dorsal VIII to XI, 23 to 27; anal 24 to 28; depth 12 to 12.5; head 3 to 3.1; eye 2 to 3.7 in postorbital part of head; interorbital 16 to 18; snout 1.5; gillrakers obsolete; scales 240.

Distribution.—Bermuda and West Indies; Florida. A common species about the reefs of Bermuda.

Family FISTULARIIDÆ

Cornetfish

Fistularia tabacaria Linnaeus

Field Characters.—Large, elongate, somewhat compressed fishes with small mouth at tip of long head and snout; body without scales; no spiny finlets in front of dorsal fin; caudal fin continued in a long filament. Greenish brown above; pale below; sides with a row of blue spots from snout to base of caudal; sides and back with about 10 cross bars, a little darker than ground color. Grows to 5 or 6 feet.

Diagnosis.—Dorsal 13 to 15; anal 13 to 15; depth 9.8 to 15; head 2.6 to 2.8; eye 9.6 to 11.7; snout long, 1.35 to 1.4 in head; maxillary 8.4 to 11.4 in head; gill-rakers obsolete; scales absent.

Distribution.—Bermuda and West Indies; Massachusetts to Rio de Janeiro. Uncommon.

SILVERSIDES

See Key, p. 285

These small, silvery-sided fish, commonly known as "fry," live in large schools of thousands and are easily mistaken for anchovies or round herrings. At close range they can be distinguished by the presence of two instead of one dorsal fin, the anterior of which is supported by spines.

In temperate oceans, to the north, silversides are caught in great numbers for the market, and are known as whitebait.

Family ATHERINIDÆ
Silversides, Blue-Fry or Rush-Fry
Atherina harringtonensis   Goode

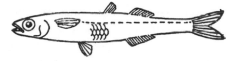

Field Characters.—Small, elongate fishes with two small, separate dorsal fins; anus under or near tips of pelvic fins, remote from anal fin. Greenish white, head and back turquoise green; a narrow silvery band from gill opening to tail; eye silvery white. Grows to 3½ inches.

Diagnosis.—Dorsal V to VI-I, 11; anal I, 12 or 13; depth 5.6 to 6.7; head 4 to 4.6; eye 2.6 to 3; snout 3.6 to 4; scales 44 to 50.

Distribution.—Bermuda. A common species about Bermuda.

Whitebait
Menidia notata   (Mitchill)

Field Characters.—Small, elongate fishes with two small, separate dorsal fins; anus close to anal fin, not under tips of pelvic fins; transparent green, back thickly covered with fine dots; a lateral silvery band, bordered above with a conspicuous greenish-black line. Grows to 5 inches.

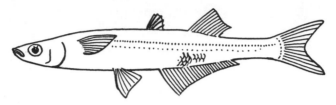

Diagnosis.—Dorsal V-I, 8 to 9; anal I, 22 or 23; depth 5 to 6; head 4.4 to 5; eye 3.3 to 3.5; snout about as long as eye; scales about 46.

Distribution.—Coast of North America from Nova Scotia to Cape May. One Bermuda record.

MULLETS
See Key, p. 285

This is a rather uninteresting group of fish, clumsy in build, blunt-headed and feeding on the organic matter in mud. The young choose animal matter but as the fish grow older they become almost exclusively vegetarian in habit. Elsewhere mullets are numerous enough to be valued as an important article of diet. In Bermuda they are usually found associated in small schools, in shallow water near mud banks.

Family MUGILIDÆ
Striped Mullet
Mugil brasiliensis Agassiz

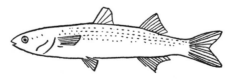

Field Characters.—Elongate, round-headed, rather robust, compressed fishes; adults with strongly developed adi-

pose eyelid; mouth small, with minute teeth; two separate
dorsal fins, the first of 4 spines, the second of 1 spine and
8 rays; anal fin of 3 spines and 8 rays; scales almost
absent on the soft dorsal and anal fins. Bluish black above,
silvery below; rows of scales on sides with distinct dark
streaks; pelvics usually pale, other fins more or less
dusky. Grows to 18 inches.

Diagnosis.—Dorsal IV-I, 8; anal III, 8; depth 4 to 4.8;
head 3.7 to 4; eye 3.75 to 4.8; snout 4.1 to 5.3; interorbital
2.15 to 2.65 in head; gill-rakers moderate in length, about
45; scales 31 to 36; fins with very few scales.

Distribution.—Bermuda and West Indies to Patagonia.
Uncommon.

Mullet
Mugil curema Cuvier and Valenciennes

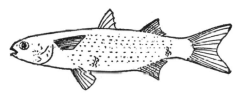

Field Characters.—Elongate, somewhat compressed,
round-headed fishes with large adipose eyelids; mouth small,
somewhat triangular, with small teeth; two separate dorsal
fins, the first of 4 spines, the second of 1 spine and 8 rays;
anal fin of 3 spines and 8 or 9 rays, young with 2 anal
spines and 9 or 10 rays; soft dorsal and anal densely covered with scales. Silvery, body without longitudinal stripes
on sides, a blackish spot at base of pectorals. Grows to 3 feet.

Diagnosis.—Dorsal IV-I, 8; anal III, 8 or 9; depth 3.2
to 4.45; head 3.1 to 4.2; eye 2.9 to 4.5; snout 4 to 5.4; gill-
rakers 65 in adult; scales 35 to 43; young of 80 mm. and
less have few or no scales on the membranes of the soft
dorsal and anal fin.

Distribution.—Bermuda, West Indies, both coasts of America, Cape Cod to Brazil and Gulf of California to Chile. A common species about Bermuda.

Fan-Tail Mullet
Mugil trichodon Poey

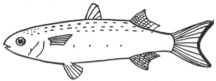

Field Characters.—Elongate, rather robust fishes with two separate dorsal fins, the first of 4 spines, the second of 1 spine and 7 to 8 rays; anal fin with 3 spines and 8 rays; adipose eyelid strongly developed in adult. Bluish above, silvery below; no dark streaks along the rows of scales; pelvics and anal pale; other fins with usually more or less dusky; base of pectorals bluish. Attains a length of 10 inches.

Diagnosis.—Dorsal IV-I, 7 to 8; anal III, 8; depth 3.2 to 3.6; head 3.3 to 4; eye 3.1 to 4; snout 4.2 to 5; interorbital 2.1 to 2.8; gill-rakers about 70, scarcely ½ length of eye; teeth in jaws small but notably larger than in related species; scales 29 to 33.

Distribution.—Bermuda and West Indies; Florida Keys to Brazil. Rare in Bermuda.

BARRACUDAS
See Key, p. 286

These large, voracious fish recall the pike and pickerel of northern waters. They are mid-water forms and fairly good game-fish, taking artificial or live fish bait when trolled from a boat. They share with sharks the reputation of being dangerous to bathers, but we have had no unpleasant experiences although they are not uncommon in many places where we swim and dive, and often come quite close to a diver.

Family SPHYRÆNIDÆ

Great Barracuda
Sphyræna barracuda (Walbaum)

Field Characters.—Medium to large sized, elongate, cylindrical fish with two small, widely separated dorsal fins; scales large, 75 to 85 in the lateral line; snout long, the lower jaw projecting; teeth large, pointed, wide set. Grayish brown above, silvery below; sides with irregularly placed, small inky-black spots; young with dark cross bars on back and quadrate blotches on the sides; soft dorsal, anal and caudal fins blackish. Reaches a length of six feet and possibly larger.

Diagnosis.—Dorsal V-I, 8 or 9; anal II, 8 or 9; depth 6.1 to 7.2; head 2.95 to 3.55; eye 4.9 to 7.2; snout 2.1 to 2.3; maxillary reaching well past anterior margin of eye, longer than snout in adult, proportionately shorter in the young, 1.9 to 2.3; gill-rakers obsolete; scales 75 to 85 in the lateral line.

Distribution.—Widely distributed in warm seas. Known from the Red Sea, the Indian and Pacific Oceans, and in the Western Atlantic from Bermuda, West Indies, South Carolina to Brazil, occasionally straying north to Massachusetts. Small individuals are not uncommon about Bermuda, swimming near the surface and over the reefs.

Northern Sennet
Sphyræna borealis De Kay

Field Characters.—Elongate, slender, little compressed fishes with long low head, and pointed snout; two small, widely separated dorsal fins; eye rather small, 5.3 to 5.7 in head; scales 132 to 138. Grayish brown above, silvery below; a dark longitudinal stripe, sometimes broken up into blotches along the lateral line to the base of the caudal; upper surface of head and snout black; dorsal and caudal fins dusky, other fins mostly pale. Grows to about 18 inches.

Diagnosis.—Dorsal VI-I, 8 or 9; anal II, 8 or 9; depth 7.8 to 10; head 3.1 to 3.3; eye 5.3 to 5.7; snout 2.2 to 2.4; maxillary 2.5 to 2.7; gill-rakers obsolete; scales 132 to 138.

Distribution.—Known from Bermuda and West Indies; Cape Cod to Panama. Uncommon.

Southern Sennet
Sphyræna picudilla Poey

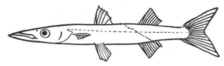

Field Characters.—Elongate, slender, little compressed fishes with long, low head and pointed snout; two small, widely separated dorsal fins; scales 123 to 130. Eye medium in size, 4.8 to 5 in the head. Light olive, darker above, silvery on sides; soft dorsal and pelvic fins yellowish. Grows to 18 inches.

Diagnosis.—Dorsal V-I, 8 or 9; anal II, 8 or 9; depth 7 to 7.9; head 3.1 to 3.3; eye 4.8 to 5.0; snout 2.2 to 2.4; interorbital ⅔ eye diameter; maxillary 2.6 to 2.7; gill-rakers obsolete; scales 123 to 130.

Distribution.—Bermuda, West Indies, south to Brazil. Not especially common about the islands.

European Barracuda
Sphyræna sphyræna (Linnaeus)
Field Characters.—Slender, more or less cylindrical fishes with two short, separated dorsal fins. Scales very small,

150 in the lateral line. Uniform greenish, lead colored, silvery beneath; the dark color of the back occasionally sending down cross bars that cross the lateral line. Grows to six feet.

Diagnosis.—Dorsal V-I, 9; anal I, 8 or 9; depth 9 to 10 in the total length; head 3.5; eye 8; scales 150.

Distribution.—Coasts of southern Europe; this fish has twice been recorded from Bermuda. Both records are questionable and it is very possible that the fish does not occur here at all.

MACKERELS
See Key, p. 286

The Mackerels and their near allies command our enthusiasm for their strength, speed and beauty as well as for the game fight they put up when being captured on rod and line, and in addition, their flesh is a great delicacy for the table.

The stream lines, the narrow tail base and wide, crescentic tail, together with strong, firm muscles, indicate great swimming powers and ability to make abrupt turns, and the large mouths and abundance of teeth indicate predacious hunters of living prey. They are, as a rule, inhabitants of the open sea, some coming inshore to spawn.

The six species recorded from Bermuda have been taken off-shore, finding their way occasionally into the bays and harbors.

Family CYBIIDÆ
Spanish Mackerel
Scomberomorus maculatus (Mitchill)

Field Characters.—Medium to large sized, elongate, compressed fishes with slender spines in the first dorsal fin; second dorsal and anal fins followed by a series of finlets. Bluish above, silvery below, sides with elliptical, bronzy spots not running into definite streaks or rows. Grows to 3 or 4 feet and a weight of 8 to 10 pounds.

Diagnosis.—Dorsal XVII or XVIII—15 to 18—VIII or IX; anal II, 15 to 17—VIII or IX; depth 4.4 to 5.7; head 3.4 to 3.8; eye 4.5 to 6; snout 2.6 to 3.1; maxillary 1.65 to 1.8; gill-rakers 10 to 12, about half as long as eye in adult; pectoral fins naked; body covered with fine rudimentary scales; lateral line wavy, descending obliquely.

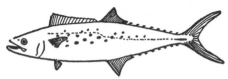

Distribution.—Bermuda, West Indies; Atlantic coast from Maine to Brazil; also found in the Pacific from Cortez Banks to the Galapagos Islands. It is uncommon in Bermuda, drifting in pelagically.

Family ACANTHOCYBIIDÆ
Kingfish; Wahoo; Queenfish
Acanthocybium petus (Poey)

Field Characters.—Large, mackerel-like fishes with long, slender, pointed head; body long, tapering toward both ends; caudal peduncle depressed, with a large lateral keel and with a small keel above and one below the larger one; eye large; teeth in a close-set series, saw-like. Metallic blue above, bright silver on sides and lower surfaces; sides occasionally with white vertical bands. Grows to 6 feet or more, and to a weight of 100 pounds.

Diagnosis.—Dorsal XXVI-12-IX; anal II, 10-IX; depth about 6.4; head 3.6 to 4; eye 9.7.

Distribution.—Bermuda, West Indies north to Key West. Uncommon in Bermuda waters, and apparently mistaken at times for Barracudas.

Family SCOMBRIDÆ
Chub Mackerel; Tinker Mackerel
Pneumatophorus grex (Mitchill)

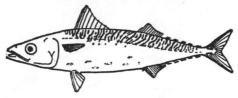

Field Characters.—Small to medium, elongate, fusiform, slightly compressed fishes with small finlets following the dorsal and anal fins; maxillary slipping completely under the preorbital; small scales present on the entire body; no median lateral keel on the side of the caudal peduncle, but a small horizontal keel on its upper and lower aspects. Silvery, the upper surface of the body with transverse angled narrow bars, more irregular posteriorly. Grows to about 14 inches.

Diagnosis.—Dorsal IX to XI—11 or 12—V; anal I-I, 10 to 12—V; depth 4.5 to 5.85; head 3.3 to 3.8; eye 3.7 to 4.8; snout 3.1 to 3.7; maxillary 2.4 to 2.8; gill-rakers nearly as long as the eye, 25 to 30 on the lower limb of the first gill-arch.

Distribution.—Western Atlantic, rather widely distributed. Occasional in Bermuda. Related forms are found all over the world.

Family THUNNIDÆ
Tunny; Horse Mackerel
Thunnus thynnus (Linnaeus)

Field Characters.—Large, robust, rather deep, compressed fishes with small finlets following the dorsal and anal fins; scales present on the entire body, those on the corselet larger than the rest. Gill-rakers slender, 20 or more on the lower limb of the first gill-arch; pectoral fins shorter than the head. Dark blue or black above with gray or green reflections; cheeks silver; sides and belly silvery-gray often with large silvery spots and bands. Said to grow to 14 feet or more and to a weight of 1600 pounds, but fish growing to 500 pounds are to be considered as giants.

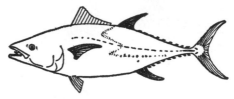

Diagnosis.—Dorsal XIII or XIV-I, 13 or 14—IX or X; anal 11 to 12—VIII or IX; depth about 4; head 3.25 to 3.75; eye 5.75 to 6; gill-rakers about 28.

Distribution.—Warmer parts of the Atlantic and Pacific. In Bermuda it is uncommon, but apparently a few individuals come about the island each year.

Family KATSUWONIDÆ
Mackerel; Little Tunny
Euthynnus alletteratus (Rafinesque)

Field Characters.—Elongate, robust, fusiform, slightly compressed fishes; scales present on anterior part of the body only, forming a corselet; dorsal fins close together, the first of 15 to 16 spines, a series of finlets back of the dorsal and anal fins. Bluish above, silvery below; sides above the lateral line with black, oblique lines or spots; region below the pectoral fins with several black spots about the size of the pupil. Grows to two or three feet and a weight of 20 pounds.

Diagnosis.—Dorsal XV or XVI—11 to 13—VIII; anal II, 12 or 13—VI or VII; depth 3.8 to 4.1; head 3.45 to 3.6;

eye 5.25 to 6.5; snout 3.25 to 3.7; maxillary 2.3 to 2.6; gill-rakers 23 to 27 on the lower limb of the first arch; anterior dorsal spines longest, the posterior ones very short.

Distribution.—A pelagic species recorded from warm seas generally. Reaches north on our coast in the Gulf Stream as far as Cape Cod. Fairly common in the late fall in Bermuda, and much watched for by fishermen.

Frigate Mackerel
Auxis rochei (Risso)

Field Characters.—Medium sized, fusiform-shaped fishes with scales present on the body in the form of a corselet close to the head, and along the lateral line, remainder of body naked; spinous and soft dorsal fins widely separated, the first with 9 to 11 spines; a series of finlets following the dorsal and anal fins. Bluish above, silvery below; sides above lateral line and behind corselet with black spots or more or less wavy bars; no markings of any kind below the lateral line. Grows to about 16 inches.

Diagnosis.—Dorsal IX to XI—10 or 11 VIII; anal II, 10 or 11—VII; depth 4 to 4.8; head 3.45 to 4; eye 5 to 5.5; snout 4.2 to 5; maxillary 3 to 3.35; gill-rakers 29 to 33.

Distribution.—Open Atlantic, at times northward to Cape Cod. Closely related if not identical forms are found distributed all over the world. Uncommon.

TAPIOCAFISH AND BERMUDA CATFISH
See Key, p. 287

These elongate fish are even more predacious than the mackerels, and their slender, swift forms and long, sharp fangs place most smaller sized fish in their power. They are fish of the deeper shore zones, from twenty-five fathoms down, so will seldom or never be seen by the ordinary observer unless especially fished for at considerable depths.

Family GEMPYLIDÆ
Tapiocafish, Oil-Fish
Ruvettus pretiosus Cocco

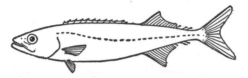

Field Characters.—Elongate, fusiform, mackerel-like fish without keels on the side of the caudal peduncle; skin with bony plates set with short spines; two dorsal and two anal finlets following the soft dorsal and anal fins; purplish brown, darkest above, with blackish patches, inside of mouth dusky. Grows to about six feet.

Diagnosis.—Dorsal XV—18—II; anal 17-II; depth 6; head 4; eye 5.

Distribution.—Bermuda; tropical parts of the Atlantic and the Mediterranean in moderately deep water from 80 to 400 fathoms, usually in the latter depths, and rarely in shallower water. This fish is also found through the tropical Pacific. Uncommon.

Bermuda Catfish
Promethichthys prometheus (Cuvier and Valenciennes)

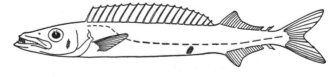

Field Characters.—Medium sized, elongate, slender, compressed, fusiform fishes; mouth large, with strong fang-like teeth in front of each jaw, both jaws with an outer row of short, strong, compressed triangular teeth; lower jaw projecting; uniform coppery brown in life with metallic iridescence and blackish cloudings; fins more or less dusky or rich brown. Grows to about 2½ feet.

Diagnosis.—Dorsal XVIII or XIX—19 to 21—II; anal 16-II; depth 6.4 to 7; head 3.6 to 4; eye 4 to 5.5; snout 2.3 to 2.4; maxillary 1.65 to 2.1; interorbital 7.4 to 7.8.

Distribution.—Bermuda and Tropical Atlantic; Hawaii. Usually taken from depths of 350 to 600 feet, but taken occasionally at 150 feet.

SWORDFISH
See Key, p. 287

These great fish are inhabitants of the open sea, recorded from Bermuda because of the accident of their being found in that part of the ocean. They are even rarer than near the continental coast, as only two species, one Spearfish and one Swordfish have been observed.

The projection of the upper jaw into a hard, bony sword, together with their great size, from ten to sixteen feet, distinguishes them from all other fish.

Family XIPHIIDÆ
Swordfish
Xiphias gladius Linnaeus

Field Characters.—Large sized, elongate fishes with the upper jaw much prolonged, forming a flat blade-like "sword"; no teeth in the adult; no pelvic fins; dorsal fin short and high; a keel along the side of the caudal peduncle. Dark metallic purplish above, dusky below; sword almost black above; fins dark with a silvery sheen. Grows rarely to 16 feet, but usually considerably smaller. Weighs up to 750 pounds,—a 13 or 13½ foot fish weighing about 600 pounds.

Diagnosis.—Dorsal 40-4; anal 18-14; depth 5.5; head 2.25; snout 3.

Distribution.—Known from open seas generally.   Rare at Bermuda.

Family ISTIOPHORIDÆ
Bermuda Spearfish
Makaira bermudæ   Mowbray

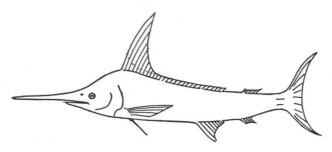

Field Characters.—Very large fish with the upper jaw prolonged into a long beak; pelvic fins present; base of dorsal fin very long, the height of its anterior part one third higher than the depth of the body; blue-black above; silvery with a bluish luster on the lower sides and underparts; four faint bluish-white bars in the pectoral region. Grows to 10 feet in length.

Diagnosis.—Dorsal XLII-7; anal 15-II; depth 4.1; head 2.5; pectoral length 2.5 in snout.

Distribution.—Off shore Bermuda waters; the only known specimen was taken in 1927 on the northern shore of Castle Harbor.

Discussion.—The drawing given above is an approximation only, as the type specimen was destroyed before it could be thoroughly examined. The species is known only from an abbreviated description and a foreshortened photograph.

DOLPHINS
See Key, p. 289

This name is confusing, for it is applied to the familiar aquatic mammals which love to play about the bows of vessels, as well as to these striking fish.

They are excellent gamefish and the shift and change of the prismatic colors on the body of Dolphins have long made them famous. Dolphins are quite independent of shore waters and their appearance near Bermuda is of no more local significance than the drifting seaweed.

Family CORYPHÆNIDÆ
Common Dolphin
Coryphæna hippurus Linnaeus

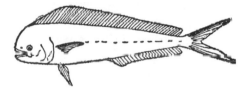

Field Characters.—Large, compressed, elongate, tapering fishes with very long, high dorsal fin beginning on the nape, entirely of flexible spines or jointless rays; anterior profile almost vertical in adult males. Brilliantly colored fishes, changing rapidly when captured and after death; gold, greens and blues; dorsal fin purplish blue, with paler oblique lines; caudal yellow; other fins tinged with blue; small black spots on the lower parts. Grows to 6 feet in length, a fish of such length weighing about 34 pounds.

Diagnosis.—Dorsal 55 to 65; anal 26 to 30; depth 5 to 6.3; head 3.75 to 5.75; eye 2.65 to 3; snout 3.9 to 4.35; maxillary 2.15 to 2.45; gill-rakers slender, 8 to 10; scales minute.

Distribution.—A pelagic species cosmopolitan on the high seas. Common off shore at Bermuda.

Little Dolphin
Coryphæna equisetis Linnaeus

Field Characters.—Similar to the Common Dolphin, but possessing a smaller number of fin rays. Dorsal 51 to 55, anal 24 to 26. Brilliantly colored as in its larger relative.

Diagnosis.—Dorsal 51 to 55; anal 24 to 26; depth 3.4 to 4; head 4.2 to 4.6; maxillary 3.8 to 4.8.

Distribution.—Open Atlantic, rare in West Indies. Recorded from Bermuda, but it may possibly have been the common dolphin to which this record refers.

PORTUGUESE MAN-OF-WAR FISH

This small species of fish gets its name from its habit of hiding from its enemies within the maze of poisonous tentacles of the Physalia or Portuguese Man-of-War Jelly. Its occurrence in a Bermuda list is due only to the drifting past of one of these jellies sheltering one of these fish.

Family NOMEIDÆ
Portuguese Man-of-War Fish
Nomeus gronovii (Gmelin)

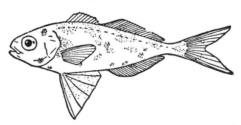

Field Characters.—Small, elongate, symmetrical, compressed, blunt-snouted, fork-tailed fishes with the pelvic fins very large and mostly black, inserted in a groove. Light brown above, silvery below; sides with large brown spots and blotches; anal fin with 3 or 4 brown spots;

pectoral brown anteriorly, white posteriorly. Grows to 6 or 8 inches.

Diagnosis.—Dorsal X or XI-I, 25 to 27; anal III, 25 to 27; depth 3.8; head 3.4; eye 3.2; snout 4.2; maxillary 1.2; scales 64 to 66.

Distribution.—Tropical parts of the Atlantic and Pacific. Found usually in company with the Portuguese Man-of-War. Uncommon.

JACKS AND BONITOS

See Key, p. 287

A large and diversified assemblage of fish, many oceanic in habitat, the young more often found near shore than the adults. Among them are the Amberfish, Jacks and Bonitos —all large, strong and affording excellent sport to lovers of game-fishing; the Pampanos—smaller, very beautiful and most delicious food fish; the Pilotfish—a sort of little-friend-of-all-the-sharks; Moonfish—like very thin, round silver dollars with long trailing fins; and finally, the little Bumpers—which when young spend much of their life hiding beneath the disks and tentacles of jellyfish. Sixteen species of this group inhabit the waters around Bermuda.

Family CARANGIDÆ
Robin; Round-Robin; Scad; Dotted Scad; Cigar-Fish
Decapterus punctatus (Agassiz)

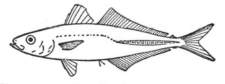

Field Characters.—Small, elongate, slightly compressed or fusiform fishes with minute teeth; long dorsal and anal fins, each of which are followed by a single detached finlet; a series of scutes along the posterior sides. Bluish black above, silvery below; a dark opercular patch; dorsal and caudal fins dusky, other fins pale; axil of pectoral black. In all but the very young there are a series of 12 small black spots along the sides. Grows to about a foot.

Diagnosis.—Dorsal VII or VIII-I, 29 to 33—I; anal II-I, 24 to 27—I; depth 4.3 to 5.3; head 3.7 to 4.3; eye 2.75 to 3.8; snout 2.75 to 3,5; maxillary 2.1 to 3; gill-rakers 32 to 35 on the lower limb of the first gill-arch, short and close set; scutes 35 to 42.

Distribution.—West Indies to Brazil, north to Cape Cod and Bermuda. It is a fairly common species in Bermuda.

Ocean Robin
Decapterus macarellus (Cuvier and Valenciennes)

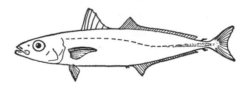

Field Characters.—Similar to the Round-Robin but with less scutes along the sides. Bright green-blue above on the sides, becoming blue black when viewed from above, lower sides bright silvery; a green streak slightly narrower than the pupil, extending from the shoulder to the caudal fin; tips of upper and lower jaws dusky; a black spot on inner base of pectoral rays, and a black spot on the posterior end of the opercle; caudal fin pinkish, the central portion of each lobe dusky. Grows to about a foot,—some fishermen claim that it attains a length of two feet.

Diagnosis.—Dorsal VIII-I, 32 to 33—I; anal II-I, 27 or 28—I; depth 5.4 to 6; head 4.25 to 5; eye 4.3; snout 2.6; maxillary 3.1; gill-rakers about 37; scutes 20 to 30.

Distribution.—Warmer parts of the Atlantic, occasionally straying northward as far as Nova Scotia. The Ocean Robin is usually found in less protected situations than its relative, and farther out to sea.

Goggle-Eyed Jack; Goggler; Big-Eyed Scad
Trachurops crumenophthalma (Bloch)

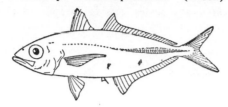

Field Characters.—Small to medium sized, elongate, fusiform fishes with large eye and well-developed adipose eyelid; a deep furrow on the shoulder girdle near the isthmus and a fleshy projection above this furrow,—these characters visible when the gill-covers are lifted. Dark greenish above becoming bright silvery below; a narrow greenish band from shoulder to upper part of caudal peduncle; all fins with dusky punctulations; a small black spot on the posterior part of the opercles. Grows to two feet.

Diagnosis.—Dorsal VIII-I, 23 to 26; anal II-I, 20 to 23; depth 3.1 to 4; head 3 to 3.4; eye 2.75 to 3.2; snout 3.3 to 3.9; maxillary 2.1 to 2.45; gill-rakers 23 to 27; scutes along sides 40.

Distribution.—Known from most tropical seas. It is found fairly commonly at Bermuda.

Gwelly
Caranx guara Bonnaterre

Field Characters.—Medium sized, compressed fishes with outlines of body evenly curved; arch of the lateral line very long and low; lips thick in adult, papillose; mouth small; lower jaw included within the upper. Bluish or greenish above and silvery below; a black opercular spot; a yellow band along the middle of the sides, wider posteriorly; another along base of soft dorsal and anal fins; soft dorsal, soft dorsal sheath and caudal fin dusky yellow; iris silvery white. Grows to two feet in length.

Diagnosis.—Dorsal VII or VIII-I, 26; anal II-I, 21 to 23; depth 2.5 to 2.9; head 2.7 to 2.9; eye 4.6 to 7.4; snout 2.2; gill-rakers 27; scales 112 in lateral line; scutes 24 to 29.

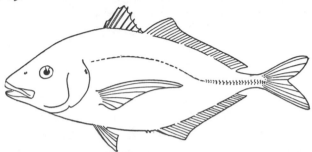

Distribution.—Tropical parts of the Atlantic and Pacific and in the Mediterranean. Uncommon in Bermuda.

Yellow Jack
Caranx bartholamæi Cuvier and Valenciennes

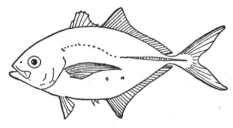

Field Characters.—Small, rather deep, compressed fishes with weak scutes along the posterior sides and with upper and lower profiles almost evenly convex, the upper slightly more so; head short and blunt. Bluish green above, sides silvery; the young strongly reticulated with gold. Grows to about 15 inches.

Diagnosis.—Dorsal VIII-I, 26 to 28; anal II-I, 22 to 24; depth 2 to 2.7; head 2.8 to 3.25; eye 2.8 to 4; snout 2.75 to 3.4; maxillary 2.25 to 2.5; gill-rakers 17 to 19 plus a few rudiments; lateral scutes 22 to 35, rather weak.

Distribution.—Bermuda, West Indies, North Carolina to Panama. Young individuals are often taken over the beaches at Bermuda.

Jack; Yellow Jack
Caranx latus Agassiz

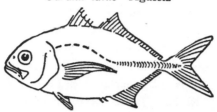

Field Characters.—Elongate, compressed, rather deep, silvery, small-scaled fishes with enlarged scutes along the posterior part of the sides. Silvery, all fins except the pectorals yellowish, tip of soft dorsal fin black. Young with vertical darkish cross bars. Grows to almost two feet.

Diagnosis.—Dorsal VIII-I, 20 to 22; anal II-I, 17 or 18; depth 2.3 to 2.6; head 2.9 to 3.2; eye 3.1 to 3.6; snout 3.4 to 3.7; maxillary 2 to 2.2; gill-rakers 13 to 16, exclusive of rudiments, rather slender; lateral scutes 35 to 38.

Distribution. Known from all tropical seas. This is the commonest Jack to be found in Bermuda.

Skip-Jack; Never-Bite
Caranx ruber (Bloch)

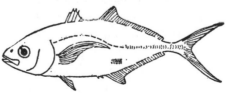

Field Characters.—Elongate, compressed fish with long tapering head and with enlarged keeled plates along the posterior middle of the sides; upper profile evenly convex, lower outline only slightly curved in front of anal. Bluish and silvery with a brilliant dark blue band on sides just below the dorsal fin; lower lobe of the caudal fin with a black bar. Grows to a little over a foot.

Diagnosis.—Dorsal VIII-I, 26 to 28; anal II-I, 23 or 24; depth 2.9 to 3.25; head 3.2 to 3.65; eye 3.6 to 4.3; snout 2.9 to 3; maxillary 2.5 to 2.8; gill-rakers 30 to 33; scutes 28 to 35, rather weak; second dorsal and anal fins slightly elevated anteriorly, each with a low sheath of scales at the base, the fins entirely covered with scales.

Distribution.—Bermuda and West Indies, North Carolina to Cozumel. This is a common species over the outer reefs off Nonsuch, where they may be found in small schools.

Hardtail
Caranx crysos (Mitchill)

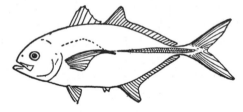

Field Characters.—Elongate, rather slender, compressed, short-headed and short-snouted fishes with strong scutes along the posterior middle of the sides; lateral scutes 38 to 52; gill-rakers 24 to 25. Bluish above, silvery below; spinous dorsal and margins of dorsal and caudal fins dusky, other fins pale; a black opercular spot. Grows to about 20 inches and to a weight of 4 pounds.

Diagnosis.—Dorsal VIII-I, 23 to 25; anal II-I, 18 to 20; depth 2.8 to 3; head 3.3 to 3.7; eye 3.2 to 4.1; snout 3.25 to 3.75; maxillary 2.3 to 2.5; gill-rakers 24 or 25, exclusive of rudiments; scutes 38 to 52, strong posteriorly.

Distribution.—Bermuda, West Indies, Cape Cod to Brazil, casually to Nova Scotia. Also known from the eastern Pacific. Not common at Bermuda.

Bumper
Chloroscombrus chrysurus (Linnaeus)

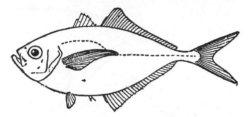

Field Characters.—Small, compressed fishes with convex dorsal and ventral outlines, the latter more convex than the former; anal and dorsal fins long and low; posterior scutes of the lateral line very weak and few, sometimes wholly wanting. Silvery, fins somewhat yellowish; specimens over an inch and a quarter with a black spot on the upper side of the caudal peduncle. Young with a blackish line along the bases of the dorsal and anal fins and along the mid-line of the posterior part of the sides. Grows to eight inches in length.

Diagnosis.—Dorsal VIII-I, 26 to 29; anal II-I, 26 to 28; depth 1.9 to 2.4; head 3.6 to 4.3; eye 2.6 to 3.2; snout 3.3 to 4; maxillary 2.44 to 2.75; gill-rakers slender, close-set, 28 to 33 on lower limb of the first arch; scales very small; scutes few and weak, sometimes altogether wanting.

Distribution.—Bermuda, West Indies, Cape Cod to Brazil. At Bermuda this fish is known only from small individuals taken floating under jelly-fish.

Moonfish; Look-Down; Horse-Head
Argyreiosus vomer (Linnaeus)

Field Characters.—Very deep, exceedingly compressed, silvery fishes with elongate anterior lobes to the second dorsal and anal fins. Edges of the body sharp; anterior profile sloping upward and backward; no scutes on the posterior part of the lateral line. Bluish-green above, sides silvery; sides with indistinct vertical bars or dusky blotches;

fins mostly pale, dorsal and caudal dusky in adult. Grows
to about a foot in length.

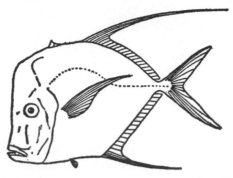

Diagnosis.—Dorsal VIII-I, 21 to 23; anal II-I, 18 to
20; depth 1.2 to 1.45; head 2.2 to 2.7; eye 4 to 5.25; snout
1.66 to 2.2; maxillary 2.7 to 3.4; gill-rakers 23 to 26 plus
one or two rudiments. Scutes absent.

Distribution.—Bermuda, West Indies, Maine to Uruguay. Rare at Bermuda.

Alewife; Gaff-Topsail Pampano
Trachinotus palometa Regan

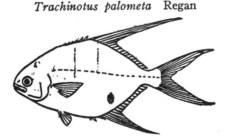

Field Characters.—Medium sized, elongate but deep,
strongly compressed fishes with small scales, blunt snout,
and with the lobes of the soft dorsal and anal fins reaching
half way to the tip of the caudal in the adult. Color
bluish-black to pale brown above, silvery below, upper sides
with 4 or 5 narrow vertical dark bars, varying in width and
intensity, absent in fishes smaller than 3 inches; dorsal and
anal lobes dark. Grows to about a foot.

Diagnosis.—Dorsal V or VI-I, 19 or 20; anal II-I, 17 or 18; depth 1.9 to 2.2; head 3 to 3.9; eye 3 to 4.1; snout 3.7 to 4.45; maxillary 2.2 to 2.75; gill-rakers very short, 8 to 10; scales small, more or less embedded.

Distribution.—Bermuda, West Indies, Virginia to Argentina. Fairly common at Bermuda.

Alewife
Trachinotus goodei Jordan and Evermann

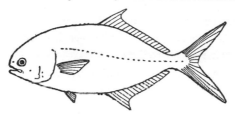

Field Characters.—Medium to large sized, oblong, moderately compressed, small-scaled, snub-snouted fishes; tips of dorsal and anal fins not reaching beyond base of caudal fin in the adult. Bluish silvery above, silvery below, dorsal, caudal and anal lobes black in adult, yellow and white in the young. Grows to a weight of 28 pounds.

Diagnosis.—Dorsal VI-I, 19 or 20; anal II-I, 17 or 18; depth 2.5 to 2.6; head 3 to 3.3; snout obliquely truncate; maxillary 2.6; gill-rakers 12 plus 2 rudiments.

Distribution.—Bermuda, West Indies, Florida. Locally common at Bermuda.

Family SERIOLIDÆ
Pilot-Fish
Naucrates ductor (Linnaeus)

Field Characters.—Small, rather elongate, compressed, cigar-shaped fishes with small mouths; spinous dorsal fin with 3 to 4 low disconnected spines; blue, young and old with 6 vertical dark cross-bands. Usually seen following sharks and vessels well off shore. Grows to about two feet.

Diagnosis.—Dorsal III or IV-I, 26 to 28; anal II-I, 15 or 16; depth 3.8 to 4; head 3.35 to 4.05; eye 3.9 to 5.85; snout 3.45 to 4.2; maxillary 2.8 to 3.15; gill-rakers 15 to 17 on the lower limb of the first arch; scales small, present on the cheeks.

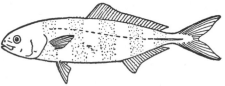

Distribution.—Cosmopolitan in all warm seas well off-shore. Near Bermuda it is seldom seen inshore.

Amber-Fish; Crevalle; Rudderfish
Seriola zonata (Mitchill)

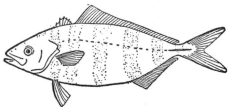

Field Characters.—Medium to large sized, fusiform, well-compressed small-scaled fish; anterior lobe of the dorsal and anal fins low, not falcate; general color bluish above, white below with a brassy tinge. A conspicuous yellow lateral band; vertical fins dark, the tip of the anal fin with a narrow white edge; dark vertical bands present on the body of the young, extending onto the fins. A band from eye to occiput. Grows to two feet and probably greater.

Diagnosis.—Dorsal VII-I, 36 to 39; anal II-I, 21; depth 3.2 to 3.3; head 3.25 to 3.5; eye 5; snout 2.6, long, conic; interorbital 2.12; maxillary 2.9; gill-rakers 16.

Distribution.—Bermuda, Atlantic coast from Cape Cod to Cape Hatteras.

Discussion.—The status of this species and its related forms is by no means certain.

Horse-Eyed Bonito
Seriola dumerili   (Risso)

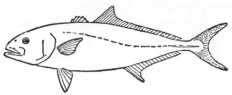

Field Characters.—Medium to large sized, somewhat fusiform fish; a golden band from eye to base of caudal, another band from eye to origin of soft dorsal fin; both of these bands may be absent or difficult to distinguish. Grows to a length of 5 or 6 feet.

Diagnosis.—Dorsal VI to VIII-I, 30 to 36; anal I or II-I, 19 or 20; depth 2.95 to 4.1; head 3.3 to 3.5; snout tapering, moderately pointed; maxillary 2.1 to 2.5; gill-rakers 11 to 14.

Distribution.—Bermuda, West Indies; Florida to Brazil, occasionally straying north to Massachusetts. Fairly common at Bermuda.

Bonito, Bermuda Salmon
Zonichthys falcatus   (Cuvier and Valenciennes)

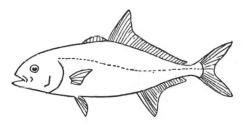

Field Characters.—Medium to large sized fish, body rather deep and compressed; head somewhat longer than deep, not conical; dorsal fin high, the anterior part of the fin falcate. Bluish silvery, darker above; vertical fins dark; a wide blackish bar which may fade out completely, from the mouth through eye to the nape; pelvic fins dark bluish, except the anterior edge which is very pale. Grows to 3 feet and possibly longer.

Diagnosis.—Dorsal VII-I, 29; anal II-I, 21; depth 3.4; head 3.8; eye 5.25; snout 2.75; interorbital space wide, convex; maxillary 3.5, reaching the front of the pupil; gill-rakers about 16 or 17; scales very small.

Distribution.—Bermuda, West Indies north to the Carolinas. Fairly common at Bermuda.

BLUEFISH

The Bluefish, well known both to anglers and to commercial fishermen and as a delicate table fish, is occasionally taken in Bermuda.

Family POMATOMIDÆ

Bluefish; Snap Mackerel; Skipjack

Pomatomus saltatrix   (Linnaeus)

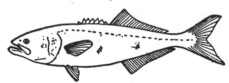

Field Characters.—Medium to large, stout-bodied, elongate, moderately compressed, fork-tailed, deep-headed, small-eyed fish. Jaws with a series of strong, compressed, unequal, widely set teeth; first dorsal fin with 8 short, weak spines; soft dorsal and anal fin equal in size, the former being slightly in advance of the latter. Deep bluish above, more or less tinged with green; silvery below. Second dorsal, caudal and pectoral fins are of the general body color, the latter with a black blotch at its base. Grows to about 3 feet in length. Thirty-inch fish will run to 10 or 12 pounds.

Diagnosis.—Dorsal VIII-I, 25; anal II-I, 26; depth 4; head 3.3; eye 8 in adult; maxillary 2.3; gill-rakers few and slender; scales about 95.

Distribution.—Widely but irregularly distributed in the warmer parts of the Atlantic and Indian Oceans. On the Atlantic coast it is found occasionally as far north as the Gulf of Maine. Uncommon in Bermuda.

CUBBY YEW

This is a fish of uncertain relationships, but the young have much the appearance of a small shark-sucker. One published record exists for Bermuda, made fifty-five years ago.

Family RACHYCENTRIDÆ

Cubby Yew; Cobia; Sergeantfish; Crab-Eater

Rachycentron canadus (Linnaeus)

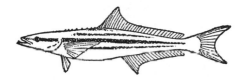

Field Characters.—Medium to large sized, slender fishes with large mouth, projecting lower jaw and moderately forked caudal fin. Spinous dorsal of 8 low, short stout spines, unconnected by membrane, and depressible in a groove. Soft dorsal long, anal similar but shorter. Dark brown on back, silvery white below; a dark lateral band, about width of eye, extending from snout to eye; below this a narrower band, fins mostly black. Grows to 5 feet in length, a specimen of this size weighing over 60 pounds.

Diagnosis.—Dorsal VIII or IX-I, 26; Anal I or II, 23 to 26; depth 5.5 to 8.1; head 4 to 5.3; eye 4.85 to 6.35; snout 2.45 to 2.85; maxillary short, 2.3 to 2.6; gill-rakers 7 to 9; lateral line wavy.

Distribution.—Known from warm seas. Rare in Bermuda.

CARDINAL-FISH

See Key, p. 289

If we watch carefully from a glass bottomed boat, or better still when in a diving helmet, grope around the ledges of a coral reef, small scarlet or coppery fish will occasionally be seen, usually in pairs. They are easily distinguishable from squirrelfish and are representatives of the present group. Five species are known from Bermuda.

The single Bermuda member of the family *Scombropidæ* has been found only in Bermuda and has never been seen alive. The three individuals which have been obtained were all taken from the stomachs of large fish caught off shore at a depth of forty fathoms.

Family APOGONIDÆ

Pigmented Cardinal-Fish

Apogon pigmentarius (Poey)

Field Characters.—Small, compressed, large-mouthed, large-scaled fishes with continuous lateral line; dorsal fins two, separated from each other, rather short and high. Coppery or bronze colored with small blackish spots on entire body, a dark blotch on the caudal peduncle; bases of soft dorsal and anal fins dark. Grows to about two inches.

Diagnosis.—Dorsal VI-I, 9; anal II, 8; depth 2.55 to 3.2; head 2.55 to 2.7; eye 2.5 to 3.2; snout 4.4 to 5.8; interorbital 3.75 to 4; maxillary 1.7 to 1.8; gill-rakers 14 to 16; scales 21 to 23.

Distribution.—Known from various islands in the West Indies, Bermuda and Panama. In Bermuda it can be found at night over certain grassy areas by dredging.

Two-Lined Cardinal-Fish
Apogon binotatus (Poey)

Field Characters.—Small, compressed, large-mouthed, large-scaled fishes with continuous lateral line; dorsal fins short and high, the spinous portion separated from the soft. Scarlet, with a narrow black band on the sides from the posterior dorsal rays to the anal fin; a second similar band across the caudal peduncle. Iris silvery. Grows to four inches.

Diagnosis.—Dorsal VI-I, 9; anal II, 8; depth 3; head 2.6; eye 2.9; interorbital 5; snout 4.6; maxillary 1.85; gill-rakers 15, including rudiments; scales 23.

Distribution.—Known from Bermuda, various islands in the West Indies, Panama and Venezuela. Rather uncommon in Bermuda.

Saddle-Tailed Cardinal-Fish
Apogon sellicauda Evermann and Marsh

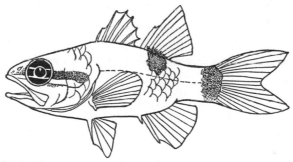

Field Characters.—Small, compressed, large-mouthed, large-scaled fish with continuous lateral line and with the dorsal fins short, rather high and separated. Scarlet with a wide black spot between the soft dorsal fin and the lateral line, and a black saddle on the caudal peduncle. A black spot on the opercle, continued forward as a band through the eye, bordered above and below by a white band; the black and white bands disappearing immediately at death. Grows to 3½ inches.

Diagnosis.—Dorsal VI-I, 9; anal II, 7 or 8; depth 3 to 3.1; head 2.6 to 2.9; eye 2.7; snout 4; maxillary 2; interorbital 4; gill-rakers 14 to 15, including rudiments, on the lower limb of the first gill-arch; scales 27 to 29.

Distribution.—Known from Bermuda, Tortugas and Porto Rico. Quite common locally.

Spotted Cardinal-Fish
Apogon maculatus (Poey)

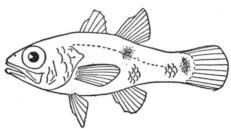

Field Characters.—Small, compressed, large-mouthed, large-scaled fishes with continuous lateral line; dorsal fins short, rather high and separated. Scarlet, with a black spot on the upper portion of the caudal peduncle, not produced into a saddle-like marking; a black dot on the sides between the soft dorsal fin and the lateral line. Grows to 4 or 5 inches.

Diagnosis.—Dorsal VI-I, 9; anal II, 8; depth 2.6 to 2.9; head 2.5 to 2.85; eye 2.7 to 3.26; interorbital 4 to 4.9; snout 4 to 5.8; maxillary 1.7 to 2; gill-rakers including rudiments 13 or 14; scales 23 to 25.

Distribution.—Bermuda, West Indies, Florida to Brazil, casually as far north as Massachusetts. Rare in Bermuda and probably confused with the preceding species.

Conchfish
Astrapogon stellatus (Cope)

Field Characters.—Small, compressed, deep-bodied, large-headed, large-scaled fishes with very long pelvic fins, the tips of which extend to the bases of the 4th to 7th anal rays; dorsal fins short, high, separated. Brown, coppery and bronze, body covered with small dark brown or black dots; three, not especially distinct, brown bands radiating backward from eye; vertical fins dusky, pelvic fins dark, often almost black. Grows to about two inches.

Diagnosis.—Dorsal VI-I, 9 to 10; anal II, 8; depth 2.45 to 3; head 2.4 to 2.66; eye 2.7 to 2.9; snout 3.7; interorbital 4.34; maxillary 1.8; gill-rakers 13; scales 24 to 27.

Distribution.—Bermuda, West Indies and Florida. Fairly common locally about the Islands.

Family SCOMBROPIDÆ
Black-Finned Scombrops
Parasphyrænops atrimanus Bean

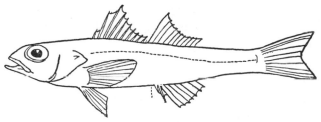

Field Characters.—Small, elongate, large-eyed, small-scaled fish; dorsal fin not quite divided into two separated fins; operculum with two flat, feeble spines, the upper larger; teeth in jaws uniserial, feeble, no canines; vomer and palate with a few teeth; preopercle serrate, serrations slightly stronger at the angle. Color in life unknown. The preserved type specimen is brownish, with a large black blotch on base of the spinous dorsal extending upward a distance about equal to the long diameter of the eye; a jet black spot behind base of pectoral. Grows to 4 inches.

Diagnosis.—Dorsal IX, 10, deeply notched, 3rd spine high, first and last two short; anal III, 7; pelvics under base of pectorals; depth 5; head 3.25; eye 3.5; maxillary short, little expanded, slipping under the edge of the pre-orbital and extending to below the middle of the eye; lower jaw slightly projecting; gill-rakers 20 to 22, long slender; scales ctenoid, about 70.

Distribution.—Known only from Bermuda, from specimens taken from the stomachs of other fishes captured in 250 feet of water.

ROCKFISH
See Key, p. 290

The fish included under this title are variously known as Hinds, Jewfish, Groupers, Soapfish and Sea-bass. They form the largest related group of Bermuda fish in point of numbers, twenty-eight having been recorded, and the most important from the fishermen's point of view in abundance, size and as first-rate food fish.

The name Rockfish is appropriate and the usual haunt of these fish is about the outer reefs, well down below the surface.

In size they vary from the tiny, two-inch Gramma or Blue and Gold Basslet to the great Jewfish with a record of eight feet and seven hundred pounds. In shape they are remarkably alike, there being a sort of Grouper or Sea-bass type of outline which all the species approximate. There is not only great diversity of color, but individual color change is very marked, spots, bands and flat ground colors appearing and disappearing with the changing emotions of the fish. A number of extreme color phases have received varietal and form names, but in this publication only specific names have been utilized.

Family EPINEPHELIDÆ

Graysby

Petrometopon cruentatus (Lacepede)

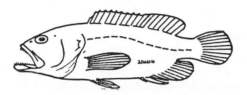

Field Characters.—Small, compressed sea-bass with nine dorsal spines and rounded soft dorsal, anal and caudal fins. Variable in color, brownish red or very pale with small dark round spots on sides and head; a jet black spot on the back just below the base of the first soft dorsal rays; sometimes with several dark spots on back just below the base of the dorsal; spots on the back may be white instead of black. Grows to about a foot.

Diagnosis.—Dorsal IX, 14; anal III, 8; depth 2.55 to 3.1; head 2.5 to 2.9; eye 5; snout 3.2 to 4.25; maxillary 1.75 to 2; gill-rakers 9 to 11 plus rudiments; scales 81 to 95; pores in lateral line 50 to 55.

Distribution.—Bermuda, Florida and West Indies to Brazil. A common Bermuda species.

Coney

Cephalopholis fulvus (Linnaeus)

Field Characters.—Small, elongate, moderately compressed sea-bass with nine dorsal spines; lower jaw strongly projecting; caudal fin gently rounded. Color variable, yellow, red, brown or cream being the ground color, the sides, head and back covered with small black, blue or white

spots. Two black spots on the upper part of the caudal peduncle and two black spots on the tip of the lower jaw.
Grows to about a foot.

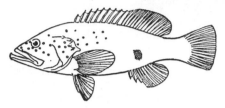

Diagnosis.—Dorsal IX, 15; anal III, 9 (rarely 8) ; depth
2.6 to 3; head 2.65 to 3; eye 3.8 to 5.3; snout 3.75 to 4.4;
maxillary 1.8 to 1.95; gill-rakers 12 to 14; scales 89 to
110.

Distribution.—Bermuda, West Indies, Florida to Brazil.
A common species at Bermuda ranging from close in-shore
down to at least 500 feet.

Black Grouper
Epinephelus mystacinus   (Poey)

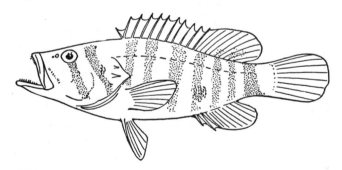

Field Characters.—Medium to large sized, somewhat
compressed sea-bass, with posterior nostril much larger than
the anterior. Dull brownish with a purplish tinge beneath;
eight to nine dark vertical bands, the anterior ones wider
than the posterior, with the exception that the band on the
caudal peduncle is widest of all. A dark mustache across

the maxillary. Grows to about three feet; a 32-inch fish weighed 33 pounds.

Diagnosis.—Dorsal XI, 15; anal III, 9; depth 2.66 to 2.9; head 2.4 to 2.7; eye 4.5 to 6.6; interorbital 4.4 to 6; maxillary 1.8 to 2.25; gill-rakers 15 including rudiments; scales 98 to 120.

Distribution.—Bermuda, West Indies to Brazil. This species is mainly taken in water from 80 to 110 fathoms deep.

Red Grouper

Epinephelus morio (Cuvier and Valenciennes)

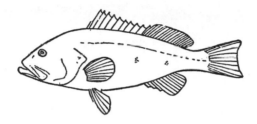

Field Characters.—Large, somewhat compressed sea-bass, with second dorsal spine almost as long as the third; caudal fin with its posterior margin straight or slightly concave. Color brownish, sometimes marbled or without distinct markings, except for well-defined dark dots about the eye; sides with more or less distinct paler blotches along the back; an indistinct black saddle-like blotch on the caudal peduncle; pectoral fins pale, the other fins colored like the body, all narrowly edged with white, the vertical fins with a submarginal dark band. Grows to three feet.

Diagnosis.—Dorsal XI, 16 or 17; anal III, 8; depth 2.6 to 2.8; head 2.5 to 2.75; eye 3.8 to 4.5; interorbital 7.5; snout 3.4 to 4; maxillary 1.95 to 2.1; gill-rakers 13 to 18; scales 100 to 140.

Distribution.—Bermuda, West Indies, Massachusetts south to Brazil. A fairly common species in the waters of Bermuda.

Rock Hind
Epinephelus adscensionis (Osbeck)

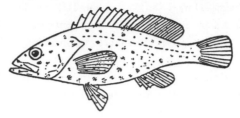

Field Characters.—Medium sized, robust sea-bass with strongly projecting lower jaw; maxillary without scales; body and head covered with red or orange spots; vertical fins without dark edges, the bases spotted like the body; body with large pale spots besides the red or orange spots; young with large black blotches at base of dorsal fin. Grows to eighteen inches.

Diagnosis.—Dorsal XI, 17; anal III, 7 or 8; depth 3; head 2.4 to 2.65; eye 4.8 to 6; snout 3.95; maxillary 1.95 to 2.3; gill-rakers short, 15 to 18 on the lower limb of the first arch; scales 90 to 110; 55 to 60 pores in lateral line.

Distribution.—Bermuda, West Indies, Florida to Brazil. An uncommon fish at Bermuda.

Red Hind; Hind
Epinephelus guttatus (Linnaeus)

Field Characters.—Small to medium sized compressed sea-bass. Variable in color but usually reddish; the entire body covered with red spots, these spots darker above, sometimes with obscure olive bands running upward and backward on the sides. Soft dorsal, anal and caudal fins broadly

RED HIND
Epinephelus guttatus

HAMLET
Epinephelus striatus

SPOTTED JEWFISH
Promicrops itaiara

edged with black or blue-black. Usually less than a foot in length, but growing to eighteen inches.

Diagnosis.—Dorsal XI, 16; anal III, 8; depth 3.33; head 2.5; eye 4.3; snout 4.3; maxillary 2.33; gill-rakers slender, 15 to 17 more or less developed on lower limb of the first gill-arch; scales 100 to 120.

Distribution.—Bermuda, West Indies, North Carolina to Brazil. A common Bermuda species.

Hamlet; Nassau Grouper
Epinephelus striatus (Bloch)

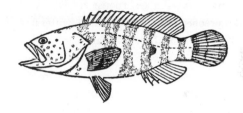

Field Characters.—Large compressed sea-bass with rays of soft dorsal somewhat longer than spines and with gently rounded posterior margin of tail. Variable in color, browns, grays or greens, either plain or with irregular vertical dark bands, a broad dark band from snout through eye to opercle and another from snout to dorsal fin, all of which may disappear. Small deep brown or black points about and on the eye; a square black blotch on the upper surface of the caudal peduncle. Grows to about 3 to 4 feet.

Diagnosis.—Dorsal XI or XII, 16 or 17; anal III, 8; depth 2.7 to 2.9; head 2.6 to 2.8; eye 3.8 to 5; snout 3.45 to 4.5; maxillary 2 to 2.2; gill-rakers short, 15 or 16 developed on the lower limb of the first gill-arch; scales 100 to 115.

Distribution.—Bermuda, West Indies, North Carolina to Brazil. One of the commonest Bermuda fish.

John Paw; Speckled Hind

Epinephelus drummond-hayi Goode and Bean

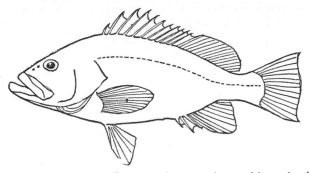

Field Characters.—Large, robust sea-bass with projecting lower jaw; preopercle evenly serrate, without a sharp angle; caudal truncate or slightly emarginate, the angles acute; light or dark umber brown, densely spotted with roundish or somewhat star-shaped white spots, except upon the lips and under part of the body; fins covered with similar spots and not dark edged. Lower side of head flushed with red and unspotted; caudal fin more densely spotted than body, the terminal spots of a fine lavender; pectoral fins with a subterminal band of orange. Grows to a weight of 52 pounds.

Diagnosis.—Dorsal XI, 16; anal III, 9; depth 2.6; head 2.6; eye 6 to 8; interorbital space slightly greater than eye; maxillary not quite reaching center of eye; scales 125; gill-rakers 16 plus 1 or 2 rudiments.

Distribution.—Bermuda; Gulf of Mexico to the Carolinas. Uncommon at Bermuda but originally described from this island.

Mutton Hamlet

Dermatolepis inermis (Cuvier and Valenciennes)

Field Characters.—Small to medium sized, deep-bodied sea-bass with a long soft dorsal fin and small embedded scales; teeth in narrow bands, small; no canines in lower jaw, one canine on each side in upper jaw only slightly larger than the other teeth. Color brownish, mottled with darker; head, body and fins covered with roundish whitish blotches, irregular in form and size, some of them larger than the eye, the spots most numerous and distinct on the tail and lower part of the head; several spots behind the eye, confluent into a pale stripe from eye toward spinous dorsal; fins all blackish, the pale spots generally less distinct than on the body; pectoral olivaceous with small, rather indistinct black spots. Grows to 20 inches.

Diagnosis.—Dorsal XI, 19; anal III, 9; depth 2.5; head 2.6; eye 5.75; interorbital 8; snout 3.66; maxillary 2.5; gill-rakers slender, about 14 in number; scales 112 to 125; about 70 pores in the lateral line.

Distribution.—Bermuda and West Indies. Rare at Bermuda.

Black Jew-Fish
Garrupa nigrita (Holbrook)

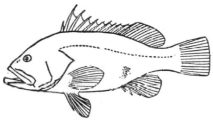

Field Characters.—Very large, robust, broad-headed, small-eyed sea-bass; interorbital area notably wider than the eye; maxillary scaly. Brown or bluish-black, uniform or with a few light spots, the lower parts scarcely paler. Grows to a length of 6 feet.

Diagnosis.—Dorsal X or XI, 14 or 15; anal III, 9; depth 2.2 to 3; head 2.5; eye 6 to 8; interorbital 4 to 6; maxillary 2; gill-rakers very short and thick, 12 to 14 in number; scales 86 to 110.

Distribution.—Bermuda, West Indies, South Carolina to Brazil. Rare at Bermuda, a 400-pound specimen having been recorded.

Spotted Jew-Fish
Promicrops itaiara (Lichtenstein)

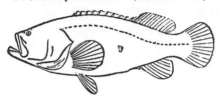

Field Characters.—Very large sea-bass with broad cranium, which is narrower in the young, depressed between the eyes. Scales of the lateral line with 4 to 6 strong radiating ridges. Variable, uniform black or brown to creamy white, sometimes ·with a greenish shade, 4 or 5 dark, broken cross bands on the sides; head, body and fins with many black spots. Grows to 8 feet and a weight of 693 pounds.

Diagnosis.—Dorsal XI, 15 or 16; anal III, 8; depth 2.85 to 3.4; head 2.4 to 3; eye 3.4 to 8.2; snout 3.7 to 5; maxillary 1.85 to 2.2; interorbital space equal to length of snout; gill-rakers short and thick, 9 or 10 developed; scales 95 to 135.

Distribution.—Bermuda, West Indies. Both coasts of tropical America, north in the Atlantic to Florida. Rare in Bermuda.

Red Nigger Hamlet; Mutton Hamlet
Alphestes afer (Bloch)

Field Characters.—Medium sized, compressed, large-eyed sea-bass with a small forward and downward projecting spine on the lower limb of the preopercle. Variable in color, usually brownish with an irregular marbling of vinaceous pink, heavily mottled with darker; many dull yellow and small turquoise spots on the body, especially on the opercles and fins. Grows to a little over a foot in length.

Diagnosis.—Dorsal XI, 17 to 19; anal III, 9; depth 2.66; head 2.57; eye 4.5; interorbital 6; snout shorter ·than eye;

maxillary 2.4; gill-rakers 14 to 16 below the angle of the first arch; scales 75 to 80; 50 to 60 pores in the lateral line.

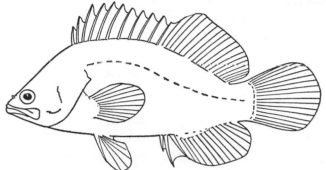

Distribution.—Bermuda, West Indies to Brazil. Fairly common in Bermuda.

Velvet Rockfish; Small-Scaled Rockfish
Trisotropis microlepis Goode and Bean

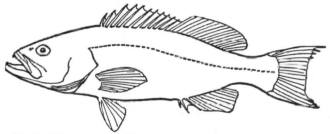

Field Characters.—Medium to large sized, rather elongate, small-scaled, considerably compressed sea-bass. Color variable, plain purplish black to gray; specimens from deeper water are plain brownish gray, paler below, without distinct rivulations or distinct spots, but with faint traces of darker spotting; dorsal dark olive, the tip of the soft part blue black, its edge narrowly white; anal deep indigo blue, olive at base, its edge white; pectoral olive, dusky toward tip, the first ray tipped with white. Specimens from shallow water among grass are greenish olive, mottled with darker

green and variously clouded, but without spots or rivulations; mustache black; fins colored as above, distinctly
bluish. Grows to a length of 3 feet and a weight of 50
pounds.

Diagnosis.—Dorsal XI, 16 to 19; anal III, 11; depth 3.5;
head 2.62; eye 6.5; maxillary 2 to 2.2; gill-rakers 12; scales
140 to 150.

Distribution.—Bermuda, South Atlantic and Gulf coasts
north to North Carolina. Uncommon at Bermuda.

Harlequin Rockfish
Trisotropis dimidiatus   (Poey)

Field Characters.—Small to medium sized sea-bass with
projecting lower jaw and equal sized nostrils placed some
distance apart from each other. Color variable, sometimes
dark brown or blackish above, sharply demarcated from the
white undersurfaces, with white top of head, black upper
and lower margin of caudal fin, yellow spinous dorsal and
with one or two black spots on the caudal peduncle; sometimes changing to a gray fish with black and brown reticulations on the sides, especially prominent on the upper part
of the body, tips of spinous dorsal yellow. The largest
specimens seen by us measured about 11 inches.

Diagnosis.—Dorsal XI, 16 to 17; anal III, 11; depth 3
to 3.5; head 2.7 to 3.1; eye 4.3 to 5.3; snout 3.4 to 4; maxillary 1.9 to 2.2; scales 110 to 135; gill-rakers 14 to 15 plus
a few rudiments.

Distribution.—Bermuda; Cuba. An uncommon Bermuda
fish.

Yellow-Finned Grouper; Red Rockfish; Monkey Rockfish
Trisotropis venenosus (Linnaeus)

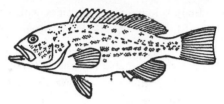

Field Characters.—Medium sized, rather strongly compressed sea-bass. Variable in color, olive green to grayish, and with a red form that is bright scarlet above, becoming gray on the lower sides and head. Sides reticulated, the enclosed darker portions red or black, having their axes horizontal. Spots on the lower portion of the body reddish salmon, this color also being found on the upper and lower lobe of the caudal fin. Tips of pectoral fins yellow or orange. Vertical fins usually with a dark edge, bordered distally with a narrow white line. Tips of membranes of spinous dorsal yellow. Grows to about three feet.

Diagnosis.—Dorsal XI, 16; anal III, 12; depth 3; head 2.6 to 2.9; eye 7; interorbital 5 to 5.7; snout 3.5; maxillary 2; gill-rakers 11; scales 120 to 125.

Distribution.—Bermuda, West Indies north to the Florida Keys, occasionally north as far as North Carolina. Fairly common.

Rockfish; Runner or Springer
Trisotropis bonaci (Poey)

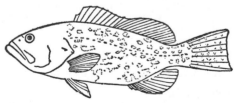

Field Characters.—Large, heavy-bodied sea-bass, tail truncate or slightly lunate, the tips sometimes produced;

colour dark olive or brownish or black, occasionally with a tinge of bluish purple fading to pale grey, the body with quadrate blotches on the sides between which are greyish reticulations. Body below and on the sides with small round bronze or yellowish spots. Vertical fins often with a black or dark blue outer border which is surmounted by a narrow white line, this especially notable in light coloured fish. Pectoral fins never with yellow tips. Grows to 4 feet in length and a weight of 100 pounds.

Diagnosis.—Dorsal XI, 16 to 18; anal III, 11 or 12; depth 3.2 to 3.4; head 2.7 to 3.2; eye 4.2 to 12; interorbital 4.8 to 6.2; snout 2.8 to 3.3; maxillary 1.9 to 2.3; gill-rakers 9 to 12, the last few usually rudimentary; scales 104-115.

Distribution.—Bermuda, West Indies, Florida to Brazil, occasionally north to Woods Hole. A common Bermuda fish.

Salmon Rockfish; Salmon; Scamp
Mycteroperca falcata   (Poey)

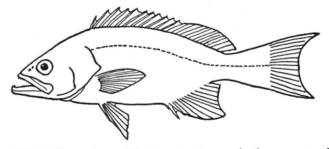

Field Characters.—Medium to large sized, compressed, large-mouthed sea-bass; posterior nostril much larger than anterior and placed close to it. Brown above, sides somewhat greyish brown, sometimes covered with darker spots; vertical fins dusky, the outer portions bluish black; pelvic and pectoral fins with a narrow outer band of white. Grows to two or three feet.

Diagnosis.—Dorsal XI, 16 to 18; anal III, 11; depth 2.8 to 3.5; head 2.8 to 3; eye 5 to 6.1; snout 3.25; interorbital

5 to 5.2; maxillary 1.9 to 2.2; gill-rakers 16 to 20, the last few rudimentary; scales 130 to 140.

Distribution.—Bermuda, West Indies. Not uncommon at Bermuda.

Princess Rockfish
Mycteroperca bowersi Evermann and Marsh

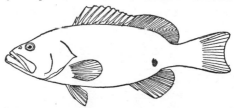

Field Characters.—Medium to large, rather long, compressed sea-bass with lower jaw projecting strongly into the profile. Body colour changeable, often dark reddish brown covered with many small, round, brown or blood-red spots between which are often greyish reticulations, these spots also present on the head, lower jaw and anal fin; soft dorsal mottled with white and black, bordered with a very narrow white edge, inside of which is a broad black band; tip of caudal narrowly white, inside of which is a broad blackish band, rest of fin mottled with white and black; anal similar to soft dorsal, but with more red spots; outer end of pectoral fin yellow. Grows to two and a half feet.

Diagnosis.—Dorsal XI, 16; anal III, 11; depth 3 to 3.4; head 2.4 to 2.9; eye 6.6 to 7.5; interorbital 4.6 to 5.2; snout 3.7 to 3.9; maxillary 2.1; gill-rakers 10 to 12 plus one or two rudiments; scales 120 to 140.

Distribution.—Bermuda, West Indies, Florida. Uncommon at Bermuda.

Gag; Rag-Tailed Rockfish
Mycteroperca tigris (Cuvier and Valenciennes)

Field Characters.—Medium-sized sea-bass, the adults with some of the dorsal, anal and caudal rays continued beyond the membranes of the fins, forming "tags." Anal fin with angular margins. Variable, but usually brownish or greenish-white with bluish-white rather regular reticulations over the entire body, especially marked on the trunk, some of these reticulations coalescing to form oblique, upward-projecting pale bars on the upper sides. Tips of pectoral fins yellow or orange. Grows to two and a half feet.

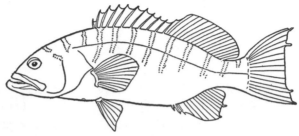

Diagnosis.—Dorsal XI, 16 or 17; anal III, 10 to 12; depth 3 to 3.6; head 2.7 to 3.1; eye 6.7 to 9; interorbital 4.8 to 6; snout 3.2 to 3.8; maxillary 1.8 to 2.1; gill-rakers 5 to 7 developed in addition to 1 to 3 rudiments; scales 125 to 135, pores in lateral line 80 to 85.

Distribution.—Bermuda and West Indies, rarely reaching the Florida Keys. At Bermuda it is quite a common fish on the outer reefs and often taken by trolling.

Two-Spined Soapfish
Rypticus bistrispinus   (Mitchill)

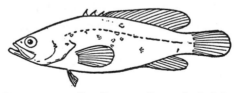

Field Characters.—Small to medium sized fishes without spines in the anal fin and with only two spines in the dorsal; the dorsal and anal fins more or less included in the skin of the body, only the tips of the rays free; scales small, embedded; body heavily covered with mucus which produces soap-like suds when the fish thrashes about; colour dusky olive, sometimes paler, sides with a few pale spots. Grows to a little longer than a foot.

Diagnosis.—Dorsal II, 25 or 26; anal 14 or 15; depth 2.9 to 3.6; head 3 to 3.2; eye 5.5 to 7; snout longer than eye in adult; maxillary 2.1 to 2.3; gill-rakers short and thick, 8 to 10; three strong preopercular spines, nearly uniform in size, the middle one sometimes slightly larger than the others; three flat opercular spines.

Distribution.—Bermuda, West Indies, north to South Carolina, accidentally reaching Rhode Island. Common locally about the islands.

Three-Spined Soapfish

Rypticus saponaceus (Bloch and Schneider)

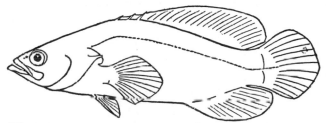

Field Characters.—Small to medium sized fishes without spines in the anal fin and with three short spines in the dorsal; dorsal and anal fins more or less embedded in the skin of the body, only the tips of the rays free; two spines on the preopercle. Body heavily covered with mucus, which produces soap-like suds. Color dusky brown, fins with blackish, and usually with a whitish edge; sides generally with pale spots. Grows to about a foot.

Diagnosis.—Dorsal III, 21 to 25; anal 15 to 17; depth 2.6 to 3.25; head 3 to 3.3; eye 4.5 to 5; snout 5.25; maxillary 2 to 2.12; about 8 developed gill-rakers; 85 to 90 pores in the lateral line.

Distribution.—Bermuda, West Indies, Florida to Brazil. West Africa. Rare in Bermuda.

Family SERRANIDÆ
Barber; Creole-Fish
Paranthias furcifer   (Cuvier and Valenciennes)

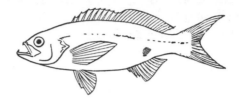

Field Characters.—Small, short-headed, short-snouted sea-bass with long, deeply-forked tail and low dorsal fin with 19 or 20 soft rays. Colour bright or dark red or salmon colour, under surfaces of head and body pale pinkish. Usually 3 small violet spots, one on side of back and one or two on the sides of the tail; centre of dorsal fin with a blackish or dark greenish-yellow streak; centre of soft dorsal yellowish and dusky. Grows to about a foot.

Diagnosis.—Dorsal IX, 19 or 20; anal III, 10; depth 2.75 to 2.9; head 3.33 to 3.6; eye 3.85 to 4.2; snout 3.85 to 4.8; maxillary 2.25 to 2.4; gill-rakers 24 to 26 on the lower limb of the first gill-arch; scales 105 to 118.

Distribution.—Bermuda, West Indies to Brazil, and on the Pacific coast from Cape San Lucas to the Galapagos Islands and Peru. Fairly common off-shore at Bermuda on the deeper reefs.

Butter Hamlet
Hypoplectrus unicolor   (Walbaum)

Field Characters.—Small, rather deep, considerably compressed sea-bass with short tapering head and slightly emarginate caudal fin. Colour and pattern highly variable, usually yellowish or greenish, with six vertical dark bands on the side, the one below the spinous dorsal widest; head and body with lavender and blue lines and spots, a conspicuous question-mark-like line around the eye and down

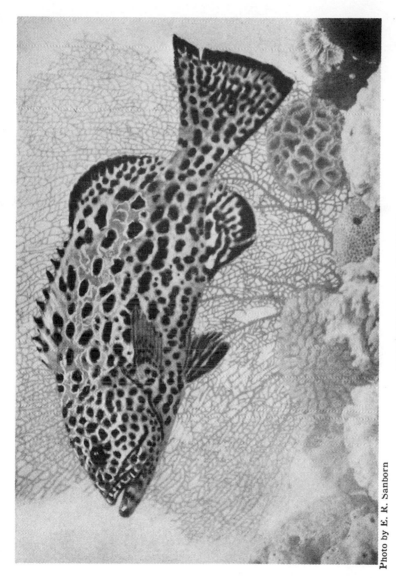

YELLOW-FINNED GROUPER
Trisotropis venenosus

Photo by E. R. Sanborn

the cheek. Other colour forms may be dark blue or purple or bright lemon and yellow, usually with some of the markings mentioned above or with a conspicuous inky-black spot or spots on the head or the caudal peduncle. Grows to about a foot. Specimens of over four inches are unusual.

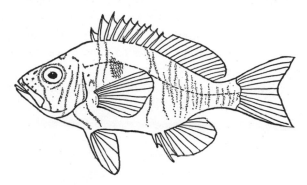

Diagnosis.—Dorsal X, 14 or 15; anal III, 7 or 8; depth 2.5 to 2.6; head 2.5 to 3; eye 3.4 to 4; interorbital 5.75; maxillary 2.66; snout 3.2; gill-rakers 12 to 13; scales 76 to 92; lateral line pores 52 to 60.

Distribution.—Bermuda, Florida and West Indies. Somewhat uncommon in Bermuda.

Aguavina
Diplectrum radiale (Quoy and Gaimard)

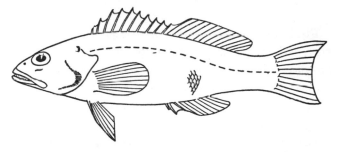

Field Characters.—Small, elongate, little compressed, large eyed sea-bass; brown above, yellowish below, sides salmon-colour; 2 dark longitudinal bands along the sides and a series of vertical faint bands on the sides, these bands wider than the interspaces; soft dorsal with blue spots encircled with darker blue rings; caudal barred with similar spots. Grows to 5 inches.

Diagnosis.—Dorsal X, 11 or 12; anal III, 7; depth 3.8 to 4.3; head 2.5 to 3.1; eye 3.1 to 3.75; snout 3.6 to 4.4; maxillary 2 to 2.25; interorbital 4.6; gill-rakers slender, 10 to 13 plus a few rudiments; scales 60 to 70 above the lateral line; 48 to 55 pores.

Distribution.—Known from Bermuda, West Indies to Brazil. Rare in Bermuda.

Tattler
Prionodes phœbe (Poey)

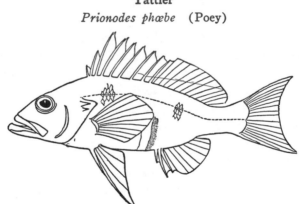

Field Characters.—Small, moderately compressed sea-bass; body rather heavy anteriorly with large eyes. Light brownish with lighter blotches and faint dusky bars; a very conspicuous sharply-defined, vertical white bar extending upward on each side from just before the vent. Grows to about 8 inches.

Diagnosis.—Dorsal X, 12; anal III, 7; depth 3.25; head 2.8; eye 3.3 to 4; interorbital 6; snout 2.8 to 3.3; maxillary 2; gill-rakers 12 to 13; scales 52-53.

Distribution.—Bermuda, West Indies and Florida. Common in Bermuda offshore in 50 to 80 fathoms.

Harlequin Serranid
Prionodes tigrinus   (Bloch)

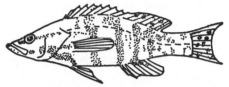

Field Characters.—Small, compressed sea-basses with pointed head and lunate caudal fin. Brownish or yellowish to greyish white, yellower beneath. A wide yellow band from maxillary and mandible under the eye to end of operculum, continued more or less in the coloration of the sides to the caudal fin, this band occasionally very dim. Body and vertical fins conspicuously barred, spotted and marked with black. Grows to about 4 inches.

Diagnosis.—Dorsal X, 11 or 12; anal III, 7; depth 3.6; head 2.8; eye 4; maxillary 2.5; gill-rakers 6 to 8, very short; scales about 68 to 70.

Distribution.—Bermuda, West Indies. An uncommon fish, found on the inner reefs of Bermuda.

Small-Scaled Anthias
Anthias tenuis   Nichols

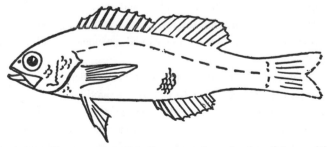

Field Characters.—Small, somewhat slender fishes with forked tail with bluntly rounded tips. Lower jaw projecting, interorbital slightly convex. Opercle with two weak flat spines at its angle, the upper the longer. Snout naked, scales extending forwards to above centre of eye. Colour in life unknown, most likely rosy. Grows to 2½ inches.

Diagnosis.—Dorsal X, 15; anal III, 9; depth 3.4; head 3.6; eye 3.3; interorbital 3.6; snout 4.7; maxillary 2; gill-rakers 26; scales 54.

Distribution.—Known only from two specimens from Bermuda, the type and a specimen taken by us from the stomach of a Hind.

Bermuda Anthias
Anthias louisi Bean

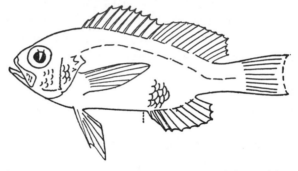

Field Characters.—Small, compressed fishes with crescentic caudal fin, none of the rays produced; maxillary with scales; pelvic fins long; gill-rakers long; pink above, shading into yellow on the sides and pearly white below. Bright golden around the eye and a similar patch of the same colour in front of the caudal peduncle. Tail golden yellow.

Diagnosis.—Dorsal X, 15; anal III, 7; depth 2.6 to 2.8; head 2.9 to 3; snout 5.3 to 6; eye 3; maxillary 2.1, reaches to below middle of eye; gill-rakers 27 to 29, the longest ⅔ of the eye; scales 35 or 36; 33 lateral line pores.

Distribution.—Known only from Bermuda, from the type and a single questionable specimen taken by us.

Blue and Gold Fairy Basslet
Gramma hemichrysos Mowbray

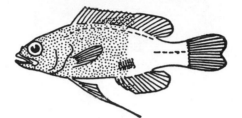

Field Characters.—Very small, compressed, sea-bass-like fish, with lateral line running parallel to the back and ending under the posterior dorsal rays, beginning again lower down on the caudal peduncle. Royal purple on the anterior half of the body, posterior half bright lemon yellow; pectorals plain with a yellowish tinge. Three stripes of greenish yellow behind the eyes, the lower extending on the opercle; premaxillary with a spot of the same colour. A black blotch on the anterior dorsal spines. Grows to about 2 inches.

Diagnosis.—Dorsal XII, 9 or 10; anal III, 9 or 10; depth 3.5; head 3.5; eye about 3.7; interorbital 3.3; gill-rakers long, slender, close together; scales 48 to 50.

Distribution.—Bermuda and West Indies. Rare in Bermuda but occasionally seen on the outer reefs. Also seen from the Bathysphere a mile off-shore.

Discussion.—This species can easily be confused with young Spanish Hogfish (*Bodianus rufus*) which it resembles closely in colour.

BIG-EYES; PEMPHERIDS
See Key, p. 294

The Big-eyes are medium sized scarlet fish uncommonly taken at Bermuda on the outer reefs.

The Pempherids are equally rare, but a school of several thousand, all barely an inch long, transparent, and floating in an open grotto six fathoms down near Gurnet's Rock, Nonsuch, were observed many times.

Family PRIACANTHIDÆ

Big-Eye

Priacanthus cruentatus   (Lacepede)

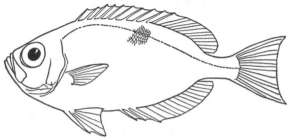

Field Characters.—Medium sized, compressed, small-scaled fish with extremely large eyes; pelvic fins moderate; margin of opercle with two indentations, one above and behind the tip of the preopercular spine, and another larger U-shaped one under tip of preopercular spine; gill-rakers 16 to 18; colour mostly brilliant red.   Grows to a foot in length.

Diagnosis.—Dorsal X, 12 or 13; anal III, 13 or 14; depth 2.4 to 2.55; head 3.1 to 3.2; eye 2 to 2.4; snout 3.3 to 3.5; maxillary 1.8 to 1.9; gill-rakers 16 to 18; scales 88 to 90.

Distribution.—Known from Bermuda, West Indies, to St. Helena and the Canaries.   Rare in Bermuda.

Blear-Eye; Glass-Eye

Priacanthus arenatus   Cuvier and Valenciennes

Field Characters.—Small to medium sized, considerably compressed fish with extremely large eyes; scales rather small, lateral line abruptly curved upward anteriorly; pelvic fins long; a single small indentation on the opercle just above the flat opercular spine; gill-rakers slender, 22 or 23 on the lower limb of the first arch.   Usually bright red, occasionally fading to pinkish and somewhat mottled. Grows to 15 inches.

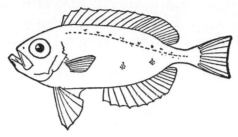

Diagnosis.—Dorsal X, 14, rarely 13; anal III, 15, rarely 16; depth 2.5 to 2.8; head 3.2 to 3.6; eye 2.15 to 2.4; snout 3.45 to 3.6; maxillary 1.8; gill-rakers 22 or 23 on the lower limb of the first arch; scales 88 to 94.

Distribution.—Bermuda, West Indies, extending north in the Gulf Stream to Rhode Island and southward to Brazil. Common locally in Bermuda, especially on the northern reefs.

Short Big-Eye
Pseudopriacanthus altus (Gill)

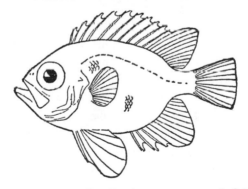

Field Characters.—Small, deep, compressed fishes with large eyes and scaly maxillary and large pelvic fins; scales large, 37 to 47. Colour red, dorsal fin red, the spinous part edged with yellow, a few blackish dots on the soft rays; caudal fin pale with blackish reticulations; anal fin red, edged with black; pelvics red at base, the rest of fins dusky or black; pectorals plain red.

Diagnosis.—Dorsal X, 11; anal III, 9 to 11; depth 1.7; head 2.45; eye 2.1; snout 3.85; interorbital 5.1; maxillary 1.85; gill-rakers slender, about 20 on the lower limb of the first gill-arch.

Distribution.—Bermuda, West Indies north to Massachusetts. Rare in Bermuda.

Family PEMPHERIDÆ
Glassy Pempherids
Pempheris mulleri Poey

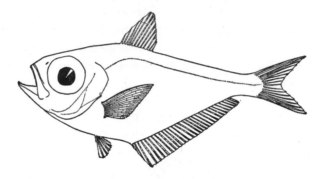

Field Characters.—Small fishes, the body deepest anteriorly, tapering posteriorly; mouth large, oblique; eye fairly large; dorsal fin very short, situated near the middle of the body on its tapering portion; anal fin very long. Colour of 1 inch fish almost transparent, with heavily pigmented red and black vertebræ. Opercles and organs of the body cavity glittering iridescent silver with copper and blue reflections. Iris powdered densely with golden bronze. Lips lemon yellow, a deep stain over the top of the head. Grows to five inches.

Diagnosis.—Dorsal V, 9; anal III, 32 to 34; depth 2.4 to 2.6; head 2.8 to 3.2; eye 2.1 to 2.3; snout 3.7 to 4.1; maxillary 1.56 to 1.75.

Distribution.—Bermuda, Tortugas, West Indies to Brazil. Locally common in Bermuda.

TRIPLE-TAILS

These fish which elsewhere grow to a considerable size and are considered a good food fish, seem not to have established themselves in Bermuda, but a few individuals of small size may, now and then, be found among the Sargassum weed floating past.

Family LOBOTIDÆ
Triple-Tail; Flasher
Lobotes surinamensis   (Bloch)

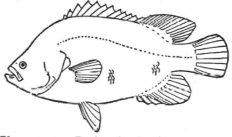

Field Characters.—Rather large, deep, compressed, bass-like fishes with small, rough scales, projecting lower jaw and serrate preopercle; head concave over eye; eye placed far forward in head. Dark brown to pale brown or greenish or creamy yellow, with more or less silvery, at least below the lateral line; an indistinct dark band from eye to occiput; two narrower bands or lines extending backward for a short distance from the interorbital space, another band from lower margin of eye to angle of preopercle; all of the fins except the dorsal, darker than the body, their bases the same colour as the rest of the body. Smaller specimens have the vertical fins tipped with white and have five black spots at the base of the soft dorsal, the 2nd and 4th much paler than the others. A black spot at the base of the posterior rays of the anal fin. Grows to three feeet in length.

Diagnosis.—Dorsal XI, I, 15 or 16; anal III, 11 or 12; depth 1.8 to 2; head 2.6 to 3; eye 4 to 6; snout 4.1 to 5; maxillary 2.6 to 3; gill-rakers 11 plus about 4 rudiments; scales 45 to 53.

Distribution.—Bermuda, West Indies, Atlantic coast from Massachusetts to Guiana, Mediterranean, Japan. Young specimens are fairly common in Sargassum weed.

SNAPPERS
See Key, p. 295

Second in importance and abundance to Rockfish, and somewhat similar in general appearance, are the Snappers, mostly dull in colour although varied with spots and bands, and some of the species from deep waters are red. They put up sufficient fight to be classed as game-fish. Eleven forms have been recorded from Bermuda.

Family LUTIANIDÆ
Blear-Eyed Snapper; Night Snapper
Etelis oculatus   (Cuvier and Valenciennes)

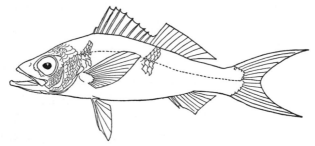

Field Characters.—Medium to large sized, elongate slim-tailed snappers with large eyes, and with the space between the eyes flat or slightly concave; dorsal fins with the posterior spines very short, the anterior rays much longer than the posterior spines. Brilliant rose-red; base of scales deeper, sides and belly abruptly paler, rosy; mouth reddish within; fins all rosy, spinous dorsal and caudal bright red, the other fins paler. Grows to 2 or 3 feet.

Diagnosis.—Dorsal X, 11; anal III, 8; depth 3.5; head 3.3 to 3.4; eye 3; interorbital 3.66 to 4; snout 3 to 3.8; maxillary 2.16; gill-rakers 16 including rudiments; scales 51 to 54.

Distribution.—Warm seas, Bermuda, West Indies to Madeira. Usually taken in deep water off-shore, uncommon.

Chub-Head Snapper; Night Snapper
Rhomboplites aurorubens (Cuvier and Valenciennes)

Field Characters.—Medium sized snappers with 12 or rarely 13 spines in the dorsal fin; gill rakers long and slender, numerous; pterygoid teeth present. Colour vermilion, paler below; faint darker lines running obliquely forward and downward from the dorsal along the rows of scales. Pale yellow, narrow, longitudinal streaks along the sides below the lateral line. Posterior margin of the caudal fin with a very narrow black edge. Grows to about 15 inches.

Diagnosis.—Dorsal XII, 11; anal III, 8; depth 2.9 to 3; head 3 to 3.3; eye 3.4 to 4.8; interorbital 3.35; snout 3; maxillary 2.8; gill-rakers 18; scales 68 to 75.

Distribution.—Bermuda, West Indies, north to Charlestown, south to Rio de Janeiro. Fairly common off-shore.

Yellow-Tail; Yelting
Ocyurus chrysurus (Bloch)

Field Characters.—Medium to large, elliptical, elongate snappers with long, deeply forked caudal fin; gill-rakers numerous, 19 to 21 on the lower limb of the first gill-arch.

Olivaceous or violet above, silvery below; a number of large, irregular, deep yellow blotches on the sides of the back; a bright yellow-bronze stripe from the snout through the eye to the caudal peduncle and fin which are bright golden yellow. Grows to about 2½ feet.

Diagnosis.—Dorsal X, 13 or 14; anal III, 9; depth 2.8 to 3; head 2.9 to 3.1; eye 3.65 to 4.5; snout 2.6 to 2.9; maxillary 2.25 to 2.55; gill-rakers 19 to 21; scales 47 to 57.

Distribution.—Bermuda, West Indies, Florida to Brazil. A common reef fish.

Silk Snapper; Spot Snapper; Lane Snapper; White-Water Snapper
Lutianus synagris (Linnaeus)

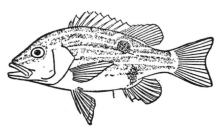

Field Characters.—Medium sized elongate, compressed snappers; rather pale in color with about 9 horizontal golden bands on the side and 3 to 4 on the head; a black spot, varying in size, on the sides on and above the lateral line, under the anterior part of the soft dorsal fin. Anal and pelvic fins golden, dorsal and caudal fins reddish, the latter with a narrow blackish edge. Vertical, dark angulate bars occasionally present on the sides. Reaches about a foot in length.

Diagnosis.—Dorsal X, 12; anal III, 8; depth 2.45 to 2.8; head 2.6 to 2.75; eye 3.2 to 4.75; snout 2.7 to 3.5; maxillary 2.25 to 4.75; gill-rakers 8 to 11; scales 46 to 55.

Distribution.—Bermuda, West Indies, Florida to Brazil. Common in certain localities.

Day Snapper; Day Red Snapper; Long-Fin Red Snapper
Lutianus vivanus (Cuvier and Valenciennes)

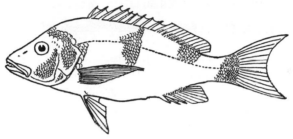

Field Characters.—Medium sized, compressed, elongate, reddish snappers with yellowish stripes along the sides; pectoral fins reaching the vertical through the origin of the anal fin; pelvic fins reaching to or past the vent. Iris bright golden yellow, very conspicuous, becoming orangey-red in older fish; caudal fin becoming yellowish toward its posterior edge and with a narrow black or dark red margin. Grows to 20 inches and a weight of 6 pounds, and said to reach 40 pounds.

Diagnosis.—Dorsal X, 14½; anal III, 8½; depth 2.6 to 3; head 2.66 to 2.95; eye 4.4 to 5; interorbital 4.7 to 4.8; snout 2.7; maxillary 2.2 to 2.6; gill-rakers, 16 to 17 including rudiments; scales 67 to 72; 50 pores in the lateral line.

Distribution.—Bermuda, West Indies. A common fish at depths of 70 to 85 fathoms during the daytime and at shallower depths at night.

Bermuda Silk Snapper; White-Water Snapper
Lutianus hastingsi   (Bean)

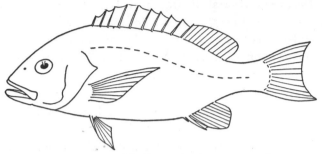

Field Characters.—Medium sized compressed snappers. Pectoral fin extending to the vent only.   Pelvic fins not reaching the vent by a space equal to one-half the eye's diameter.   Iris bright golden yellow; body vermilion or paler, upper parts overlaid with coppery brown; brownish spots on the scales, forming many oblique streaks above the lateral line.   Some specimens with a dark lateral blotch. Four or five narrow golden stripes below the lateral line. Grows to about 15 inches.

Diagnosis.—Dorsal X, 14; anal III, 8; depth 3; head 3; eye 4; interorbital 4; snout 3; maxillary 3; 9 gill-rakers on the lower limb of the first arch; scales 65.

Distribution.—Known only from Bermuda, and may possibly prove to be a variation of the preceding species.

Black-Fin Snapper; Red Snapper
Lutianus buccanella   (Cuvier and Valenciennes)

Field Characters.—Small to medium sized, slender snappers with long pointed snout; crimson, silvery below flushed with crimson; axil and base of pectorals with a conspicuous black spot; eye orange; dorsal fin crimson, its edge scarlet as is also part of the caudal peduncle; last rays of soft dorsal, most of the anal and pelvics, yellow; pectorals, base of anal and pelvic spines, pinkish.   Occasionally this fish is pale greyish pink with the black pectoral spot remaining as a conspicuous color pattern. Grows to a little over a foot.

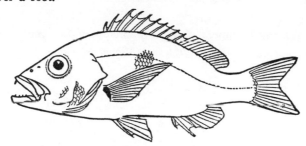

Diagnosis.—Dorsal X, 14; anal III, 8; depth 2.8; head 2.4; eye 3.5; interorbital 5.7; snout 3.2; maxillary 2.4; gill-rakers 12 plus 5 or 6 rudiments; scales 63.

Distribution.—Bermuda, West Indies, rarely north to Florida. An uncommon Bermuda fish.

Schoolmaster
Lutianus apodus (Walbaum)

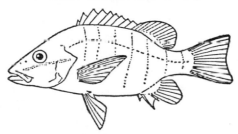

Field Characters.—Medium sized, elongate, compressed snappers with long, sharply pointed snout; margin of caudal fin without a black margin; sides greenish or greyish with 8 to 9 vertical pale bars, which may disappear in older specimens; no lateral spot; a blue stripe on the head below the eye. Fins pale yellow to green, the pelvics sometimes orange. Grows to about 8 pounds.

Diagnosis.—Dorsal X, 14; anal III, 8; depth 2.45 to 2.7; head 2.5 to 2.65; eye 3.45 to 4.25; snout 2.4 to 3.25; maxillary 2.25 to 2.6; gill-rakers 7 or 8; scales 37 to 41.

Distribution.—Bermuda, West Indies, Massachusetts to Brazil. A fairly common Bermuda fish.

Grey Snapper; Mangrove Snapper; Lawyer
Lutianus griseus (Linnaeus)

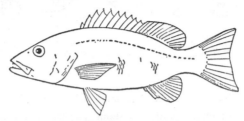

Field Characters.—Large, elongate, compressed snappers. Colour variable, generally grey, and with a blackish oblique band along the side of the head and through the eye,—this band may be completely absent. Some individuals, especially small fish, may be dark green above, chest and abdomen dark red, scales on the sides with rusty centres, forming lines along the sides. Fins all red, vertical fins darkest. No black lateral spot. Iris coppery brown with a golden pupil rim. Grows to 3 feet and a weight of 18 pounds.

Diagnosis.—Dorsal X, 14, rarely 13; anal III, 8; depth 2.65 to 3.3; head 2.6 to 3; eye 3.45 to 5.2; snout 2.25 to 3.2; maxillary 2.35 to 2.55; gill-rakers 7 or 8; scales 39 to 50.

Distribution.—Bermuda, West Indies, Massachusetts to Brazil. One of the commonest of Bermuda fish.

GRUNTS
See Key, p. 296

This large group of thirteen Bermuda species differs from the snappers chiefly in the slighter dentition, although most of them are deeper in the body. Yellow colour is found in most of the species, and often a splash of scarlet on the inside of the mouth. They are small to medium sized fish and hardly to be reckoned as game-fish. The group name is

YELLOW-TAIL
Ocyurus chrysurus

YELLOW GRUNT
Hæmulon flavolineatum

derived from their ability to produce deep muffled sounds
by means of their pharyngeal teeth or the complex swim-
bladder.

Family HÆMULIDÆ
White Grunt
Bathystoma aurolineatum (Cuvier and Valenciennes)

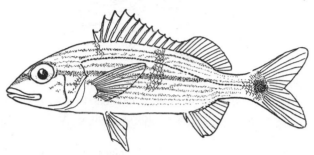

Field Characters.—Small, rather elongate, red-mouthed
grunts with 13 dorsal spines; mouth rather small; greyish
with yellowish longitudinal streaks, one from snout through
eye to base of caudal most conspicuous, a second from interorbital to posterior end of the soft dorsal fin,—between these
two are other, less conspicuous horizontal lines of similar
colour; no black spot under the preopercle; a dusky spot
sometimes present at the base of the caudal fin. Grows to
about 8 inches.

Diagnosis.—Dorsal XIII, 14 or 15; anal III, 8 or 9;
depth 3.3 to 3.7; head 2.8 to 3.3; eye 3.36 to 4; snout 2.6 to
3; interorbital 4; maxillary 1.9 to 2; gill-rakers 12 to 16
on lower limb of the first gill-arch; scales 50 to 59.

Distribution.—Bermuda, West Indies, Florida Keys to
Brazil. One of the commonest Bermuda fish.

White Grunt
Bathystoma striatum (Linnaeus)
Field Characters.—Small, elongate, compressed, red-
mouthed grunts; maxillary rather short, not or scarcely
reaching to the vertical of the middle of the eye; gill-rakers

rather long, 18 on the lower limb of the first gill-arch. Silvery white with a number of greenish yellow stripes along the sides. No black under the preopercular edge. Grows to about 7 inches.

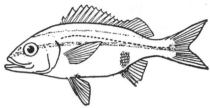

Diagnosis.—Dorsal XIII, 14; anal III, 8; depth 3.4 to 3.9; head 3.5; eye 2.6 to 3.35; snout 3.5 to 3.6; maxillary 2.25 to 2.4; gill-rakers 18 on lower limb of the first gill-arch; scales 65 to 72.

Distribution.—Bermuda, West Indies, south to Brazil. Uncommon in Bermuda.

Yellow Grunt
Hæmulon flavolineatum   (Desmarest)

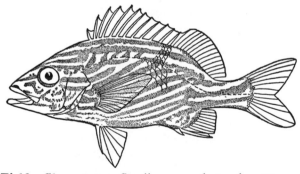

Field Characters.—Small, somewhat elongate, compressed, fairly large-mouthed grunts with very large and deep scales on the sides below the lateral line. Sides with yellow stripes, more or less parallel with the lateral line above it, those below the lateral line quite oblique anteriorly; angles of mouth black, red inside; a black spot under the preopercular edge. Grows to about a foot in length.

Diagnosis.—Dorsal XII, 14 or 15; anal III, 7 or 8; depth 2.5 to 2.85; head 2.8 to 3.1; eye 3 to 3.5; snout 2.4 to 2.9; interorbital 3.25; maxillary 2.1 to 2.4; gill-rakers 13 to 14 on the lower limb of the first arch, rather short; scales 47 to 53.

Distribution.—Bermuda, West Indies, Florida Keys to Brazil. The commonest grunt of Bermuda, found almost everywhere.

Comical Grunt
Hæmulon melanurum (Linnaeus)

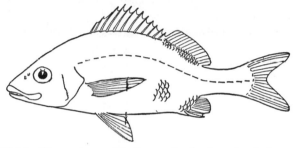

Field Characters.—Medium sized, long-headed grunts. Variable in color, bluish silvery, occasionally with large, dark, vertical blotches, and with about 9 longitudinal golden stripes on head and sides, the one from snout through eye to caudal fin wider and often darker than the others. A black spot under the preopercular edge; a wide black band on the body at the base of the dorsal fin which is continued onto the caudal fin, where it divides and is then found on each lobe, the outer edges of the caudal lobes greyish. This black band may also be absent. Inner corner of mouth reddish. Grows to about one foot.

Diagnosis.—Dorsal XII, 15 or 16; anal III, 8; depth 2.7 to 3; head 3; eye 4.7 to 5; interorbital 3.2 to 4; snout 2.25 to 2.75; maxillary 2; gill-rakers 12 to 14; scales 50 to 53.

Distribution.—Bermuda, West Indies to Brazil. Fairly common occasionally.

Blue-Striped Grunt; Yellow Grunt; Boar Grunt
Hæmulon sciurus (Shaw)

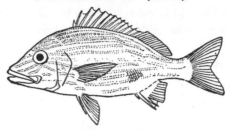

Field Characters.—Medium sized, somewhat elongate, compressed, large-mouthed, long-snouted grunts; yellowish, sometimes with irregular dark vertical bars; sides of head and body with horizontal blue stripes, one below the eye starting at the mouth, arching upward toward the eye and backward toward the pectoral base. Fins usually yellowish or translucent, but they may be greenish or black and the caudal may be black with a wide greenish or yellow posterior margin. Mouth red inside. Young with a dark blotch on the caudal peduncle. Grows to eighteen inches.

Diagnosis.—Dorsal XII, 16 to 17; anal III, 8 or 9; depth 2.6 to 2.7; head 2.7 to 2.8; eye 3.6 to 4.3; snout 2.2 to 2.4; maxillary 1.9 to 2; gill-rakers 16 to 18 on lower limb of first gill-arch, rather short; scales 48 to 60.

Distribution.—Bermuda, West Indies, Florida to Brazil. A fairly common Bermuda species.

Black-Tail Grunt; Black Grunt
Hæmulon carbonarium Poey

Field Characters.—Medium sized, red-mouthed grunts. Bluish silvery-grey or greyish brown with longitudinal yellow or bronze stripes, narrower than their interspaces; larger ones on upper half of the body and smaller ones on the lower half, with additional narrower ones between those on the upper half of the body. A large dark spot at base of the caudal. Dorsal translucent with a yellowish base and with orange and black tips. Pectorals dusky. **Pelvics**

dusky especially toward the tip. Caudal dusky toward base.
A black spot under the preopercular edge. Grows to about
a foot.

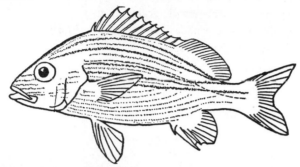

Diagnosis.—Dorsal XII, 15 or 16; anal III, 8; depth
2.7 to 2.85; head 2.9 to 3.1; eye 3.3 to 4.5; snout 2.3 to 2.6;
maxillary 2.5 to 2.6; gill-rakers 11 to 13 plus a few rudiments; scales 55 to 56.

Distribution.—Bermuda, West Indies, Florida Keys to
Brazil. Uncommon.

Margate Fish
Hæmulon album Cuvier and Valenciennes

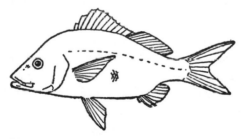

Field Characters.—Medium to large sized deep, compressed grunts, back elevated and sharply compressed. Color
pearl grey or grey, with or without three longitudinal bands,
one from snout through eye to caudal, where it often ends
in a round dark blotch; two narrower bands above this.
Mouth orange within; a faint dusky spot under the preopercle. Reaches a length of two feet or more.

Diagnosis.—Dorsal XII, 16; anal III, 8; depth 2.5 to 2.7; head 2.7 to 3; eye 5 to 7; interorbital 3.75; snout 2.25 to 2.4; maxillary 2.3 to 2.8; gill-rakers 12 to 13 on lower limb of the first arch, small; scales 46 to 51.

Distribution.—Bermuda, West Indies, Florida Keys to Brazil. An uncommon species.

Streaked Grunt, Striped Grunt, Grey Grunt, Sow Grunt
Hæmulon macrostomum   Günther

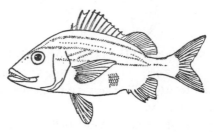

Field Characters.—Medium sized, rather deep, long-snouted, large-mouthed grunts. Greenish silvery above, becoming clearer silver below; scales mostly with pearly centres, under surface of head dusky. Conspicuous dark streaks along the sides,—a median streak from tip of snout to dorsal; one from above eye along side of back to last ray of soft dorsal; two above this from upper portion of eye to posterior portion of soft dorsal, the upper one more or less interrupted posteriorly; another from eye to base of caudal. Spinous dorsal fin brownish green, soft dorsal and anal greenish yellow. Caudal fin dusky, greenish yellow distally. Grows to about 14 inches.

Diagnosis.—Dorsal XII, 15 to 17; anal III, 8 or 9; depth 2.4 to 2.55; head 2.6 to 2.8; eye 3.1 to 4.9; snout 2.2 to 2.5; maxillary 1.9 to 2.3; gill-rakers short, 16 or 17 on lower limb of the first arch; scales 50 to 60.

Distribution.—Bermuda, West Indies, Florida to Panama and Colombia. Recently introduced into Bermuda, but there is a previous record of its having been found on the island.

Photo by E. R. Sanborn

YELLOW GRUNT
Hæmulon flavolineatum

Photo by E. R. Sanborn

BLUE-STRIPED GRUNT
Haemulon sciurus

Black Grunt
Hæmulon bonariense Cuvier and Valenciennes

Field Characters.—Medium sized, moderately deep, compressed, rather long snouted grunts; dark greyish above, silvery below, rows of scales on the sides marked by rusty brown lines following the rows of scales; young with 3 or 4 black longitudinal stripes, the lower one extending from snout through eye to base of caudal broadest and most distinct. Young have a distinct caudal blotch which may persist in fish up to 5 or 6 inches long. Grows to a foot or slightly less.

Diagnosis.—Dorsal XII, 15 to 17; anal III, 8 or 9; depth 2.3 to 2.7; head 2.7 to 2.9; eye 3 to 4.7; snout 2.3 to 3.2; maxillary 2.3 to 3; gill-rakers 12 to 14 on lower limb of the first gill-arch, short; scales 43 to 50.

Distribution.—Bermuda, West Indies south to Buenos Aires. Known in Bermuda, only from a questionable published record.

Sailor's Choice; Pig-Fish
Orthopristis chrysopterus (Linnaeus)

Field Characters.—Medium sized, compressed, long-snouted grunts with 12 to 13 rays in the anal fin, body somewhat elevated at the shoulders. Blue above shading to silvery below; each scale on body with a blue centre, the edge of the scale with a bronze spot, these forming orange-brown stripes on back and sides following the lines of scales, those above the lateral line extending obliquely upward and backward, those below nearly horizontal; snout and head with bronze spots and lines; inside of gill-cavity touched with golden; dorsal translucent with about three bronze horizontal shades, composed of spots, those of the soft dorsal most distinctly spot-like; edge of fin dusky; caudal yellowish at base, dusky toward tip; anal whitish, its edge dusky, its base shaded with bronze; pectorals and pelvics yellowish, the latter darker at the tip. Grows to about fifteen inches.

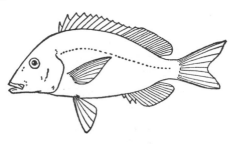

Diagnosis.—Dorsal XII or XIII, 15 or 16; anal III, 12 or 13; depth 2.6 to 2.75; head 3 to 3.15; eye 5; snout 2.4; maxillary 3.3; gill-rakers 12 on the lower limb of the first arch, short; scales about 60.

Distribution.—Bermuda, South Atlantic and Gulf coasts of the United States; young common as far north as New York. Apparently a much rarer fish now than formerly.

PORGIES

See Key, p. 298

Still deeper at the shoulder than the Grunts are the Porgies, of which there are five in the waters of Bermuda. One peculiarity which they all share is the division of the teeth into distinct canines and molars, this character changing with age and a corresponding shift of diet.

The several *Calamus* are often caught by the fishermen and attaining a large size are prized as food. The smaller Bream, with its characteristic black spot at the base of the tail, is one of the commonest of Bermuda fish.

Family SPARIDÆ
Blue-Bone Porgy, Jolt-Head Porgy
Calamus bajanado (Bloch and Schneider)

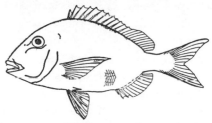

Field Characters.—Medium to large sized, compressed, very deep fishes with molar teeth posteriorly in the small mouth which is placed very low in the head. Colour brassy, rather dull, with little blue marking; a blue stripe below the eye, extending forward on the preorbital; a second duller streak above this, the two meeeting on the forehead; pre-orbital dull coppery, often with irregular and obscure blue lines, these sometimes forming obscure veinings, and grow-ing duller with age; lower jaw dull purplish; angle of mouth purplish and orange yellow; axil yellowish; no violet border on base of pectoral; fins plain, the pelvics sometimes slightly dusky, the caudal obscurely barred. Grows to a little more than two feet, and to a weight of 14 pounds.

Diagnosis.—Dorsal XII, 10 to 12; anal III, 10 to 11; depth 2.2 to 2.5; head 2.75 to 3.7; eye 2.75 to 3.3; maxillary 2.5 to 2.7; gill-rakers 6, short and blunt; scales 51 to 54.

Distribution.—Bermuda, West Indies, Florida to Brazil. A common species.

Sheepshead Porgy; Saucer-Eyed Porgy; Goat's Head Porgy
Calamus calamus (Cuvier and Valenciennes)

Field Characters.—Small to medium sized, very deep fishes with molar teeth posteriorly in the small, low mouth. Silvery with bluish reflections; the base and central portions

of each scale golden, forming longitudinal stripes, the space
between pearly or bluish; rows of scales on cheeks and
opercles with the pearly stripe median, the golden marginal;
a deep violet streak below eye; preorbital deep blue violet
like the snout, the ground color forming reticulations around
conspicuous, round, brassy spots which cover half the surface; naked part of preopercle sometimes similarly marked,
more often colored like the body; edge of opercle gilt;
lower jaw dusky violet; base of pectoral above with a
violet bar, axil golden; fins all pale, vaguely blotched with
dull orange; pelvics more or less dusky on inner rays; gape
yellow; iris golden. Grows to eighteen inches.

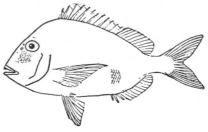

Diagnosis.—Dorsal XII, 12; anal III, 10 or 11; depth
1.9 to 2.3; head 3.1 to 3.3; eye 3.3 to 3.6; snout 1.5 to
1.7; maxillary 2.3 to 2.7; gill-rakers 6 to 7, small and
blunt; scales 50 to 54.

Distribution.—Bermuda, West Indies to Florida Keys.
Fairly common at Bermuda.

Pin-Fish; Spanish Porgy
Lagodon rhomboides (Linnaeus)

Field Characters.—Small to medium sized, compressed
elliptical fishes with notched incisor teeth anteriorly and
with molar teeth posteriorly. Dark green above, silvery
below; a round dark spot on the shoulder about the size
of the eye; 4 to 6 dark vertical cross-bars on body, each
about the width of the eye; numerous longitudinal golden
stripes; dorsal spines purplish or bluish silvery, the mem-

brane pale yellow; anal fin yellow with a broad light blue margin; caudal and pectoral fins pale yellow. Grows to slightly less than a foot.

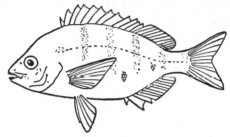

Diagnosis.—Dorsal XII, 11; anal III, 11; depth 2 to 2.6; head 3.25; eye 4; maxillary 3.3; gill-rakers 18 to 20; scales 65 to 70.

Distribution.—Bermuda, Gulf and Atlantic coasts from Cape Cod to Cuba. Rare, known only from a published record.

Bream
Diplodus argenteus (Cuvier and Valenciennes)

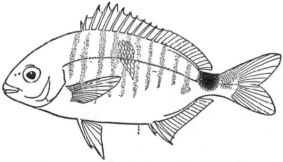

Field Characters.—Small to medium sized, compressed fishes with incisor teeth anteriorly and molars posteriorly. Steel blue above, silvery on sides and below; a conspicuous black spot on the anterior part of the caudal peduncle; five or six narrow vertical or slightly oblique blackish cross bars, between which are similar narrower bars,—these bars may be completely absent. Grows to about 20 inches.

Diagnosis.—Dorsal XII, 14 or 15; anal III, 13 or 14; depth 1.8 to 2.2; head 3.2 to 3.35; eye 3.2 to 4.1; snout 2 to 2.25; maxillary 3; gill-rakers 10 to 11 on the lower limb of the first arch; scales 60 to 65.

Distribution.—Bermuda, West Indies, Florida to Argentina. A very common Bermuda species.

CHUBS

Only one species of these steel-grey, small-mouthed fish occurs at Bermuda, but it is common and schools of hundreds are to be seen when diving on the outer reefs. They are called Rudderfish elsewhere from their habit of following close behind ships, sometimes for hundreds of miles.

Family KYPHOSIDÆ
Chub, Rudderfish
Kyphosus sectatrix (Linnaeus)

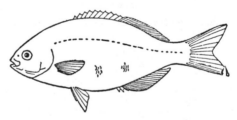

Field Characters.—Medium sized, rather deep, compressed fishes with small mouths, flattened incisor teeth anteriorly, these teeth with a conspicuous horizontal process or root; and with the soft dorsal and anal fins scaly in the adult. Brownish to steel grey, plain with small lozenge-shaped spots or with horizontal dark and light lines, these two patterns often interchanging in a short time; a diffuse pale streak below the eye, a yellowish one above and below this; fins all dull grey; pelvic and anal fins somewhat blackish; edge of opercle slightly darker. Grows to about 18 inches.

COLOUR-PHASES OF THE BERMUDA CHUB
Kyphosus sectatrix

Photo by E. R. Sanborn

Diagnosis.—Dorsal XI, 12; anal III, 11; depth 2.1 to 2.3; head 3.4 to 3.8; eye 3.1 to 3.4; snout 2.9; maxillary 3.1; gill-rakers 14 to 16; scales 55.

Distribution.—Bermuda, West Indies, Cape Cod to Brazil. Common.

BOGAS

These elongate fishes are exceedingly rare, although they have been reported in schools of large numbers off the coast of Cuba. They are accidental stragglers in Bermuda.

Family INERMIIDÆ
Boga
Inermia vittata Poey

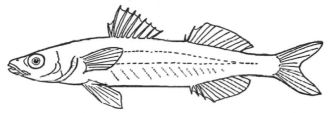

Field Characters.—Small, elongate, slightly compressed fusiform fish with excessively protractile mouth; no teeth in the jaws; dorsal fins separate. Three darkish longitudinal bands on the upper surfaces of body; a series of oblique lines on the lower part of the sides. Grows to about eight inches.

Diagnosis.—Dorsal XI-III-I, 10; anal III, 9; depth 4.75; head 4; eye 3.33; snout 3; scales about 100.

Distribution.—Bermuda and West Indies. Rare everywhere.

MOJARROS OR "SHAD"
See Key, p. 299

Shad is the local Bermuda name for fish of this group although they have nothing in common with the true shad of other countries. These fish have exceedingly protractile mouths which aid them in feeding on organisms in the sand. We sometimes catch hundreds in a single haul of a seine along sandy shores. Their scales are of the most intense glittering silver, although it is difficult to recognise these fish when looking down at them, for at this angle the silver is visually completely oxidized into dark gray. There are six species in this region.

Family GERRIDÆ
Shad; Gray Mojarra
Xystæma cinereus (Walbaum)

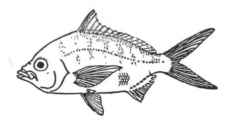

Field Characters.—Medium sized, compressed fishes with extremely protractile mouth; preopercle without serrations; 3 anal spines. Bright silvery, dark above, pale below; sides with broken vertical bluish bands, these often very faint; no dark lines along the rows of scales; dorsal and caudal dusky; pectoral fins pale, pelvic and anal fins yellowish in life; snout dusky. Grows to 12 or 15 inches.

Diagnosis.—Dorsal IX, 10; anal III, 7; depth 2.25 to 2.6; head 2.75 to 3.8; eye 2.64 to 3.25; snout 2.75 to 3.75; maxillary extending to past anterior margin of eye to pupil margin; gill-rakers 7 below the angle; premaxillary groove broad and free from scales; preorbital and preopercle entire; scales 41 to 45, a sheath of scales at base of dorsal and anal.

Distribution.—Bermuda, West Indies, Florida to Columbia; Pacific coast from Lower California to Peru. Uncommon.

Shad

Eucinostomus gula   (Cuvier and Valenciennes)

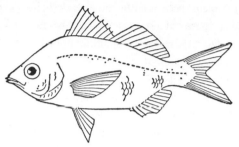

Field Characters.—Small, compressed, bright silvery fishes with extremely protractile mouths; anterior interhæmal bone in the shape of a long hollow cone; premaxillary groove closed or nearly closed by scales in front. Silvery with bluish reflections above; dorsal, caudal and anal fins more or less dusky; pectorals and pelvics pale; spinous dorsal with a black margin. Grows to five inches.

Diagnosis.—Dorsal IX, 10; anal III, 7; depth 2.2 to 3; head 2.8 to 3.4; eye 2.4 to 2.9; snout 3.1 to 3.8; maxillary reaching to or slightly past the anterior margin of the eye; gill-rakers 7; scales 44 to 48.

Distribution.—Bermuda, West Indian fauna, Carolinas to Brazil, young occasionally taken as far north as Massachusetts. Common.

Shad

Eucinostomus californiensis   (Gill)

Field Characters.—Small to medium, elongate, compressed, silvery fishes with extremely protractile mouthparts; anterior interhæmal bone shaped like a hollow cone. Premaxillary groove open and linear, occasionally slightly restricted by scales on the sides. Greenish above, with bluish reflections; bright silvery below and on the sides; smaller specimens occasionally have dark blotches and bars on the sides; pectoral fins pale, all other fins dusky; anal and pelvic fins often pale; spinous dorsal with a black margin. Grows to about 8 inches.

Diagnosis.—Dorsal IX, 10; anal III, 7; depth 2.5 to 3.3; head 2.7 to 3.5; eye 2.4 to 3.5; snout 2.7 to 3.8; gill-rakers 7, occasionally 8, below the angle of the first arch; scales 44 to 48; preorbital and preopercle entire.

Distribution.—Bermuda, West Indies, Atlantic coast from Carolina to Brazil; Pacific coast from California to Ecuador. Fairly common.

Shad
Eucinostomus havana (Nichols)

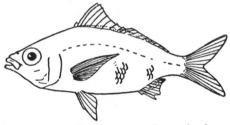

Field Characters.—Small to medium sized, compressed, silvery fishes with extremely protractile mouths; anterior interhæmal bone with a small depression or groove on its lower, anterior end, into which the posterior end of the air-bladder descends and is fastened; 3 anal spines. Silvery, no cross-bars, rows of scales on centre of sides with faint longitudinal streaks. Spinous dorsal tipped with blackish. Grows to 6 or 7 inches long.

Diagnosis.—Dorsal IX, 10; anal III, 7; depth 2.7 to 3.3; head 3.1 to 3.5; eye 2.75 to 2.9; interorbital 3.2 to 3.3; snout 3.1 to 3.3; gill-rakers 7; scales 42 to 45.

Distribution.—Bermuda, Porto Rico, Cuba and Florida. Quite common.

Mowbray's Shad
Eucinostomus mowbrayi Beebe and Tee-Van

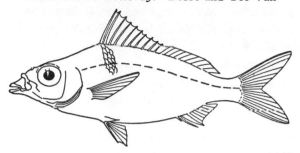

Field Characters.—Small, somewhat elongate, compressed, bright silvery fishes with extremely protractile mouth parts; interhæmal spine with a cup-shaped depression on its lower anterior side into which the tip of the air-bladder is fastened; third anal spine twice as large in diameter as the second and slightly longer; first anal spine very small. Bright silvery, darker above, no traces of cross-bars; a dusky spot at the tip of the anterior rays of the dorsal fin. Fins, except the clear pectorals, slightly dusky.

Diagnosis.—Dorsal IX, 10; anal III, 7; depth 2.98; head 3.4; eye 2.9; snout 2.96; interorbital 3.46; maxillary 2.96; gill-rakers 7; scales 48.

Distribution.—Known only from Bermuda, from the type specimen.

Long Bone Shad; Grass Shad
Ulæma lefroyi (Goode).

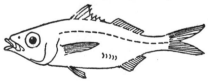

Field Characters.—Small to medium sized, elongate, compressed fishes with extremely protractile mouth-parts; preopercle entire; only two anal spines; premaxillary groove narrow, free from scales. Brilliant silver, darker above, everywhere with fine dusky punctulations, bars and cross-bars, especially when viewed from above; top of spinous dorsal black to dusky; dorsal and caudal dusky; anal, pelvic and pectoral fins paler, but with dusky punctulations. Grows to 8 inches.

Diagnosis.—Dorsal IX, 10; anal II, 8; depth 2.95 to 3.3; head 3.2 to 3.4; eye 2.7 to 3.1; snout 3 to 3.3; maxillary reaching to or slightly past anterior margin of eye; gill-rakers 7; scales 46 to 49.

Distribution.—Bermuda, West Indies, Florida to Brazil. Uncommon.

GOATFISH
See Key, p. 300

These are easy fish to identify for they are almost always to be seen swimming slowly along close to the bottom with the two long chin barbels advanced, both playing vigorously about, stirring up the sand into a small cloud as the sensitive tips search for food.

Goatfish are most brilliant in coloration, a single individual showing tints of yellow, red, violet, blue and green. A closely related species was made famous by Roman gourmands who, before cooking it, exhibited to their guests the marvellous interplay of colour in the dying fish. We found two species at Bermuda, and another was reported many years ago.

Family MULLIDÆ
Northern Goatfish
Mullus auratus Jordan and Gilbert

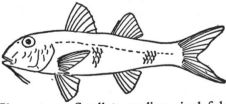

Field Characters.—Small to medium sized fish with two slender barbels at the chin; teeth absent in the upper jaw.

Scarlet,—sides with two distinct longitudinal stripes; first dorsal fin with an orange band at base and a yellow band higher up, rest of fin pale; second dorsal fin pale, mottled with scarlet; sides of head with a silvery lustre. Grows to eight inches.

Diagnosis.—Dorsal VII-I, 8; anal II, 6; depth 3.75 to 4; head 3.4; maxillary 2.75; gill-rakers slender; scales about 40.

Distribution.—West Indies to Cape Cod. Rare in Bermuda, known only from one published record.

Spotted Goat-Fish
Upeneus maculatus (Bloch)

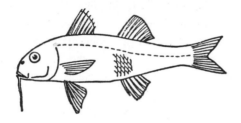

Field Characters.—Elongate, robust fishes with two long barbels at the chin; 30 to 32 scales in a lateral series. Colour variable, red, green and yellowish with violet, blue or green spots and lines, and with a series of 3 or 4 large brown blotches along the middle of the sides. Young have a lateral band from snout through eye to caudal, which breaks up into the lateral blotches. Colour changing with habitat, so that fish from sand may lack practically all colour and be plain grey. Grows to 9 or 10 inches.

Diagnosis.—Dorsal VIII-I, 8; anal I or II, 6 or 7; depth 3.6 to 4; head 3.1 to 3.2; eye 3.65 to 4.8; snout 1.8 to 2.3; maxillary 3.3 to 3.6; gill-rakers 15 to 17 plus 3 or 4 rudiments; scales 30 to 32.

Distribution.—Bermuda, West Indies, Florida Keys to Brazil. Fairly common.

Yellow Goatfish
Upeneus martinicus   Cuvier and Valenciennes

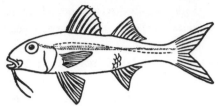

Field Characters.—Elongate, somewhat compressed fish with two long barbels at the chin, 37 to 40 scales along the sides. Pinkish with a yellow band on the sides from eye to caudal fin; pectorals pinkish; other fins yellowish. Grows to a foot in length.

Diagnosis.—Dorsal VII-I, 8; anal II, 6; depth 3.5 to 4.2; head 3.25 to 3.6; eye 3.4 to 3.7; snout 2.35 to 3; gill-rakers 16 or 17 plus 3 or 4 rudiments; scales 37 to 40.

Distribution.—Bermuda, West Indies, Florida and Panama. Less common than the preceding species.

RIBBONFISH
See Key, p. 300

The name of this beautiful little fish applies not to the general form, but to band or ribbon-like markings on the body. It is not uncommon around the reefs and may at once be recognised by the extremely high dorsal fin. A second species is included on the strength of a single specimen washed ashore thirty years ago. They are extremely local in their choice of a home, and may be found week after week in the same hollow or crevice of coral.

Family SCIÆNIDÆ
Lance-Shaped Ribbonfish
Equetus lanceolatus   (Linnaeus)

Field Characters.—Small, compressed fishes, deepest anteriorly, tapering to a narrow caudal peduncle; spinous dorsal base short, the spines long; soft dorsal long and low.

Ground colour pale yellowish; a narrow brownish band from the corner of the mouth across eye meeting its fellow on top of the head; another broader band edged with a narrow white line on each side from the nape down and back over the opercle, meeting its fellow between the pelvic fins and extending to the tips of their outer rays; a third and still broader band, also bordered with white, extending from tips of the dorsal spines to their base, then downward and backward to the tips of the middle caudal rays. Grows to about 8 inches.

Diagnosis.—Dorsal XIV to XVI-I, 53; anal II, 5; depth 2.4; head 4; eye 4; gill-rakers about 9.

Distribution.—Bermuda, West Indies to Florida. Rare at Bermuda, known from one published record.

Cluck; Ribbonfish; Sword-Fish; Croaker; Cubbbyu
Pareques acuminatus   (Bloch and Schneider)

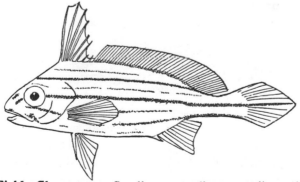

Field Characters.—Small to medium, small-mouthed, compressed fishes, deepest anteriorly; the profile rather

steep; spinous dorsal fin base short, the spines long, forming a conspicuous high fin; soft dorsal long and low.
Silvery grey to brownish with about 7 narrow brownish
horizontal bands along the sides, the one from snout through
eye to tip of caudal most prominent; snout, pectorals, spinous
dorsal, tips of soft dorsal rays and distal portions of anal
and pelvic fins dusky. Grows to about a foot.

Diagnosis.—Dorsal VIII or IX-I, 37 to 41; anal II, 6
or 7; depth 2.8 to 3.1; head 3.1 to 3.3; eye 3.2 to 4.3;
snout 3.6 to 4.2; maxillary 2.6 to 2.9; gill-rakers 12, including rudiments; scales 56 to 65; tip of lower jaw with
a fleshy knob.

Distribution.—Bermuda, West Indian fauna, South Carolina to Brazil. Fairly common.

WHITEY

This is an elongate, almost eel-shaped fish with vertical
fins extending far along the body, and with delicate and
beautiful colouring. The single species is not uncommon,
and can be found from close inshore on sand and grass
banks to the deeper waters of 90 to 100 fathoms.

Family MALACANTHIDÆ
Whitey
Malacanthus plumieri   (Bloch)

Field Characters.—Medium sized, elongate, slightly compressed, small-scaled fishes with conical snouts; preopercle
entire; dorsal and anal fins long; caudal fin deeply lunate,
its tips produced. Variable in colour; sides often with
irregular vertical greenish or brownish bars; purplish lines
on the head; base of caudal yellowish and dark green,

outer border pale, upper and lower edges dark. Grows to about 15 inches and occasionally to almost two feet.

Diagnosis.—Dorsal VI, 49 to 55 (the spines difficult to determine) ; anal 48 to 50; depth 6.5; head 3.66; eye 5.5; maxillary 2.8; snout 2.5; well-developed canines in front of jaw; scales 130.

Distribution.—Bermuda, West Indies, Fernando de Noronha. Common locally.

ANGEL AND BUTTERFLYFISH
See Key, p. 300

The common Angelfish seems to have become a sort of symbol of Bermuda, although it is no more common here than throughout the West Indies. Next to the Sergeant Major it is the most conspicuous fish about the wharves. The magnificent Black Angelfish are seen only about the outer reefs, and the West Indian and French Angelfish are here only by artificial introduction by man.

The Four-eyes or Butterflyfish are often seen about the inner reefs and harbours. Some of these have a large eye-like spot near the tail, which gives them the appearance of swimming backward. Eight species of this interesting group are found in Bermuda waters.

Family CHÆTODONTIDÆ
Banded Butterflyfish
Chætodon striatus Linnaeus

Field Characters.—Small, deep-bodied fishes with a single dorsal fin of spines and rays; vertical fins densely scaled; mouth small, teeth fine and brush-like. Vertical black bands present on body, one from nape through eye and over cheek; second from anterior part of spinous dorsal to abdomen; third from posterior part of spinous dorsal to middle of anal, and a fourth band usually present on posterior part of soft dorsal and anal crossing the caudal peduncle. Rows of scales usually marked with dark streaks. Grows to six inches.

Diagnosis.—Dorsal XII, 19 or 21; anal III, 16 to 18; depth 1.4 to 1.6; head 2.4 to 2.85; eye 2.5 to 3.1; snout 2.7 to 3.1; gill-rakers rudimentary; scales 39 to 44.

Distribution.—Bermuda, West Indies, Panama, rarely to Florida. Uncommon.

Four-Eyed Butterflyfish
Chætodon capistratus Linnaeus

Field Characters.—Small, deep-bodied fishes with single dorsal fin composed of spines and rays; vertical fins covered with scales; mouth small, teeth fine; scales below middle of sides passing downward and backward, the scale rows with

FOUR-EYED BUTTERFLYFISH
Chatodon capistratus

blackish streaks; yellowish, a black band from nape through eye over cheek, a large black ocellus on the sides below the soft dorsal. Very young with two black ocelli, one on anterior rays of dorsal, and one on side below posterior rays of dorsal, and with a broad dusky band from anterior dorsal spines to abdomen. Grows to six inches.

Diagnosis.—Dorsal XIII, 19 or 20; anal III, 16 to 18; depth 1.35 to 1.7; head 2.5 to 3.4; eye 2.55 to 2.9; snout 2.6 to 3.3; gill-rakers very short; scales 36 to 44.

Distribution.—Bermuda, West Indies, Florida, Panama, occasionally straying north to Woods Hole. Common.

Two-Spotted Butterflyfish
Chætodon ocellatus   Bloch

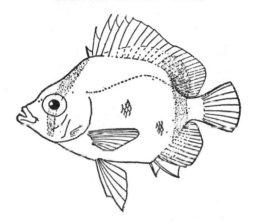

Field Characters.—Small, deep-bodied fishes with a single dorsal fin composed of spines and rays; vertical fins densely scaled; mouth small, teeth fine and brush-like; scales below middle of side running obliquely upward and backward. Grey on sides, lower parts yellowish; a black bar from origin of dorsal, through eye to lower margin of opercle. Base of soft dorsal with a large, non-ocellated black spot, which in some specimens is continued downward as a dark band across the caudal peduncle to the posterior portion of the anal fin; a blackish point on the outer tip of the soft dorsal. Grows to about 8 inches.

Diagnosis.—Dorsal XII, 19 to 21; anal III, 16 to 18; depth 1.35 to 1.6; head 2.5 to 3; eye 2.5 to 3.5; snout 2.5 to 2.85; gill-rakers rudimentary; scales 27 to 35.

Distribution.—Bermuda, West Indies, north in the Gulf Stream occasionally to Rhode Island. Uncommon.

Least Butterflyfish
Chætodon sedentarius Poey

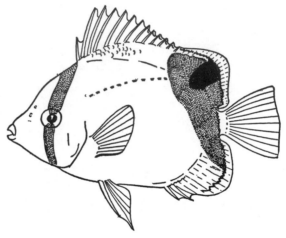

Field Characters.—Small, deep-bodied fishes with a single dorsal fin of spines and rays; vertical fins densely scaled; mouth small, teeth fine and brush-like; scales below axis of body horizontal. Body yellowish, dusky above; ocular band dusky, very broad above, narrower below, edged with whitish above in front, with yellow behind above; a broad, dark brown, vertical band from extremity of dorsal across tail over posterior half of soft dorsal and anal. Grows to about 4 inches.

Diagnosis.—Dorsal XIII, 23; anal III, 19; depth 1.75; head 3.2; snout scarcely as long as eye; scales 38.

Distribution.—Bermuda, West Indies. Rare in Bermuda.

Black Angel; Rock Beauty
Holacanthus tricolor (Bloch)

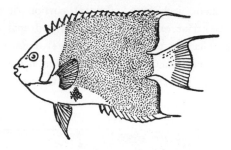

Field Characters.—Small to medium sized robust fishes with dorsal and anal fins completely covered with scales; mouth small, teeth brush-like. Head, anterior third of body and tail rich orange, rest of body black; snout sometimes greenish. Young with much less black, the black concentrated under the posterior portion of the dorsal and spreading forward with age. A small white ocellus in this black spot disappears with growth. Grows to a foot in length.

Diagnosis.—Dorsal XIV (rarely XV), 17 or 18; anal III, 17 to 19; depth 1.5 to 2; head 3.5 to 3.9; eye 3.1 to 4.4; snout 2.2 to 2.75; gill-rakers short; scales 44 to 48.

Distribution.—Bermuda, West Indies south to Bahia. A fairly common reef fish.

Angelfish
Angelichthys bermudensis (Goode)

Field Characters.—Medium sized, compressed, robust fishes with small mouth; teeth fine, brush-like. Dorsal and anal fins produced posteriorly into long streamers. Variable in colour, an 8-inch fish being as follows: scales of the sides purplish brown with yellow green edges, the general effect being greenish with a slight bluish tinge. Head greenish. Top of eyeball, preopercular spines, edge of opercle, isthmus and thoracic part of body, base of pectoral fin, nape, pelvic spine, posterior edges of dorsal and anal fin, as well as snout, rich blue. Central portion of pectoral, pelvic fins, posterior extensions of dorsal and anal fins, and outer edges of caudal yellow. Upper edge of dorsal with a subterminal brown band. No distinct blue ocellus on the nape. Young with vertical white bands. Grows to about 18 inches long.

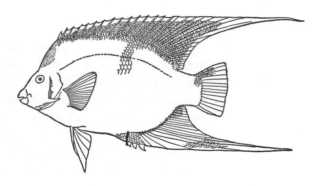

Diagnosis.—Dorsal XIV, 18; anal III, 19; depth 1.6; head 3.4; eye 3.5 (young); snout 2.85.

Distribution.—Bermuda, West Indies, Florida. A common Bermudian fish.

DOCTOR OR SURGEONFISH
See Key, p. 302

These are medium sized, round, usually dark fish seen singly or in small schools around the reefs. They are mainly dark brown or rich dark blue with very small mouths. On the side of the body near the base of the tail is a stout prostrate spine, sharp-edged and pointed. When needed, this can be raised and slashed along the side of an enemy, lashing with sharp, clean cuts, the rather far-fetched simile to a surgeon's knife providing the common name. Four Bermuda Surgeons have been seen by us.

Family ACANTHURIDÆ
Blue Doctorfish
Acanthurus cœruleus Bloch and Schneider

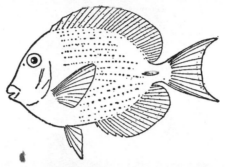

Field Characters.—Small, compressed, deep fishes with a small, erectile spine on either side of the caudal peduncle; body deep, 1.5 to 1.75 in length. Brown washed with deep blue, with undulating longitudinal pale blue streaks on the body. Dorsal fin with blue and brown slightly oblique horizontal lines. Grows to a foot or slightly more.

Diagnosis.—Dorsal IX, 25 to 27; anal III, 24 to 26; depth 1.55 to 1.75; head 3.2 to 3.5; eye 3 to 4.5; snout 1.2 to 1.5; scales about 160.

Distribution.—Bermuda, West Indies, Florida to Brazil. Common.

Yellow Doctorfish
Acanthurus heliodes (Barbour)

Field Characters.—Small, compressed deep fish with small, movable spine on side of caudal peduncle; body deep, 1.45 to 1.67; brilliant yellow with lighter yellow undulating horizontal stripes on the sides; darker greenish-yellow oblique stripes on the dorsal fin anteriorly, roughly following the upper margin of the fin. A narrow blue margin along the outer edge of the dorsal and anal fins. Anterior margin of the pelvic fin and upper edge of the caudal fin blue. Grows to six inches.

Diagnosis.—Dorsal IX, 26 to 27; anal III, 24 to 26; depth 1.45 to 1.67; head 3.15; eye 3.33; snout 1.45; interorbital 3.17.

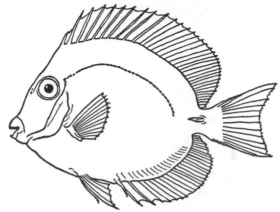

Distribution.—Bermuda and the Bahamas. This is probably the yellow phase of the Blue Doctorfish. Uncommon.

Ocean Tang; Tank
Acanthurus bahianus Castelnau

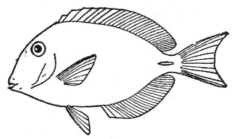

Field Characters.—Medium sized, compressed fishes with a small erectile spine on each side of the caudal peduncle; caudal fin deeply emarginate, the upper tip lengthened in older fish. Dark brown, young with a lighter area at the base of the caudal; dorsal fin with about eight dark lines running parallel to its outer edge for its whole length. Grows to about a foot.

Diagnosis.—Dorsal IX, 24 to 26; anal III, 21 to 23; depth 1.8 to 2.1; head 3.2 to 3.6; eye 2.9 to 3.7; snout 1.3 to 1.75; scales about 150.

Distribution.—Bermuda, West Indies, Florida to Brazil and occasionally northward to Massachusetts. Fairly common.

Doctorfish
Acanthurus hepatus (Linnaeus)

Field Characters.—Medium sized, compressed fishes with small, erectile spine on each side of caudal peduncle; caudal fin moderately concave, the upper lobe not much produced and not much longer than the lower. Uniform brownish, young often with narrow cross-bars and the base of the caudal yellowish green; a bluish blotch surrounding the caudal spine. Grows to 10 inches.

Diagnosis.—Dorsal IX, 23 to 25; anal III, 22 to 23; depth 1.75 to 2.1; head 2.8 to 3.6; eye 2.5 to 4; snout 1.4 to 1.75; scales about 140.

Distribution.—Bermuda, West Indies, Massachusetts to Brazil. Fairly common.

SCORPIONFISH
See Key, p. 302

This great family of fishes is almost unknown in Bermuda, three of the four species being represented so far by one individual each, and the fourth is by no means a common fish. They are very spiny, especially about the head.

Family scorpænidæ
Agassiz's Scorpionfish, Prickly Hind
Scorpæna agassizi   Goode and Bean

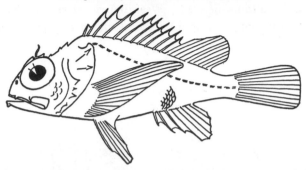

Field Characters.—Small, robustly-built, large-eyed fish with head armed with short spines; scales of body with a few dermal fringes and flaps; eye large, 2.5 to 2.9 in head. Colour light orange yellow, creamy below lateral line, fins pale. Grows to 4 to 6 inches.

Diagnosis.—Dorsal XII, 9 to 10; anal III, 5; depth 2.7 to 3; head 2.2 to 2.33; eye 2.5 to 2.9; snout 4; interorbital 5 to 5.5; maxillary 2; 6 to 7 gill-rakers on lower limb of first gill-arch; scales 47 to 48; 24 to 28 tubes in the lateral line.

Distribution.—Bermuda, and ocean east of Cuba.   Rare.

Prickly Hind; Plumier's Scorpionfish
Scorpæna plumieri   Bloch

Field Characters.—Small to medium sized robust fishes with conspicuous dermal flaps and tentacles on head and body; head very rugose; a small but distinct pit below the anterior border of the eye. Variable in colour, browns, yellows, greys, etc.; axil of the pectoral fin black with conspicuous white or blue spots. Grows to about a foot.

Diagnosis.—Dorsal XII, 9 or 10; anal III, 5 or 6; depth 2.4 to 2.9; head 2.2 to 2.5; eye 3.6 to 5.5; snout 3.2 to 3.8; interorbital 4.2 to 5; maxillary 1.85 to 1.95; gill-rakers short and coarse, about 7 developed on the lower limb of the first arch; scales 43 to 47.

Distribution.—Bermuda, West Indies, Massachusetts to Brazil. Uncommon.

Lion-Fish; Long-Horned Scorpionfish
Scorpæna grandicornis Cuvier and Valenciennes

Field Characters.—Small fishes with rough spiny head and with many conspicuous dermal flaps and tentacles on head and body; the tentacle above the eye always much longer than the diameter of the eye. Greyish brown above, ςaler below; a dark vertical band below eye extending over interorbital; one across base of pectoral and spinous dorsal; a third band from tips of pectorals to last spines of dorsal, one from base of second anal spine to near middle of soft dorsal; a bar on caudal peduncle; fins with dark bars, pelvics with black tips; axil of the pectoral fin grey with small bluish or white spots enclosed in black rings. Grows to about 8 inches.

Diagnosis.—Dorsal XII, 9 or 10; anal III, 5 to 6; depth 2 to 2.6; head 2 to 2.6; eye 3 to 3.85; snout 3.2 to 3.85; interorbital 5.5 to 6.3; maxillary 1.9 to 2.1; gill-rakers short and blunt, spinose, about 6 developed on lower limb of the first arch; scales 41 to 45.

Distribution.—Bermuda, West Indies, Massachusetts to Brazil. Rare.

Small-Scaled Scorpionfish
Pontinus microlepis Bean

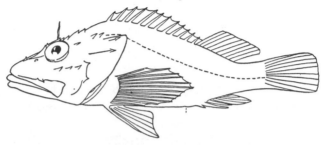

Field Characters.—Small, long and large-headed compressed fish with short low spines on head, a bony stay across cheek below the eye; pectoral rays unbranched; two slender tentacles above each eye, the first minute, the second about two-thirds the diameter of the eye. Colour in life unknown, rosy in preserved specimen. Grows to 9 inches.

Diagnosis.—Dorsal XII, 10; anal III, 5; depth 3.33; head 2.2; eye 4.66; interorbital 3 in snout; snout 3.5; maxillary reaches to almost behind the hind margin of the eye; gill-rakers 6, well-developed, with about 8 rudiments; scales 48; 33 lateral line pores.

Distribution.—Known only from Bermuda. Rare,—only one published record.

FLYING GURNARDS

These are probably the most versatile fish in the world for they can swim, glide, float, fly and walk, using their fins in turn as hands, feet, oars and wings. The flight is less strong than that of flyingfish, the head being encased in almost solid bony armour.

The moment the Gurnard touches the bottom the two

pelvic fins are lowered and the fish steps daintily ahead or to one side, one fin after the other exactly like legs.

It is not a common fish anywhere.

Family DACTYLOPTERIDÆ

Flying Gurnard

Dactylopterus volitans (Linnaeus)

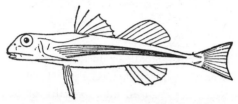

Field Characters.—Small to medium sized fishes with the head enclosed in a bony armature, the bony head shield produced backward and ending in a spine; pectoral fins long, large, wing-like, used for flight; first one or two spines of the dorsal fin nearly free from the others. Coloration variable, sometimes greenish olive and brown above, below pale, marked irregularly with dusky and bright brick red; pectoral fins mottled. Grows to about a foot.

Diagnosis.—Dorsal II-IV-8; anal 6; depth 5.25 to 5.5; head 3.65 to 3.9; eye 2.7 to 3.2; snout 2.5 to 3; interorbital 1.45 to 1.95 in head; maxillary 2.75 to 3.1; scales 56 to 60; no lateral line.

Distribution.—Bermuda, West Indies, both coasts of the Atlantic straying as far north as Massachusetts. A stray and rare fish at Bermuda.

LUMP-SUCKERS

This group of thick, clumsy fish occurs only very rarely and accidentally in Bermuda. The skin is covered with bony warts or low spines, and the pelvic fins are joined together to form an effective sucking disk, by which these fish cling to rocks.

Family CYCLOPTERIDÆ

Lump-Sucker

Cyclopterus lumpus Linnaeus

Field Characters.—Small to medium sized fishes with sucking disk on the ventral surface, formed with the altered pelvic fins which are changed into six pairs of fleshy knobs in the centre of a disk which is surrounded by a roughly circular flap of skin. Body with conical tubercles arranged in longitudinal ridges. Colour variable, more or less matching the surroundings, sometimes with dark blotches. Reaches a length of twenty inches, although usually not over fifteen.

Diagnosis.—Dorsal VI to VIII, 11 (the first dorsal disappearing in large specimens) ; anal 9 or 10; depth about 2; head 5; eye about 4.

Distribution.—Both sides of the North Atlantic, north to Greenland and Hudson's Bay, south to New Jersey and occasionally to Chesapeake Bay, mainly on the bottom and among sea-weed, but also found floating in weed. Rare in Bermuda, only one record.

DEMOISELLES

See Key, p. 303

These brilliant little fishes are very abundant in Bermuda. Some are dark with yellow tails, others have a scattering of turquoise spots, and still others are gorgeous in bright blue and gold. Even the tiny young in the tidepools in August and September glow like living jewels.

Demoiselles are the very opposite in habits of the nomadic

fish like mackerel and sharks. They live throughout the year in pairs, selecting a hollow, or little cave or crevice among the coral, and spend all their time in or near it, defending it against all intruders, large or small.

Ten species have been recorded from Bermuda.

Family POMACENTRIDÆ
Brown Chromis
Demoisellea marginatus (Castelnau)

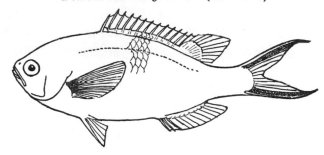

Field Characters.—Small, oblong, compressed, with the body tapering gradually backward; teeth conical, in bands; anal fin low, its longest ray much shorter than the length of the base of the fin. Colour brown and black; upper and lower lobe of caudal fin greyish with a black band.

Diagnosis.—Dorsal XII, 12; anal II, 10 to 12; depth 2.3 to 2.4; head 3.3 to 3.6; eye 2.8 to 3; interorbital 2.66 to 2.8; snout 3.8 to 4; maxillary 2.8; gill-rakers 25.

Distribution.—West Indies. The single record upon which this species is included in the Bermuda fauna may be an error.

Blue Chromis
Demoisellea cyanea (Poey)

Field Characters.—Small, oblong, compressed fishes with body tapering gradually backward; teeth conical, in bands; anal fin rather high, its longest ray equal to or longer than the base of the fin. Sides bluish and black, axillary spot absent, but a scattering of small spots across upper base of pectoral. Upper and lower lobe of caudal with a black band.

Diagnosis.—Dorsal XII, 12; anal II, 11 to 12; depth 2.2 to 2.4; head 3.2 to 3.3; eye 2.8 to 3; snout 3.7 to 4; interorbital 2.5 to 2.8; maxillary 2.6 to 2.8; gill-rakers 18 or 19; scales about 29 to 30.

Distribution.—Bermuda, West Indies. An abundant species off-shore, hundreds of specimens having been seen while diving with the Bathysphere.

Bermuda Chromis
Heliases bermudæ   (Nichols)

Field Characters.—Small, oblong, compressed, small-mouthed fishes lacking a lateral line on the caudal peduncle; teeth conical, in bands; interorbital space almost flat. Colour in life unknown; in spirits purplish above, paler below; axil of pectoral black; paired fins, caudal fin and caudal peduncle yellowish. Grows to 2 and ⅖ inches.

Diagnosis.—Dorsal XIV, 11; anal II, 11; depth 2.5; head 3.1; eye 2.7; interorbital 3; snout 4; maxillary 3.5; gill-rakers 19 on lower limb of first arch; scales 27.

Distribution.—Known only from the type specimen taken at Bermuda.

Yellow Demoiselle
Eupomacentrus chrysus Bean

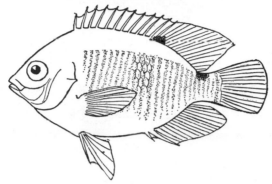

Field Characters.—Small, compressed, deep fishes with one row of teeth in each jaw; preopercle and suborbital serrate; depth of body 2 or less than 2 in the length. Bright yellow changing to greenish yellow or dark green, with narrow vertical dark stripes on the sides; a large black spot bordered with blue on the posterior base of the spinous dorsal; a black spot on the upper side of the caudal peduncle; a very small spot at base of upper pectoral rays; scattered small blue spots on head, anterior anal fin and the body near the anal fin. Grows to 2 inches.

Diagnosis.—Dorsal XII, 16; anal II, 15; depth 1.9 to 2; head 3.25; eye 3.5; snout 3.2; interorbital 3; maxillary barely reaching front of eye; gill-rakers 12 on lower limb of first gill-arch; scales 28; 18 lateral line pores.

Distribution.—Bermuda, Porto Rico. Uncommon.

Scarlet-Backed Demoiselle
Eupomacentrus rubridorsalis Beebe and Hollister

Field Characters.—Small, compressed, rather deep fishes with one row of teeth in each jaw. Dark blue in general with top of head, upper sides and spinous dorsal scarlet;

two ocelli, black with a turquoise border, one between the spinous and soft dorsal, and the other on the upper aspect of the caudal peduncle. Grows to two or three inches.

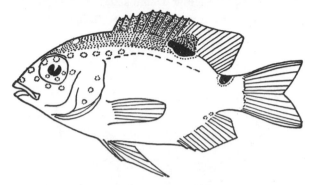

Diagnosis.—Dorsal XII, 16; anal II, 13½; depth 2.06; head 2.58; eye 2.74; snout 3.53; maxillary 3.53; scales 29.

Distribution.—Bermuda, Leeward Islands. A few individuals seen on the outer reefs.

Demoiselle

Eupomacentrus fuscus (Cuvier and Valenciennes)

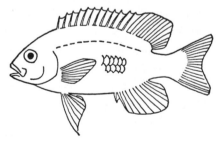

Field Characters.—Small, compressed, rather deep fishes with one row of teeth in each jaw; preopercle and suborbital serrate. Colour variable, dark green or brown to nearly black, edges of scales darker, forming narrow vertical cross-bars; fins all dark brown or black, the caudal sometimes dusky or yellowish; a black axillary spot. Grows to about 6 inches.

Diagnosis.—Dorsal XII, 15; anal II, 13; depth 2.2 to 2.5; head 3.5; eye 3.4; scales 28.

Distribution.—Bermuda, West Indies. Common.

Yellow-Belly; Beau Gregory
Eupomacentrus leucostictus (Muller and Troschel)

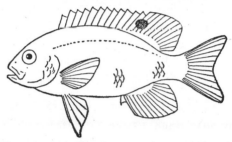

Field Characters.—Small, compressed, rather deep fishes with one row of teeth in each jaw; preopercle and suborbital serrate. Posterior half of the body unlike the anterior half, being usually bright yellow, anterior upper portion of body dark blue or black; blue lines and spots on head and body; caudal fin bright yellow; a blue spot on posterior base of the anal fin; last rays of the soft dorsal black. Young with a large black ocellus on the dorsal fin. Grows to about 3 inches.

Diagnosis.—Dorsal XII, 13 to 15; anal II, 12 to 14; depth 2.16 to 2.25; head 3.3 to 3.5; eye 3.3; snout less than eye; gill-rakers' 9 to 10; scales 28 to 29.

Distribution.—Bermuda, West Indies, Florida. Common.

Sergeant-Major; Cow-Pilot; Nuisance; Cock-Eye
Pilot
Abudefduf marginatus (Bloch)

Field Characters.—Small, deep, compressed fishes with small terminal mouth; preopercle and suborbital without serrations. Somewhat variable as to ground colour, usually bluish green with yellow above and below; upper parts of head dusky; sides with five or six black, vertical bands;

pectorals light green with black axil, other fins usually same colour as body. Grows to six inches.

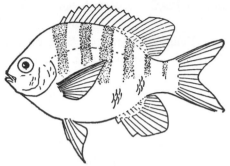

Diagnosis.—Dorsal XII, 13 (rarely 12) ; anal II, 11 or 12 (rarely 10) ; depth 1.55 to 1.9; head 2.75 to 3.45; eye 2.4 to 3.6; snout 3.2 to 4.25; maxillary scarcely reaching anterior margin of eye in adult; gill-rakers 16 to 21; scales 28 to 30.

Distribution.—Bermuda, West Indies, Rhode Island to Uruguay; Pacific Coast from Lower California to Peru. One of the commonest Bermuda fishes.

Yellow-Tailed Demoiselle
Stegastes chrysurus (Cuvier and Valenciennes)

Field Characters.—Small, deep, compressed, brownish fishes with small, terminal mouth and with small, close-set, movable teeth in jaws. Brownish, caudal fin yellowish or orange or same colour as rest of body, other fins bluish-black. Small round spots of blue on upper part of body. Grows to six inches.

Diagnosis.—Dorsal XI, 14 or 15; anal II, 12 or 13; depth 1.75 to 1.85; head 2.85 to 3.15; eye 3.6 to 4.35; snout 2.3 to 2.5; gill-rakers, 13 or 16 more or less developed, very short; scales 27 or 28.

Distribution.—Bermuda, West Indies, Panama. Uncommon, found on the outer reefs.

Turquoise-Spotted Demoiselle
Stegastes niveatus   (Poey)

Field Characters.—Small, deep, compressed fishes with small, close-set, movable teeth in the jaws. Uniform velvety black, the sides with rich turquoise-blue spots surrounded by a lavender ring,—these spots becoming greenish in some lights. Grows to 4 inches.

Diagnosis.—Dorsal XII, 16; anal II, 13½; depth 2; head 2.75 to 2.85.

Distribution.—Bermuda, West Indies. Uncommon,—this may be the same as the preceding species.

WRASSES
See Key, p. 304

This heading includes two families rather unlike in external aspect. The Hogfish and its allies are fairly stout, deep and of large size, boldly marked with masses of such colours as maroon and yellow.

The Wrasses proper, as exemplified by the Slippery Dicks, number nine Bermuda species. They are usually small and slender, and among the most abundant of the island fish.

They exhibit great variety in pattern and colour, not only in the separate species but in the course of individual growth, from young to adult. In the studies of Bermuda fish which we have made we have had to discard five species of Wrasse which were based solely on changes of colour and pattern.

Wrasse live in and about coral reefs, feeding on small animal life, and their numbers about Bermuda are incalculable. A glance into the water anywhere will be sure to reveal one or more Wrasse. These fishes sleep on the sand or in the hollows of coral, lying on their sides.

Family LABRIDÆ
Purple-Tailed Wrasse
Clepticus parræ   (Bloch and Schneider)

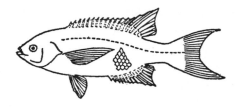

Field Characters.—Medium sized, robust, compressed fish; head and vertical fins enveloped in small scales; teeth weak. Head and irregular anterior two-thirds of body deep purple and violet; tail fin rich maroon; remainder of body, including pelvic, anal and posterior soft dorsal fins, belly and caudal peduncle, bright yellow mottled with violet and purple. Grows to a maximum of 12 inches, but usually considerably smaller.

Diagnosis.—Dorsal XII, 10; anal III, 12; depth 3.66; head 2.87; scales 35; tail deeply forked.

Distribution.—Bermuda and the West Indies. Rare in Bermuda and found on the deeper, outer reefs.

Hogfish
Lachnolaimus maximus   (Walbaum)

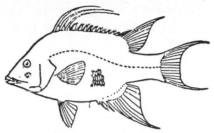

Field Characters.—Large, deep, heavy-bodied wrasses
with three or four anterior spines of the dorsal fin
lengthened; tips of the soft dorsal, anal and the caudal fins
produced.   Colour highly variable, usually pinkish or red,
often with the top of the head sharply demarcated in red;
a dark spot present on the body at the base of the soft
dorsal fin.   Reaches a length of over 2 feet and a weight
of over 20 pounds.

Diagnosis.—Dorsal XIII or XIV, 11; anal III, 10; depth
2.3; head 3; eye 4 to 5.4; snout 2.5; scales 39 to 40; males
with the cleft of the mouth very much wider than in the
females.

Distribution.—Bermuda and the West Indies, Panama
and Key West, straggling north on the Atlantic Coast as
far as North Carolina.   Uncommon in Bermuda, except in
certain local situations.

Spanish Hogfish
Bodianus rufus   (Linnaeus)

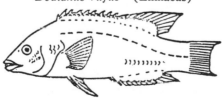

Field Characters.—Small to medium sized wrasses with a
scaly sheath at the base of the soft dorsal and anal fins,

these fins and the lobes of the caudal fin somewhat produced behind; anterior canines strong, posterior canines present. Colour extremely variable, but well marked patterns exist; often red above and in front and yellow or orange behind and below; these colours may change but the arrangement of the two contrasting colours is a common one in the species. Grows to 2 feet in length.

Diagnosis.—Depth 2.76 to 3.5; head 2.9 to 3; dorsal XII, 9 to 10; anal III, 11 or 12; eye 6.3; snout 2.24; maxillary 2.5; gill-rakers 10 or 11; scales 30 to 33.

Distribution.—Bermuda, Florida and the West Indies to Brazil. In Bermuda common on all rocky reefs.

Family CORIDÆ
Deep-Water Wrasse
Iridio bathyphilus Beebe and Tee-Van

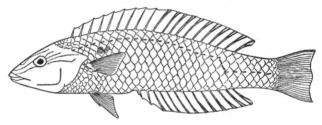

Field Characters.—Small, elongate wrasse from deep water with the posterior margin of the caudal fin double concave. Brilliant in coloration, with a band of green or yellow from the snout to the eye, which bifurcates posterior to eye, the upper bifurcation extending to the nape, the lower continued along the sides as a broken band of yellow, the yellow alternating on two scale rows. A large black or brilliant turquoise-green patch on the upper anterior sides, sometimes a small black patch on the body at the base of the middle caudal rays. Grows to about six inches.

Diagnosis.—Dorsal IX, 11; anal III, 12; depth 4.25; head 3.3 in length; snout 3 in head; interorbital 4.8 in head;

eye 6 in head; scales 28 to 29; gill-rakers 11 on lower half of the anterior arch.

Distribution.—Known only from deep water (85 fathoms) off Nonsuch Island, Bermuda.

Variegated Wrasse
Iridio garnoti (Cuvier and Valenciennes)

Field Characters.—Small, rather elongate wrasses with complete lateral line; posterior canines well developed. Colour highly variable; short, conspicuous, black or dark blue lines radiating back and up from the eye; small black spots on the nape; body often with a vertical or slightly oblique dark bar down the middle of the sides; behind this and before it the coloration is usually markedly different. Smaller examples are often bright yellow with a bright blue longitudinal band along the middle of the sides; caudal fin in older fish with narrow, curved, vertical, blue lines. Grows to about 8 inches.

Diagnosis.—Dorsal IX, 10 or 11; anal III, 11 or 12; depth 3.7 to 4.3; head 3.3 to 4.3; eye 5 to 6; snout 3.3 to 3.5; scales 26 or 27; pelvic fins with the outer rays exserted; caudal fin rounded or subtruncate; scales before the dorsal not crossing the median line.

Distribution.—Bermuda and the West Indies. A fairly common species in Bermuda.

Nichols' Wrasse
Iridio similis Nichols

Field Characters.—Small wrasses with the outer pelvic rays exserted and with only 2 canines in each jaw. A conspicuous, broad, black band on the sides from the snout to the caudal fin; colour in life unknown; in spirits with a black spot in the axil of the pectoral fin; an elongate black blotch on the spinous dorsal and a dusky, lengthwise streak in the centre of the dorsal behind the same. Reaches 4 inches.

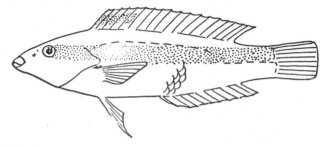

Diagnosis.—Dorsal IX, 11; anal II, 11; depth 3.6; head 3.1; eye 5; interorbital 5; snout 3; maxillary 4.6; scales 26; about 8 rows of scales before the dorsal, the anterior reduced in size, and some of them crossing the centre of the back; caudal subtruncate, its angles slightly rounded.

Distribution.—Known only from a single specimen taken in Bermuda. Possibly same as *maculipinna*.

Slippery Dick
Iridio bivittata (Bloch)

Field Characters.—Slender, elongate, compressed wrasse with rounded or truncate tail and with the outer rays of the pelvic fins not especially lengthened. Usually greenish or greyish with two lateral bands, the upper from the snout through the eye to the base of the caudal fin, the lower from the pectoral base to above the anal fin, these stripes sometimes bordered with red; reddish or brownish bands on the head, often with one from each eye meeting over the nape and continuing as a single longitudinal band to the dorsal fin; a violet or black spot on the opercle edged by green and orange; lower jaw with a single or double red cross band; a black spot in the centre of the dorsal fin, less marked or absent in older fish; dorsal in older fish may be dusky in addition to its bright reds, yellows and greens; caudal fin variable in colour, with oblique reddish or bluish bands in adult, plain in the young. Grows to 6 or 8 inches.

Diagnosis.—Dorsal IX, 11; anal III, 12; depth 3.6 to 4.3; head 3.6 to 4; eye 5 to 6; snout 2.2 to 3; scales 26 to 28.

Distribution.—Bermuda and the West Indies to Brazil and north on the North American coast as far as North Carolina. An abundant fish everywhere in Bermuda on the shallow reefs and especially in weed-covered bottoms.

Band-Headed Wrasse
Iridio maculipinna (Muller and Troschel)

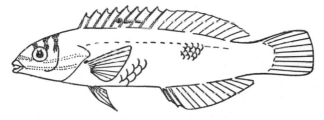

Field Characters.—Small, elongate, rather heavily built, thick-lipped wrasses with two small, forward-pointing teeth in each jaw. Greenish or yellowish with or without a dark band along the middle of the sides, over which are short, slightly oblique red lines; three conspicuous brown cross bands on top of the head, the anterior two between the eyes, the posterior one behind the eyes. Series of oblique reddish stripes on lower sides of the body. A small black spot on membrane of the dorsal fin between the 5th to 8th spines.

Diagnosis.—Dorsal IX, 11; anal III, 11; depth 3.6 to 4; head 3.1 to 3.5; eye 3.8 to 6; snout 3.3 to 3.8; scales 26 to 28; gill-rakers 9-10; scales not meeting in the middle line of the nape.

Distribution.—Bermuda, West Indies, questionably north as far as North Carolina. In Bermuda it is fairly common, especially on the outer reefs, where it is often found with other small wrasses.

Pudding-Wife or Blue-Fish
Iridio radiata   (Linnaeus)

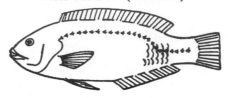

Field Characters.—Medium to large sized wrasses with the outer rays of the pelvic fins lengthened, more than twice as long as the inner. Colour variable, especially with age, the sexes, when adult, different in coloration;—generally bluish or bronzy with blue stripes and spots; a conspicuous colour pattern, present in fish from 3½ inches long upward, is two oblique short bands, usually yellow, orange or reddish, bordered with blue, extending downward and backward from in front of and behind the base of the pectoral; young of 1 or 1½ inches lack these bands, but possess black blotches on the dorsal fin and dorsal surface of the body and at base of the tail; this is also true of the intermediate stages; anal fin with longitudinal bands and groups of spots of varying colour. Grows to 18 or 20 inches.

Diagnosis.—Dorsal IX, rarely VIII, 11; anal III, 12; depth 2.7 to 3; head 3.4 to 4; eye 6.5 to 10.4; snout 2.5; scales 28.

Distribution.—Bermuda, Florida Keys, and the West Indies south to Brazil. Common in Bermuda.

DOCTOR-FISH
Acanthurus hepatus

BLUE-FISH; PUDDING-WIFE
Iridio radiata

King Slippery Dick or Blue Head
Thalassoma bifasciatum (Bloch)

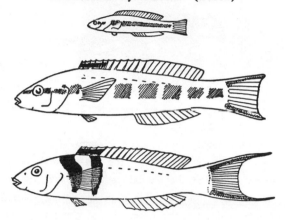

Field Characters.—Small, elongate, small-mouthed wrasses; tail varying in shape from rounded in small specimens to deeply cleft and with lengthened tips in the adult males. Coloration highly variable, not only as to differences due to growth stages, but also in the individual fish, which may change its coloration completely in a few seconds or minutes; adult male with head blue or green followed by two wide vertical black bands separated by a blue interspace, posterior part of the body green; females, and young males and young, greenish or bright yellow, with or without a wide lateral dark band which may be broken up into large spots; in one phase the paler interspaces between these spots may appear as pale vertical bands extending from the dorsal fin almost to the ventral surface; a brown stripe from snout through eye to opercle; a dark spot on anterior membranes of the spinous dorsal; outer edges of the caudal with a black border. Grows to 6 inches.

Diagnosis.—Dorsal VIII, 13; anal III, 11; depth 3.5 to 4.2; head 3.1 to 3.5; eye 3.7 to 5.1; snout 3.1 to 3.5; scales 26 or 27.

Distribution.—Bermuda and the West Indies; Southern Florida. Common in Bermuda.

Razor-Fish
Xyrichthys rosipes   Jordan and Gilbert

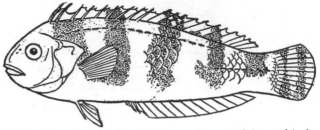

Field Characters.—Small, deep, elongate fishes with lateral line abruptly broken under the soft dorsal, beginning again lower down on the caudal peduncle; first two dorsal spines longer and more flexible than remaining spines, and slightly separated from the remainder of the fin; pelvic fins short. Greenish and brownish with irregular, darker, vertical bars continued onto the fins; these bars merge somewhat with each other on the middle of the sides; first two dorsal spines and anterior portion of ventral fins dark. Grows to 3 inches.

Diagnosis.—Dorsal IX, 12 or 13; anal III, 12; depth 3 to 3.2; head 3 to 3.5; eye 3.6 to 4.6; snout 3 to 3.5; maxillary 3.5; gill-rakers 11; scales 23 to 27.

Distribution.—Bermuda; Florida; Curaçao. Uncommon in Bermuda.

Splendid Razor-Fish
Xyrichthys splendens   Castelnau

Field Characters.—Small, elongate, very much compressed fishes with lateral line abruptly broken under the soft dorsal, beginning again lower down on the caudal peduncle; first two dorsal spines slightly longer than the remainder; pelvic fins with their outer ray considerably lengthened. Greenish, with an ill-defined green stripe along the middle of the sides; a few small pale blotches along the dorsal surface of the body; a small, black blotch on the sides; head with vertical blue lines; vertical fins with a narrow, distal, reddish band, outside of which is a very narrow blue line; dorsal and anal fins mottled. Grows to 4 inches.

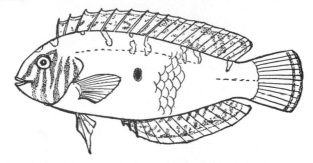

Diagnosis.—Dorsal IX, 12 or 13; anal III, 12; depth 3.1; head 3.4; eye 4.6; interorbital 4.9; snout 2.8; maxillary 3.8; gill-rakers 12; scales 27.

Distribution.—Bermuda; Bahamas; Yucatan. Rare in Bermuda.

PARROTFISH

See Key, p. 307

Next to the Angelfish the most conspicuous and brilliant fish in Bermuda waters are the Parrotfish. To see them at their best one should take a small boat with a plate of glass sunk into the bottom and drift for hours over the reefs, or if one is in a diving helmet these fish often come close to the glass.

They bear some general resemblance to Wrasse, but beside being heavier and deeper, may always be told by the teeth being fused into a solid beak. They are vegetarians and browse on the seaweed and gnaw at the algæ-covered coral for sustenance. Their colours are often very brilliant, blues, yellows and greens, and some have the power of changing pattern at will.

The larger forms go into groups or schools and are sluggish in their movements, often feeding so close to shore that their backs are out of water. They seem to have few or no enemies. The farther we go from shore over the reefs, the larger do we find the Parrotfish. Eighteen species are found in Bermuda waters.

Family SPARISOMIDÆ
Many-Toothed Parrotfish
Cryptotomus roseus Cope

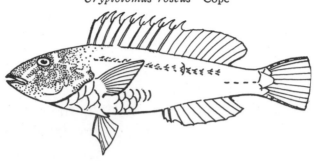

Field Characters.—Small parrotfish with the anterior teeth of the jaws more or less canine-like, the sides of the jaw with a fused cutting edge; scales of the breast notably enlarged. Colour greyish brown to green, all fins more or less pale except the caudal which has cross bars; sides with 4 darker cross shades; a black blotch at base of pectoral. Grows to about 5 inches.

Diagnosis.—Dorsal IX, 9; anal III, 9; depth 3.75 to 4.2; head 3 to 3.2; eye 5; snout pointed, more or less conical, 3 to 3.75; mouth small, its angle not reaching to vertical of front of eye.

Distribution.—Bermuda and the West Indies; Brazil. Uncommon in Bermuda.

Red Parrotfish
Sparisoma abildgaardi (Bloch)

Field Characters.—Small to medium sized parrotfish with upper jaw included in the lower when the mouth is closed, and with a small posterior canine on the upper jaw. Brownish or greenish or greyish above, the edges of the scales

dark; lower parts bright red; membranous edge of the
opercle black; dorsal and anal fins dark; intensity and
deposition of pigment variable. Grows to about a foot.

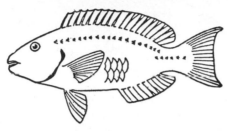

Diagnosis.—Dorsal IX, 10; anal III, 9; depth 2.5 to 2.9;
head 2.85 to 3.3; eye 4.3 to 6.4; snout 2 to 2.5; interorbital
space flat; scales 24 or 25.

Distribution.—Bermuda, Florida, and the West Indies to
Brazil. Common in Bermuda on the outer reefs.

Mud-Belly
Sparisoma radians (Cuvier and Valenciennes)

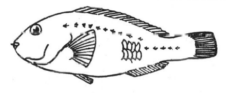

Field Characters.—Small parrotfish with upper jaw included in the lower when the mouth is closed, and with
from 1 to 4 lateral canines; caudal fin truncate or rounded.
Colour highly variable, but not especially brilliant; browns,
greens, etc., mottled; no black spot at base of pectoral fin.
Grows to a little over a foot in length.

Diagnosis.—Dorsal IX, 10; anal III, 9; depth 2.6 to 2.9;
head 3 to 3.6; eye 3.5 to 4.6; snout 2.6 to 3.1; interorbital
space convex; scales 24 to 26.

Distribution.—Bermuda, Florida and the West Indies to
Brazil. A common species in Bermuda, constantly taken,
especially among grass.

Red-Banded Parrotfish
Sparisoma aurofrenatum   (Cuvier and Valenciennes)

Field Characters.—Small to medium sized parrotfish with pale upper jaw included in the lower when the mouth is closed, and with a posterior canine tooth on each side of the upper jaw. Purplish above, becoming reddish on the sides and vivid green below; a reddish line from mouth under the eye almost to top of gill-opening; a yellow spot surmounted with black on the anterior sides; tail with outer angles tipped with black. Grows to 8½ inches, and possibly larger.

Diagnosis.—Dorsal IX, 10; anal II, 9; depth 2.5 to 2.7; head 3.25; eye 4.6 to 5.5; snout 1.7 to 2.3; scales 24.

Distribution.—Bermuda and the West Indies. Occasionally taken in Bermuda.

Dark Green Parrotfish
Sparisoma viride   (Bonnaterre)

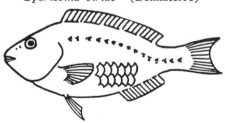

Field Characters.—Small to medium sized parrotfish with upper teeth included within the lower when the mouth is closed. Greenish with brown edges to the scales; head with brownish top and lines along the sides; a small, yellow spot on the opercle and a large one on the caudal peduncle;

caudal fin with a subterminal orange crescent, outside of which is a bluish crescent; dorsal and anal fins pinkish red, the latter with a bluish terminal and basal band. Grows to 18 inches.

Diagnosis.—Dorsal IX, 10; anal III, 9; depth 2.3; head 2.9; eye 8; snout 1.9; interorbital 4.2; scales 25.

Distribution.—Bermuda and the West Indies; southern Florida. Common on the outer reefs of Bermuda.

Stocky Parrotfish
Sparisoma flavescens (Bloch and Schneider)

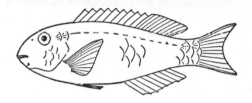

Field Characters.—Small to medium sized parrotfish with upper jaw included in the lower when the mouth is closed; no posterior lateral canines; body robust, moderately compressed. No black spot at base of upper pectoral rays; olive grey to brownish above, orangy below, to pale; sometimes with one or more indistinct pale streaks along the sides; often more or less clouded with darker blotches or bars; lower jaw brownish or dusky, crossed by a pale band; dorsal and caudal pale olivaceous, each barred and spotted with brown; anal red with faint spots or bars of brown. Grows to about a foot.

Diagnosis.—Dorsal IX, 10; anal III, 9; depth 2.64 to 3.2; head 3.25 to 3.66; eye 3.55 to 5.2; snout 2.4 to 3.3; interorbital space transversely strongly convex; scales 24 to 26.

Distribution.—Bermuda, Florida, and the West Indies to Brazil. Uncommon about Bermuda.

Grey Parrotfish
Sparisoma squalidum (Poey)

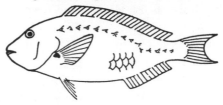

Field Characters.—Small to medium sized parrotfish without posterior canines on the upper jaw, and with the lower jaw including the upper when the mouth is closed; snout somewhat long; interorbital space slightly concave. Greyish green to pinkish grey, somewhat mottled; a whitish cross band on the chin; a conspicuous black spot at the base of the upper pectoral rays; fins mottled, the caudal orange with traces of cross-bars, most noticeable along the upper and lower edge. Grows to 6 inches, possibly larger.

Diagnosis.—Dorsal IX, 10; anal III, 9; depth 2.8; head 3.35; snout 2.25; eye 4.6.

Distribution.—Bermuda and the West Indies; Panama to Venezuela. Common in Bermuda waters.

Red-Tailed Parrotfish
Sparisoma brachiale (Poey)

Field Characters.—Medium sized parrotfish without lateral canines and with the upper jaw included within the lower when the mouth is closed. Bluish; pectorals with a very distinct black spot at the base; centre of the caudal fin clear peach red, as well as the dorsal and anal fins, the latter two sometimes brownish. Grows to a foot.

Diagnosis.—Dorsal IX, 10; anal III, 9; depth 2.85 to 3; head 3.2 to 3.5; eye 4.5 to 5.8; snout 2.25 to 3; scales 24.

Distribution.—Bermuda; Cuba; Haiti. Uncommon in Bermuda.

Family SCARIDÆ
Dotted-Finned Parrotfish
Scarus punctulatus Cuvier and Valenciennes

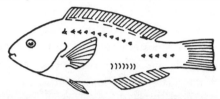

Field Characters.—Small, compressed parrotfish with pale teeth and with one or two posterior canine teeth; lower jaw included in the upper when the mouth is closed. Orange brown, centre of scales bright bluish green; a light yellow longitudinal band, occasionally almost obsolete, above the level of the green stripes on the head, from the upper part of the gill-opening to the caudal; below this a dark greyish line, bordered above and below by bright green; these green stripes extend forward on the head and snout, one above and one below the eye, the lower meeting its fellow of the opposite side on the upper lip, the upper on the forehead; a grass green band around the lower jaw; lower half of head bright green; dorsal and anal bright green at base and tip, mesially orange, the orange with a median more or less interrupted band of blue, the corresponding band on the anal forming a row of spots; caudal bright greenish blue; outer rays entirely blue, inner with their membranes orange. Grows to 9 inches.

Diagnosis.—Dorsal IX, 10; anal III, 9; depth 2.6 to 3; head 2.8 to 3.3; eye 5 to 6.1; snout 2.35 to 2.6; mouth small, reaching less than half way to the eye.

Distribution.—Bermuda and the West Indies; Panama. Rare in Bermuda.

Painted-Tail Parrotfish
Scarus tæniopterus Desmarest

Field Characters.—Small to medium sized parrotfish with the lower jaw included within the upper when the mouth is closed, and with posterior canine teeth. Orange brown above, changing to blue below; two horizontal green stripes on the head, the interspace yellowish brown; a yellow stripe above the pectoral, below the level of the green stripes on the head; dorsal and anal fins greenish blue at base, then a broad band of orange, and tipped with a rather broad bluish band; no spots in the membrane of either fin; caudal fin with outer rays orange, the upper and lower edge with a narrow black band. Apparently does not reach a foot in length.

Diagnosis.—Dorsal IX, 10; anal II, 9; depth 2.66; head 3; eye 6; snout 2.8; scales 24.

Distribution.—Bermuda and the West Indies; Florida. Rare in Bermuda.

Blue Fish; Blue Parrot or Blumber
Scarus vetula Bloch and Schneider

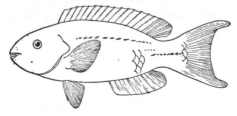

Field Characters.—Medium to large sized parrotfish with lower jaw included within the upper when the mouth is closed; canine teeth present posteriorly. General colour

dark sky blue; scales brown-, orange- or lilac-edged; eye
with blue spots and bands above and behind; a green band
from the angle of the mouth, bordered above and below
by red or orange; fins chiefly blue or green, the dorsal and
anal with orange or lilac bases, within which are spots of
green and blue; a lilac, orange or red band near the edge
of the caudal, and one near the upper edge of the pectoral;
pelvics mostly orange, yellow or red, their anterior border
blue; upper jaw with red and blue edgings. Grows to about
2 feet.

Diagnosis.—Dorsal IX, 10; anal II, 9; depth 2.7; head
2.7; eye 7; interorbital 2.8; scales 25.

Distribution.—Bermuda; Cuba; Porto Rico; Florida.
Found commonly on the outer reefs of Bermuda.

White-Banded Parrotfish
Scarus gnathodus (Poey)

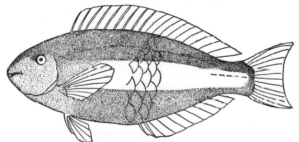

Field Characters.—Medium sized parrotfish with lower
jaw included in the upper when the mouth is closed and with
three canines on the posterior surface of the upper jaw;
lateral line canals greatly divergent. General colour dark
vinaceous brown, the belly somewhat paler; a broad white
band along the sides from pectoral fin to the caudal; fins
pinkish and brownish, the dorsal and caudal darkest. Grows
to 14 inches.

Diagnosis.—Dorsal IX, 10; anal II, 9; depth 2.8 to 2.9;
head 3.1 to 3.2; eye 7.2 to 7.7; snout 2.2 to 2.4; interorbital
2.8; scales 24.

Distribution.—Bermuda; Cuba. A fairly common species on the outer reefs of Bermuda.

Blue Parrot or Clamacore
Scarus cæruleus (Bloch)

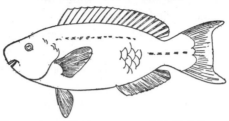

Field Characters.—Large, compact-bodied parrotfish without posterior canine teeth, the lower jaw included within the upper when the jaw is closed; large individuals have the snout swollen; lateral line simple, the tubes not divergent. General colour bright blue, the scales occasionally with brownish bases and with a purplish overcast; a reddish bar on the lower lip, not present in the young; dorsal and anal with a bright blue outer margin. Grows to 3 feet.

Diagnosis.—Dorsal IX, 10; anal III, 9; depth 2.8 to 3.2; head not much longer than deep, 3 to 3.6; mouth small, reaching about half way to eye; snout 2.35 to 3.25; interorbital 3.1; scales 24 to 26.

Distribution.—Bermuda and the West Indies; Maryland to Trinidad. A common species in Bermuda, especially on the off-shore reefs.

Mud-Belly
Scarus acutus Poey

Field Characters.—Small parrotfish with lower jaw included in the upper when the mouth is closed; 3½ rows of scales on the cheeks; no posterior canine teeth; posterior medio-lateral scale of the lateral line short and broad. Brownish with horizontal pale and dark bands. Grows to a foot.

Diagnosis.—Dorsal IX, 10; anal II, 9; depth 3.5; head 3.5; eye 7; scales 24.

Distribution.—Bermuda; Bahamas; Cuba. Rare in Bermuda.

Mud-Belly
Scarus croicensis Bloch

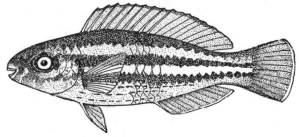

Field Characters.—Small parrotfish with lower jaw included in the upper when the mouth is closed; no posterior canines; posterior medio-lateral scale elongate, considerably longer than wide. Brownish with longitudinal stripes along the sides; these stripes alternately light and dark, varying considerably in intensity, usually a pale stripe from above the eye and one from below it, continued to the caudal. Grows to 7 inches.

Diagnosis.—Dorsal IX, 10; anal III, 9; depth 3.1 to 3.65; head 2.9 to 3.3; eye 3.6 to 4.85; snout 2.84 to 3.6; mouth small, not reaching to the eye; scales 22 to 25.

Distribution.—Bermuda and the West Indies; Florida to Brazil. A common species about Bermuda.

Rainbow Parrotfish
Pseudoscarus guacamaia (Cuvier)

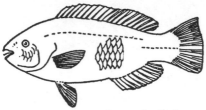

Field Characters.—Large, heavy-bodied parrotfish with green teeth, the lower jaw included within the upper when the mouth is closed. Variable in colour, sometimes olive green with each scale edged with brown, the lower parts reddish; sometimes rich reddish-brown with green blotches; vertical fins edged with deep blue or green; smaller specimens are not as conspicuously coloured and may be greenish, rather pale, with a brown spot at the base of each scale. Grows to over 3 feet in length.

Diagnosis.—Dorsal IX, 10; anal II, 9; depth 2.25 to 3; head 2.7 to 3.2; eye 5 to 10; snout 2.3 to 2.8; interorbital 2.8 to 3; scales 25.

Distribution.—Bermuda and the West Indies; north to Florida Keys, south to Rio de Janeiro. A common species about Bermuda. Three-foot specimens at numerous times have been seen in shallow water along shore, and four-foot ones were observed from the Bathysphere 150 feet down.

Wine-Coloured Parrotfish
Pseudoscarus plumbeus Bean

Field Characters.—Medium to large sized parrotfish with green teeth; the lower jaw included in the upper when the mouth is closed. Purplish brown, wine-coloured; chin, upper lip and lower part of subopercle vivid greenish blue; nape bluish green; a spot of bluish green at the insertion of the spinous dorsal; a few scales on the sides with similar green; margin of dorsal, anal, tips of caudal, upper ray of the pectoral and first ray of the pelvic fin with a narrow stripe of bluish green. Grows to 18 inches.

Diagnosis.—Dorsal IX, 10; anal 11; depth 2.66; head 3; eye 4 in snout, 8.5 in head; snout 2.25; interorbital 2.6; scales 25.

Distribution.—Bermuda; Florida. Uncommon in Bermuda.

GOBIES
See Key, p. 310

These interesting little fish are found in the shallowest tide-pools, yet they can never hope to become land animals because their pelvic fins, which might have evolved into legs, have become fused together into a sucker which clings to the rocks and holds the fish safely when heavy surges wash the shore.

Gobies are adapted to withstand very unfavourable conditions of living, such as vitiated tidepools and thick mud, and can survive in a neglected aquarium after all other fish have died. Ten species have been recorded from Bermuda.

Family ELEOTRIDÆ
Sleeper
Eleotris pisonis (Gmelin)

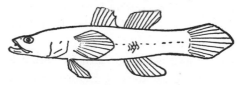

Field Characters.—Elongate, low, posteriorly-compressed fishes with two separate, short but high dorsal fins; head broad, depressed; scales small, present on the head; pelvic fins not united into a cup-shaped sucking-disk. Dark brown or blackish, sides with faint, narrow, dark lines alternating with narrow light ones; fins with dark wavy lines. Reaches 6 inches.

Diagnosis.—Dorsal VI-9; anal I, 8; depth 3.7 to 3.8; head 2.9; eye 7; snout 5; interorbital 3.6; maxillary 2.75; gill-rakers 9, very short; scales 57 to 66.

Distribution.—Bermuda and the West Indies; Florida to Rio de Janeiro. Rare,—one Bermuda record.

Bronze-Headed Goby

Eviota personata Jordan and Thompson

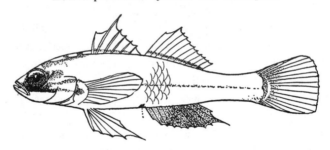

Field Characters.—Very small, compressed fishes with pelvic fins close together, but not forming a sucking-disk; head. Nape, base of pectoral fin and breast naked, rest of body covered with finely ctenoid scales. Pinkish orange, the edges of the scales especially well-marked; side of head with an orange band below the eye surmounted by a dark pigment patch, above which is another narrow orange line which terminates at the pectoral base; a red line along the base of the spinous and soft dorsal; anal fin dusky. Grows to an inch or a little more.

Diagnosis.—Dorsal VI-I, 10; anal 11; depth 4.3 to 4.7; head 3.7 to 3.9; eye 2.9 to 3; snout 6.9; maxillary 2.7 to 2.8; scales 25 to 27.

Distribution.—Bermuda, Tortugas. Rare in Bermuda.

Family GOBIIDÆ
Sheep's-Head Molly Miller
Bathygobius soporator (Cuvier and Valenciennes)

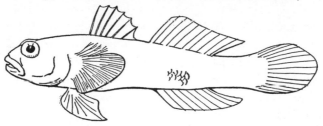

Field Characters.—Small to medium sized fish with pelvic fins united to form a sucking disk; head broader than deep; body compressed posteriorly; pectoral fins with the upper rays free almost to their bases, thread-like. Variable in colour, usually greenish or greyish to pale straw colour, mottled, occasionally with cross bars. Grows to 6 inches.

Diagnosis.—Dorsal VI-I, 8 or 9; anal I, 8; depth 3.7 to 5.3; head 2.95 to 3.4; eye 3.5 to 4.9; snout 3 to 4.1; gape reaching anterior margin of pupil; scales 35 to 40.

Distribution.—Bermuda and the West Indies; ranging north to the Carolinas. One of the commonest Bermuda fish, found everywhere; especially common in tide pools.

Crested Goby
Lophogobius cyprinoides (Pallas)

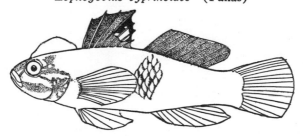

Field Characters.—Small, rather robust, short, compressed fishes with a prominent dermal crest extending from interorbital area to origin of dorsal fin. Blackish green in life; spinous dorsal blackish, often with an irregularly-shaped orange blotch; soft dorsal, pelvic and anal fins dark, plain; caudal finely mottled. Grows to 2 inches, possibly longer.

Diagnosis.—Dorsal VI-10; anal 9; depth 2.88 to 3.6; head 3 to 3.6; eye 3.35; snout 4.45; interorbital scarcely half as wide as eye; scales 27.

Distribution.—Bermuda and the West Indies; Florida; Panama. We have taken this species mainly from brackish inland lakes.

Translucent Goby
Lophogobius glaucofrænum (Gill)

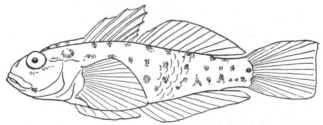

Field Characters.—Small, somewhat compressed fishes with pelvic fins joined together to form a sucking-disk; lower jaw slightly projecting; a small dermal crest along top of head extending almost to dorsal fin, low and broad. Colour more or less pale translucent white, posterior portion of body often transparent. Sides usually with groups of spots along the base of the dorsal fin, from upper part of opercle to caudal and along lower part of the sides. A narrow band from eye to upper angle of opercle where it is present as a markedly distinct spot. One or two additional horizontal streaks on the head. Blue marks on head and dorsal fins often present. Occasionally two dark spots connected by a vertical bar on the base of the caudal fin. Grows to about two inches.

Diagnosis.—Dorsal VI-10; anal 10; depth 4.3 to 4.4; head 3.3 to 3.6; eye 3.3; scales 23 to 28.

Distribution.—Bermuda, West Indies, Florida Keys. Fairly common in tidepools.

Thompson's Goby
Gnatholepis thompsoni Jordan.

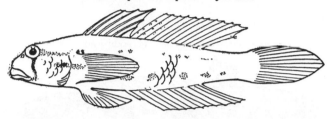

Field Characters.—Small, scaled fishes with pelvic fins joined together, forming a sucking-disk; scales present on the opercles and cheeks. Greyish yellow with dusky blotches on the sides; a conspicuous, narrow dark line downward over the cheek from the eye. Grows to 2.25 inches.

Diagnosis.—Dorsal VI or VII-I, 11; anal I, 10 or 11; depth 4.2 to 4.4; head 3.6 to 3.7; eye 3.5 to 3.6; snout 3 to 3.5; maxillary 2.7; scales 28 to 30.

Distribution.—Bermuda, West Indies. Uncommon in Bermuda.

Mowbray's Goby
Rhinogobius mowbrayi Bean

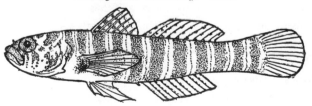

Field Characters.—Very small, scaled fishes with pelvic fins forming a cup,—the membrane crossing the base of the fin, delicate and easily broken. Scales absent on nape and cheeks. Red or greyish with 12 to 14 dark vertical cross-bands, a minute vertical dark line in the interspaces; a large dark blotch at the base of the pectorals.   Grows to about an inch.

Diagnosis.—Dorsal VI, 10 to 11; anal 9; depth 4.5 to 4.9; head 3.55 to 3.7; eye 3.6 to 4; snout 6.2; scales 26 to 31.

Distribution.—Bermuda, Haiti and Curaçao.   Uncommon.

Spot-Tailed Goby
Gobionellus stigmaturus   (Goode and Bean)

Field Characters.—Small sized, blunt-headed, little compressed fishes with the pelvic fins forming a sucking-disk; region from the dorsal fin to top of head scaled, no narrow naked groove; pale greenish to greyish-white, the body and head marbled with pearly white and brownish. Five more or less diffuse spots along middle of body, the last one at base of tail; from the anterior 3 or 4 of these diffuse narrow bars are carried downward and slightly forward. Diffuse spots on cheek under eye, from eye to upper lip, at angle of preopercle, on opercle, and one shoulder spot over angle of gill-opening,—all of these spots of about the same intensity. Grows to about 2 inches.

Diagnosis.—Dorsal VI-12; anal 13; depth 4.5 to 5.2; head 4; snout about equal to eye; eye 4; scales 29 to 33.

Distribution.—Known from Bermuda, the Bahamas and Florida. Uncommon at Bermuda.

Darting Goby
Gobionellus boleosoma   (Jordan and Gilbert)
Field Characters.—Small, slender, little-compressed fish with a sucking-disk formed by the pelvic fins; space before the dorsal fin both above and below, without scales; green-

ish, mottled with darker, usually 5 rather diffuse longitudinally elongate spots on the mid line; the 2nd, 3rd and 4th of these spots tending to be somewhat V-shaped; a dark spot behind the gill-opening and over the base of the pectoral fin, sometimes rather indistinct. Grows to two and a half inches.

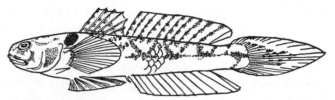

Diagnosis.—Dorsal VI-10 to 12, usually 11; anal 11 to 13, usually 12; depth 5.25; head 4; eye about 4; scales 29 to 33.

Distribution.—Bermuda, North Carolina to Panama, Brazil. Rare in Bermuda.

Naked Goby
Gobiosoma longum Nichols

Field Characters.—Elongate, small, scaleless fish with pelvic fins forming a sucking-disk; eyes small and placed toward the top and anterior part of the head. Colour in life greyish white with small, irregular, dull orange spots on the body and fins, those on the caudal fin in the form of irregular, narrow, vertical bands. Grows to 3½ inches.

Diagnosis.—Dorsal VII-14; anal 13; depth 7 to 8.7; head 4.6 to 5; eye 4 to 5; maxillary 2.3.

Distribution.—Known only from near Key West and Bermuda. A single specimen taken from a small trap set in sand in Castle Harbour, Bermuda, this being the second known example of this fish.

SHARKSUCKERS

See Key, p. 311

This is a small, isolated group of fishes which go through life clinging to the surface of sharks and sea-turtles. The first dorsal fin is transformed into an efficient vacuum sucker and by means of this the Sharksuckers are able to glide swiftly over the skin of the sharks without losing hold, or to cling so tightly that they can withstand a pull of a hundred pounds. Natives in certain parts of the West Indies and elsewhere take the advantage of this and by tying a cord to the tail of the Sucker they pay it out and allow it to take firm hold of a sleeping turtle, and then haul in both Sucker and turtle.

Sharksuckers leave their shark to feed and will now and then take a hook. Two species have been captured in Bermuda waters, their presence of course dependent upon the occurrence in offshore waters of their pelagic hosts.

Family ECHENEIDÆ
Suck-Fish
Echeneis naucrates Linnaeus.

Field Characters.—Medium sized, slender fishes with oval sucking disk on top of head composed of 20 to 28 laminæ. A black band from snout through eye to caudal; dorsal and anal dark brown, the distal parts of anterior rays pale; caudal fin dark with outer rays pale; colour may change so that the fish is almost black or greenish grey. Grows to 38 inches.

Diagnosis.—Dorsal 31 to 35; anal 30 to 34; depth 12.3 to 14.6; length of disk 3.5 to 3.9.

Distribution.—Known from all warm seas. Commonly seen on sharks about Bermuda. One specimen observed on side of a large parrotfish, *Pseudoscarus guacamaia*.

Photo by E. R. Sanborn

RED PARROTFISH
Sparisoma abildgaardi

MARK'S BLENNY
Emblemaria markii

Off-Shore Remora or Shark-Pilot
Remora remora (Linnaeus)

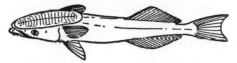

Field Characters.—Robustly-built fishes with a sucking-disk on top of head composed of about 18 laminæ. Colour nearly uniform dark brown. Grows to about 15 inches.

Diagnosis.—Dorsal 23; anal 25; depth about 6.6; head 4; sucking-disk longer than the dorsal or anal fin, of 18 lamellæ.

Distribution.—Occurs in all warm seas. Fairly common on sharks about Bermuda.

DRAGONETS
See Key, p. 311

Two species of these fantastic little fish are occasionally brought up in the shallow water dredge in Bermuda. Their pattern and colours, the elaborate development of fin structure, the curious flattened head, all give a strange, weird appearance and make them worthy of the name Little Dragons.

The extreme development of fins and ornamentation in the males suggests that these fish have a more or less elaborate courtship and this has been observed and described in a European species. In one form where the fins are eyed like the tail of a peacock the fish live in pairs and the male has an elaborate display.

Family CALLIONYMIDÆ
Bermuda Dragonet
Callionymus bermudarum Barbour

Field Characters.—Small, somewhat depressed, protractile-mouthed fishes with preopercle ending in a small spiny process,—two spines pointing upward and backward, and one pointing backward; a lateral fleshy keel along the posterior ventral surface of the body; 4 or 5 anal rays; spinous dorsal in the male very high, the spines filamentous, the fin of the female much lower. Yellowish grey mottled with orange and brown, the two latter colours are not very distinct. Two brownish cross-bands on the dorsal surface, sometimes almost absent. Small, very dark brown spots on body, especially marked on sides along lateral line and on inferior dermal keels. A large black spot on the opercle posterior to the preopercle. Two elongate black marks along the edge of the first dorsal fin. Grows to a little over an inch and a quarter in length.

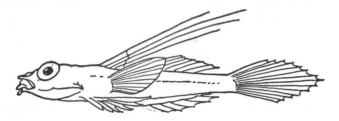

Diagnosis.—Dorsal IV to V, 7; anal 4 to 5; depth 5.55 to 6.5; eye 2.8 to 3; snout 3.5; scales absent.

Distribution.—Known only from Bermuda and the Bahamas. Uncommon in Bermuda.

West Indian Dragonet
Callionymus boeki Metzelaar

Field Characters.—Small, somewhat compressed, protractile-mouthed fishes, with 8 or 9 anal rays; preopercular process with three spines above, and one forward pointing spine below; males with spines of the dorsal very long and filamentous, often reaching to the centre of the caudal fin. Males considerably darker than females; body mottled, irregularly banded; spotted. Grows to about 3 inches.

Diagnosis.—Dorsal IV, 9 or 10; anal 8 or 9; depth 5.25 to 5.5; head to gill opening 3.25 to 3.75; eye 3 to 3.5;

interorbital very narrow; maxillary scarcely reaches eye; lateral lines connected on the nape.

Distribution.—Bermuda; Bahamas; St. Eustatius; Curaçao. Commonly taken in Bermuda by dredge in depths of 20 to 30 feet.

BLENNIES
See Key, p. 311

In action and appearance these seem to be the most intelligent of the small Bermuda fish. This is perhaps unfairly enhanced by the hand and foot-like use of the pelvic fins, and the conspicuous, intelligent looking eyes. Both in the tidepools and two to three fathoms down, which are their natural haunts, and in aquariums, they are quick, keen and fearless. They pay little attention to the approaching diver or to any one watching close to the glass of the aquarium.

Their colours are changeable, their heads often decorated with fleshy fringes, and the pelvic fins consist of a few stout rays. Seven species are on record as occurring in the waters of Bermuda.

Family CLINIDÆ
Fajardo Blenny
Auchenopterus fajardo Evermann and Marsh.

Field Characters.—Small, compressed, scaled blennies with a single soft ray at the posterior end of the dorsal fin;

lateral line complete. Reddish, mottled, with dark cross bars which extend onto the dorsal and anal fins; an ocellus sometimes present on the dorsal fin. Grows to a little over 1½ inches.

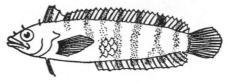

Diagnosis.—Dorsal XXIX, 1; anal II, 17; depth 4.8; head 3.25; eye 4.2; snout 4.8; interorbital 5.5; maxillary 1.7; scales 34.

Distribution.—Bermuda; Bahamas; Porto Rico and Haiti. One published record from Bermuda.

Molly Miller
Labrisomus nuchipinnis   (Quoy and Gaimard)

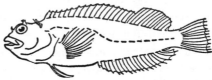

Field Characters.—Small, rather robust, scaled fishes with pelvic fins composed of 1 spine and 2 rays; a transverse fringe of tentacles on the nape; teeth in an outer large series and an inner smaller series. Colour variable, brownish, sometimes with red or orange or green on head and body, with indistinct crossbars and blotches; a black spot on the opercle and on the anterior rays of the spinous dorsal. Grows to 8 inches.

Diagnosis.—Dorsal XVIII, 12; anal II, 17 or 18; depth 3.5 to 3.9; head 3.2 to 3.5; eye 3.8 to 4.7; snout 3 to 3.33; maxillary 1.95 to 2.25; scales 68 to 80 in lateral line.

Distribution.—Bermuda and the West Indies; Florida to Brazil. One of the commonest Bermuda fishes in tide pools and along shore.

Short-Finned Molly Miller
Labrisomus lentiginosus Bean

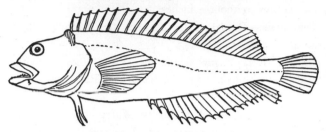

Field Characters.—Small, rather robust, scaled fishes with pelvic fins composed of 1 spine and 2 rays; a fringe of tentacles on the nape; pelvic fins very short. No black spot on the opercle or on the dorsal fin. Grows to 4½ inches.

Diagnosis.—Dorsal XVIII, 12; anal 19; depth 4; head 3; eye 4.5; snout 4.5.

Distribution.—Bermuda and Grenada. Two published records and we have taken one specimen. Rare,—and it is possible that this form may be a variation of the preceding species.

Family BLENNIIDÆ
Soft-Toothed Tide-Pool Blenny
Salariichthys textilis (Quoy and Gaimard)

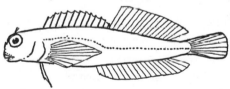

Field Characters.—Small, elongate, small-headed fish with pelvic fins of 1 spine and 3 rays; a cirrus on the nostril, eye, and one on each side of the nape; no longitudinal cirri down the middle of the nape; teeth very small, freely movable, implanted on the skin of the lips, not on the bone of the jaw. Olive green to purplish, variable; sides with vertical dark bars often in pairs, the interspaces and a series of widely scattered dots whitish to silvery; caudal fin with 5 to 7 more or less regular dark vertical bars. Grows to about 4 inches.

Diagnosis.—Dorsal XII, 16; anal 18; depth 4.6 to 4.9; head 4.6; eye 4.25; snout 3.

Distribution.—Bermuda and the West Indies to southern Florida. A common tide-pool blenny in Bermuda.

Scaleless Molly Miller
Blennius cristatus Linnaeus.

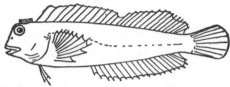

Field Characters.—Small, blunt-headed fishes with pelvic fins of 1 spine and 3 rays; a fringe of tentacles on the middle of the nape extending from between the eyes to the dorsal fin; lower jaw with two stoutish posterior canine teeth. Colour variable, some uniform dark brown, nearly black above and only slightly lighter below; others lighter with cross bars on back and side. Grows to 4 inches.

Diagnosis.—Dorsal XI, 16; anal 19; depth 4; head 4; snout blunt; interorbital ⅔ width of eye; maxillary 3; scales absent.

Distribution.—Bermuda and the West Indies; Florida to Brazil. Common in Bermuda.

Bermuda Blenny
Hypleurochilus bermudensis Beebe and Tee-Van.

Field Characters.—Small, short-headed, scaleless fish with small pelvic fins of three rays each; gill openings confined to the sides only, the membrane fully attached to the isthmus below. A short multifid tentacle above the eye and a similar one on the anterior nostril. Colour brownish to yellow-buff, heavily mottled with dark brown. Vertical and

paired fins with small brown spots on the rays. Grows to
about two inches.

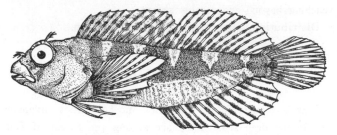

Diagnosis.—Dorsal XII, 13; anal I, 15; depth 4.05; head
3.2; eye 3.6; snout 3; interorbital 8.2; maxillary 2.9; scales
absent.

Distribution.—Known only from Bermuda.

Family EMBLEMARIIDÆ
Mark's Blenny
Emblemaria marki Mowbray

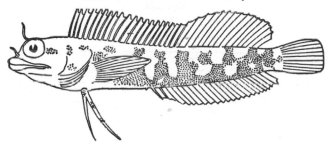

Field Characters.—Small, scaleless fish with pelvic fins
of 1 spine and 2 rays; no canines in jaws; no cirri on
nape; a nasal and an ocular cirrus; dorsal in males with
6th, 7th and 8th spines very long, their height being about
3 in the total length; the fin generally very much higher
than is shown in the illustration. Brown with 6 to 10 more
or less irregular vertical bands, the outer border of each
band with a dark spot, the band usually broken on the
upper side; vertical fins dusky with black blotches and
marks. Grows to 2½ inches long.

Diagnosis.—Dorsal XXII, 14 or 15; anal 25; depth 5.16; head 3.66; eye 4; snout slightly less than 4; maxillary reaching beyond eye; scales absent.

Distribution.—Bermuda. Rather uncommon.

BROTULIDS
See Key, p. 312

This is a large family of fishes, most of whose members live in the deep sea. They are among the rarest of Bermuda fish. Three species have been recorded, all the individuals under three inches in length living in crevices of coral. We have taken a very few individuals both in Somerset and off Nonsuch. The scales are very small, the colours dull and the pelvic fins are reduced to a single filament.

Family BROTULIDÆ
Brotula
Brotula barbata   (Bloch and Schneider)

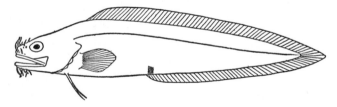

Field Characters.—Small to medium sized, elongate, compressed fishes covered with minute scales; lower jaw included in the upper; each jaw with 3 barbels on each side; dorsal fin long and low, the dorsal and anal joined to the caudal; pelvic fins each reduced to a single ray, ½ as long as head; fins enveloped in thick skin. Nearly uniform brown. Grows to 18 inches.

Diagnosis.—Dorsal 125; anal 93; depth about 5; head 4.5.

Distribution.—Bermuda and the West Indies. One record from Bermuda in 1877.

Verrill's Brotulid
Ogilbia verrillii (Garman)

Field Characters.—Very small, moderately robust, compressed fishes; pelvic fins each of one long filament; scales thin, embedded; dorsal and anal fins long, free from the caudal fin. Light olivaceous, dotted with brown, centres of scales darker; fins whitish; each flank with 3 longitudinal yellow streaks a single scale in width, separated from each other by spaces 5 scales in width, beginning behind the shoulder and ending forward of the caudal; lowest one longer; indications of similar streaks at bases of dorsal and anal fins. Grows to less than 2 inches.

Diagnosis.—Dorsal 70; anal 50; depth 6.4; head 4; eye 10; snout twice as long as eye, 5; maxillary nearly half as long as head; gill-rakers short, compressed, 12; scales about 100.

Distribution.—Bermuda only. Rare.

West Indian Brotulid
Ogilbia cayorum Evermann and Kendall.

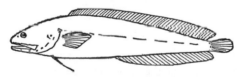

Field Characters.—Very small, moderately elongate, compressed fishes, covered with small embedded scales; snout blunt; eye very small, high up; dorsal and anal fins long and low, not connected to the caudal fin by membrane. Colour uniform pale olivaceous or light brown, finely dotted with minute brown specks. Grows to 2½ inches.

Diagnosis.—Dorsal 65 to 68; anal 50 to 55; depth 4.6; head 4 to 4.6; eye 8.5 to 9.2; interorbital 4.3; snout rather blunt, 4; maxillary 1.7; scales about 87 to 90.

Distribution.—Bermuda; Key West; Panama. One record from Bermuda in 1906.

PEARLFISH

A species of this strange Fierasfer or Holothurian-fish has been described from Bermuda, but no adult has since been recorded from the island in the literature. In deep sea trawls we have occasionally taken the sea-serpent-like larva of one of this group.

The eel-like form, the greatly elongate anal fin, absence of pelvic fins and the habit of living within a shell or a live sea-cucumber will identify this remarkable fish.

Family CARAPIDÆ
Pearlfish
Carapus bermudensis (Jones)

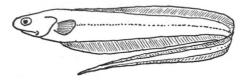

Field Characters.—Small, elongate, eel-shaped, naked fishes, the body tapering into a long and slender tail; vent at the throat; the anal fin originating immediately in back of the anus, so that the fish has an inordinately long anal; pectoral fins well developed; no pelvic fins; gill membranes little connected, leaving isthmus bare. Colour pale brownish, a bluish streak across the nape between the opercles; 4 pale points on the back; usually found living in shells, or in sea-puddings or sea-cucumbers. Grows to 4 to 6 inches.

Diagnosis.—Head 8½; eye 4, longer than snout; mouth large, the maxillary reaching beyond the orbit; pectoral 2½ in head.

Distribution.—Bermuda; Porto Rico. Rare in Bermuda.

TRIGGERFISH
See Key, p. 313
The Triggerfish and Filefish are of all sizes and colours, usually with leathery skins and small, protruding mouths.

A single conspicuous character found in all is the first dorsal element elongated into a long, sharp spine. This may be smooth or serrated and is relatively much larger in the young than in the full-grown fish.

Several are oceanic and found only under sargassum weed. The big, two foot Queen Triggers are strikingly marked, and almost always to be seen alive in the Aquarium. The little, two and three inch Filefish are common in every dredge haul made on grassy shallows.

Fourteen species are recorded from Bermuda waters.

Family BALISTIDÆ

Queen Triggerfish; Bastard Turbot; Queen Turbot

Balistes vetula Linnaeus

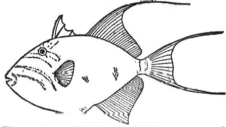

Field Characters.—Medium sized, compressed fish, with small mouth; skin leathery but the scales very evident; dorsal fins separate, the first of 3 spines, the first spine much the longest and heaviest; cheeks with two broad curved bands of blue, and a series of small narrower bands above these. Grows to 15 inches.

Diagnosis.—Dorsal III-29 or 30; anal 26 to 28; depth 1.7 to 2; head to upper angle of gill-slit 2.6 to 2.75; eye 3.5 to 4.7; snout 1.35 to 1.45; scales 60 to 62; a groove before the eye.

Distribution.—Bermuda and the West Indies; Massachusetts to Brazil. Also recorded from the Azores and Ascension Island. Occasionally taken off shore by the fishermen of Bermuda. A school of 22 seen 150 feet down from the Bathysphere.

Ocean Turbot; Spotted Trigger
Balistes forcipatus Gmelin

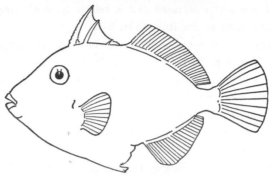

Field Characters.—Small to medium sized compressed fishes with small mouths; skin leathery, but the scales evident; dorsal fins separate, the first of three spines. Brownish above, yellow beneath, upper surfaces with brownish mottlings; entire body, dorsal and anal fins covered with blue spots, those on the fins and lower surface of the body much paler than the others. Grows to at least 15 inches.

Diagnosis.—Dorsal III-29; anal 23; depth 1.8; head 2.8; eye 3.3; snout 1.6.

Distribution.—Known from both coasts of the tropical Atlantic. Rare in Bermuda.

Turbot
Balistes capriscus Gmelin

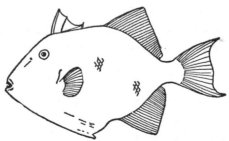

Field Characters.—Medium sized, compressed, deep fishes with rather heavy plate-like scales; eye placed high and

Photo by E. R. Sanborn

QUEEN TRIGGERFISH
Balistes vetula

with a narrow, naked groove before it; vertical fins falcate, especially the caudal. Olive grey, the interspaces between the scales paler, the head and upper part dusky; tips
of soft dorsal, anal and the entire caudal fin dusky; base
of pectoral below dark brownish green. Grows to about a
foot.

Diagnosis.—Dorsal III-27 to 29; anal 23 to 26; depth
1.7 to 2.25; head to upper angle of gill-slit 2.8 to 3.1;
scales 54 to 62.

Distribution.—Bermuda; tropical parts of the Atlantic;
occasionally northward in the Gulf Stream. Fairly common
in Bermuda.

Ocean Triggerfish

Canthidermis sobaco (Poey)

Field Characters.—Compressed, rather deep, leathery-
skinned fishes, the scales of the trunk each with a median
keel or spine; dorsal fin with 26 or 28 soft rays; anal fin
with 24 or 25 rays. Dark brown, the vertical fins dusky;
young are mottled, the mottlings darker and much more
irregular than in similar sized examples of *maculatus.*
Grows to 2 feet.

Diagnosis.—Dorsal III-26 to 28; anal 24 or 25; depth
2; head 4; eye 5.5 in head, 4 in snout.

Distribution.—Bermuda and the West Indies, occasionally north to Massachusetts. Rare,—three small specimens
taken by us off Bermuda.

Ocean Turbot

Canthidermis maculatus (Bloch)

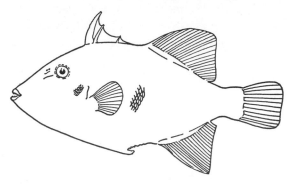

Field Characters.—Compressed, rather deep, leathery-skinned fishes, the scales of the posterior trunk keeled but without an especially well-marked median keel or spine; dorsal fin with 22 to 24 rays, anal fin with 19 to 21 rays. Brownish, with slightly darker reticulations on side of body, soft vertical fins with pale bluish spots; membrane of spinous dorsal very dark. Grows to at least 8 inches and possibly larger.

Diagnosis.—Dorsal III-22 to 24; anal 19 to 21; depth 2.5 at vertical of origin of spinous dorsal; head 2.9; eye 4.6; snout 1.65.

Distribution.—Bermuda; warmer parts of Atlantic. A fairly common species off shore in Bermuda.

Red-Tailed Triggerfish

Xanthichthys ringens (Linnaeus)

Field Characters.—Small, compressed fishes with small mouth; lower jaw projecting; 3 naked, narrow grooves on cheeks from gill opening to chin. Colour variable, each scale of the sides with a violet point at its intersection with the other scales; the naked grooves on the cheeks violet black; body yellow, green, blue or violet; membrane of the first dorsal fin black; soft dorsal and anal fin pinkish;

caudal entirely or with its upper, lower and posterior edges scarlet. Grows to 10 inches.

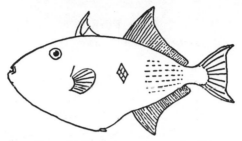

Diagnosis.—Dorsal II-31 to 33; anal 28 or 29; depth 1.6 to 2; head 3 to 4; eye 5.3 in snout; snout 1.33.

Distribution.—Bermuda and the West Indies, southward. Common under sargassum weed, but only a single fish taken by us off Bermuda.

Family MONACANTHIDÆ
Orange-Spotted Filefish
Cantherines pullus (Ranzani)

Field Characters.—Small to medium sized, leathery-skinned, small-mouthed fishes, with large dorsal spine, situated immediately above the eye; no barbs on posterior side of spine. Dark brown, entire body covered with small, round, dull orange spots with a dark centre; on the breast toward the snout these spots become irregular wavy bands; five narrow blue stripes from eye to snout. Reaches a weight of 6 pounds and a length of at least 12 inches.

Diagnosis.—Dorsal II-35; anal 31; depth 2; head 3.3 to 3.6; scales absent; skin leathery.

Distribution.—Bermuda and the West Indies; Florida; Brazil. Rare in Bermuda.

False Filefish
Cantherines amphioxys (Cope)

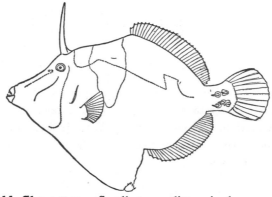

Field Characters.—Small to medium sized, compressed, leathery-skinned fishes with smooth or slightly granular spine placed immediately above the eye; pelvic spine fixed, not movable. Reddish or orange brown to blackish and greenish brown, with or without rather large, lozenge-shaped spots of whitish or buffy brown; a large, elongate, saddle-shaped patch of grey or greenish on the back between the dorsal fins; caudal fin almost black; pectoral, soft dorsal and anal fins greenish yellow. Grows to over a foot.

Diagnosis.—Dorsal I-34 to 35; anal 30; depth 2 to 1.6 (at 5 to 6 inches); head 2.6 to 2.7 (at length of 2 to 3 inches); to 3.4 (at 5 to 6 inches length); eye 3 to 4 in snout, 4.5 in head; skin leathery.

Distribution.—Bermuda and the West Indies. Rare in Bermuda.

Tucker's Filefish
Monacanthus tuckeri Bean

Field Characters.—Small, leathery-skinned, rather elongate, compressed fish with small mouth, and with a long, barbed dorsal spine over the eye; small recurved spines present on the caudal peduncle on fishes of over 2 inches. Greenish, abdomen somewhat silvery, often with hieroglyphic-like markings. Grows to about 3 inches.

Diagnosis.—Dorsal I-33 to 35; anal 34 to 36; depth 2.7 to 3; head 2.8 to 3; eye 3 to 3.4 in head; snout 1.3.

Distribution.—Bermuda; West Indies. A common species about Bermuda.

Common Filefish
Monacanthus hispidus (Linnaeus)

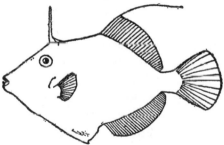

Field Characters.—Small, compressed, leathery-skinned fishes with small mouth and with a long, barbed, dorsal spine over or nearly over the eye; ventral flap never extending beyond tip of pelvic spine; first dorsal ray in adult sometimes produced as a filament; no recurved spines on the caudal peduncle. Colour variable, from plain grass green to very dark green and marbled with black. Grows to 10 inches.

Diagnosis.—Dorsal II-31 to 35; anal 31 to 35; depth 1.7 to 2.2; head 3.4; eye 3.5 to 4.

Distribution.—Bermuda and the West Indies; Cape Cod to Brazil. Fairly common in Bermuda.

Leather-Fish
Monacanthus ciliatus (Mitchill)

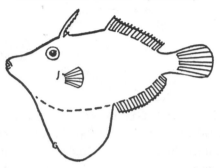

Field Characters.—Small, compressed, leathery-skinned fishes with small mouth and with a long, barbed spine near eye; ventral flap in adult greatly developed, extending far beyond the pelvic spine; strong, recurved, forward-pointing spines on the caudal peduncle in older fish. Colour variable and changing with the surroundings, markings not well defined and changing. Grows to 8 inches.

Diagnosis.—Dorsal I-29 to 35; anal 29 to 35; depth 2 to 2.6; head 2.9 to 3.4; eye 3.3 to 3.8; snout 1.3 to 1.5.

Distribution.—Bermuda and the West Indies; North Carolina to Brazil. Fairly common over weed covered areas in Bermuda.

Orange Filefish
Alutera schœpfi (Walbaum)

Field Characters.—Medium sized, ungainly, leathery-skinned fishes with small, terminal mouth; dorsal fin consisting of a single spine, followed after a wide space by the soft dorsal which has 35 to 38 rays. Orange to dark brown; sides with dark, round spots more numerous in larger examples. Reaches a length of 2 feet.

Diagnosis.—Dorsal I-35 to 38; anal 39 or 40; depth 2.3 to 2.7; head 3 to 3.4; eye 4 to 5; snout 1.1 to 1.2.

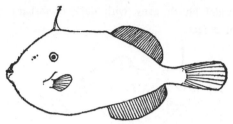

Distribution.—Bermuda and the West Indies; Maine to Brazil. Rare in Bermuda.

Scrawled Filefish
Alutera scripta (Osbeck)

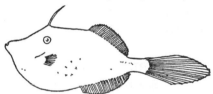

Field   Characters.—Elongate,   compressed,   ungainly, leathery-skinned fishes; a single, separate dorsal fin of one spine, followed after a wide space by the soft dorsal; caudal fin elongate, with rounded angles. Head and body olivaceous, with irregular, conspicuous, light blue spots and curved streaks, and with numerous round black spots about size of pupil. Grows to 3 feet.

Diagnosis.—Dorsal I-47 to 49; anal 48 to 51; depth 2.65 to 4; head to upper angle of gill opening 3.15 to 4.6; eye 3.25 to 5; snout 1.1 to 1.3.

Distribution.—Bermuda and the West Indies; South Carolina to Brazil; East Indies. Uncommon.

Unicorn Filefish
Alutera monoceros (Osbeck)

Field Characters.—Compressed, velvety fishes with a single dorsal spine, followed at a distance by the soft dorsal.

Dull bluish grey above, yellowish white to white below; head and body covered with blackish marks of various shapes; caudal bluish grey with dark cross-bars. Reaches a length of 2 feet.

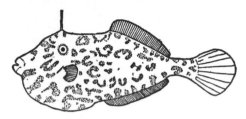

Diagnosis.—Dorsal I-48 to 50; anal 50 to 52; depth 2.4 to 2.75; head 4; eye 4 in head.

Distribution.—Bermuda and the West Indies; East Indies; recorded as a straggler from Massachusetts. One published record from Bermuda.

TRUNKFISH
See Key, p. 314

These fish are completely enclosed in a mosaic box of bone, divided into six-sided scutes. There are holes in the armour through which the jaws, eyes, fins and tail function. Trunkfish are slow swimmers and are frequently brightly coloured, having nothing to fear from their enemies. They are considered as good eating and are often baked in the shell.

Four species occur in Bermudian waters.

Family OSTRACIIDÆ
Smooth Trunkfish: Coker; Cokerfish
Lactophrys triqueter (Linnaeus)

Field Characters.—Body enclosed in a bony box; carapace without spines. Brown or greenish, thickly studded with small greenish blue spots; base of dorsal, caudal and pectoral fins black, fins otherwise plain or bright yellow. Reaches ten inches.

Diagnosis.—Dorsal 10; anal 10; depth at nape 1.7; head 2.8; snout 1.25; eye 2.4; interorbital 1.45.

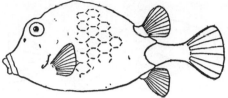

Distribution.—Bermuda and the West Indies; Florida to Brazil. Rare in Bermuda.

Cuckold; Buffalo Cowfish
Lactophrys trigonus (Linnaeus)

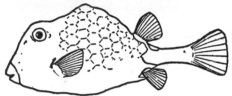

Field Characters.—Body enclosed in a bony box; the carapace open behind the dorsal fin; ventral ridges ending in a large flat spine; no spines in front of eye. Olive grey, a very faint blue spot in centre of most of the scales; boundaries of upper scutes blackish, of lower bluish. Grows to nine inches.

Diagnosis.—Dorsal 10; anal 10; depth at nape 2.65 to 2.8; head 3.8.

Distribution.—Bermuda and the West Indies; Massachusetts to Brazil. Uncommon.

Cowfish
Lactophrys quadricornis (Linnaeus)

Field Characters.—Body enclosed in a bony case; a spine on each side continuing the ventral ridge and a spine on each side in front of eye; caudal fin truncate, its outer rays sometimes produced. Colour brown, yellow, blue or green with irregular blue blotches. Grows to a foot or more.

Diagnosis.—Dorsal 9 or 10; anal 10; depth at nape 1.75 to 2; head 2.9 to 3.1; eye 2.1 to 2.4; snout 1.1 to 2; interorbital 1 in eye.

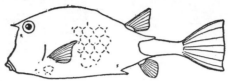

Distribution.—Bermuda and the West Indies; Carolinas to Brazil, occasionally to Massachusetts. Occasional in Bermuda.

Bermuda Cowfish

Lactophrys saxatilis Mowbray

Field Characters.—Fish with body enclosed in a bony box; two horn like projections in front of each eye, and a horn like projection on the lower sides; caudal fin rounded; plates of entire body covered conspicuously with papillæ. Dark olive green, the edges of the plates lighter, the centre of each plate in the pectoral region with a snow white centre, varying in size, the largest almost as large as the pupil; no bright blue or green spots anywhere as in *quadricornis*. Dorsal and anal yellow green; caudal olive yellow, with darker spots on the rays, which gives the caudal a vertical barred effect. Grows to 12 inches.

Diagnosis.—Dorsal 10; anal 10; depth 2 to posterior base of plates; head 4.35.

Distribution.—Known only from the two type specimens, taken among the coral reefs of Bermuda.

PUFFERS

See Key, p. 315

Three families of these small or medium sized fishes are so closely related that they may be included in one general group. Their structure and activities are subordinated to one ability—that of filling themselves with air or water and

HOME OF THE SHORE FISHES OF BERMUDA

swelling themselves up into more or less of a sphere. More than once we have seen this feat save them when about to be swallowed by some large fish. When inflated, they are helpless and float, upside down, on the surface.

The skin is smooth or covered with spines which stand erect when the fish is inflated. The pelvic and spiny dorsal fins have disappeared and the vertical fins are reduced in extent. The gills are reduced to mere slits, and the teeth are fused into cutting plates.

Five species, belonging to three families, are recorded from Bermuda.

Family TETRAODONTIDÆ
Jugfish; Elongate Pufffish
Lagocephalus pachycephalus (Ranzani)

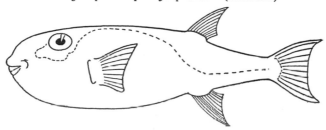

Field Characters.—Smooth-skinned, robust, rather elongate fish capable of inflating the abdomen with air or water; jaws beak-like, with a median suture; lower parts covered with short, three-rooted spines; olive green above, silvery white on sides. Reaches a length of two feet.

Diagnosis.—Dorsal 13 or 14; anal 12 or 13; depth 4.3 to 4.5; head 3.25 to 3.3; eye 4.8; snout 2.1; interorbital 2.3.

Distribution.—Bermuda; West Indies; Massachusetts to Brazil. One record from Bermuda.

Southern Puffer
Sphæroides spengleri (Bloch)
Field Characters.—Small to medium sized oblong fish capable of swallowing air and water and distending the body

for purposes of protection; teeth fused into a beak-like structure; dark greenish or brown above, mottled; a row of well-defined, round, black spots extending along the sides from mouth to tail; white below; caudal fin with two dark, vertical bands. Reaches a length of two feet.

Diagnosis.—Dorsal 7 or 8; anal 6 or 7; depth 3.6 to 5.15; head 2.2 to 3.1; eye 4 to 5.5; snout 1.85 to 2.2; interorbital 7 to 12.

Distribution.—Bermuda and the West Indies, Massachusetts to Brazil. Common in Bermuda, taken in almost every haul of the seine.

Family CANTHIGASTERIDÆ
Sharp-Nosed Puffer
Canthigaster rostratus (Bloch)

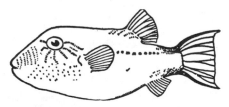

Field Characters.—Small, smooth-skinned fishes with jaws beak-like, with a median suture; body from eye to dorsal fin compressed and ridge-like; lower parts with small prickles, sometimes occurring on the back; brownish above, mottled; cream colour below; upper and under surface of caudal peduncle black; radiating lines around the eye; vertical lines on the snout; a line of small dark dots along sides of body. Less than six inches in length.

Diagnosis.—Dorsal 9 to 10; anal 8 to 9; depth 2.35; head 2.5; eye 4.3; snout 1.6; interorbital 3.5 to 3.7.

Distribution.—Bermuda and the West Indies; Florida, Madeira. Fairly common in Bermuda.

Porcupinefish
Diodon hystrix   Linnaeus

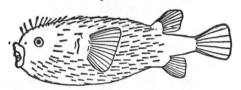

Field Characters.—Small to medium sized, short and robust fishes, body covered with sharp, erectile, movable, quill-like spines. Olivaceous, white or dusky below, body with black bars, blotches and spots. Reaches a length of three feet.

Diagnosis.—Dorsal 13 or 14; anal 12 or 13; depth 2.45 to 3; head 2.2 to 2.4; eye 2.85 to 3.45; snout 2.8 to 3.1; interorbital 1.4 in head.

Distribution.—All warm seas, drifting north rarely to Massachusetts. Fairly common in Bermuda.

Sea Porcupine
Chilomycteris atinga   (Linnaeus)

Field Characters.—Small fishes with skin covered with short stiff spines, more or less immovable; mouth small, transverse; no spines on the forehead; body and fins almost covered with small, round, black spots; a large black blotch before and around dorsal; another on each side above gill-opening and pectoral; spots on the back more or less ocellated, and of the size of the pupil, those of the fins much smaller.

Diagnosis.—Dorsal 12 or 13; anal 12 or 13; depth 2.66; head 2.66.

Distribution.—Bermuda and the West Indies; Florida Keys. One record from Bermuda in 1877.

ANGLERS OR FROGFISH
See Key, p. 315

These little creatures are probably the strangest looking fish of any living in Bermuda waters. Their true character of fish is disguised by a bizarre shape, camouflaged mouth, and dorsal fin changed into isolated peaks and tentacles. Often the body is decorated with waving shreds of skin, while the amazingly ruptive pattern and colours accentuate the general appearance of being less a fish and more a bit of seaweed or coral rock.

The anterior dorsal spine is usually in the shape of a delicate tentacle, with a dangling, fleshy, terminal bait which can be wriggled violently and has been observed to act as a successful lure in attracting living fish near enough to be seized.

Anglers are the most voracious of surface fish, and are so cannibalistic that two cannot be kept together in the same aquarium without one being swallowed.

The paired fins are mobile and have great clasping power enabling the fish to cling to whatever substance its appearance simulates.

Nine species have been recorded from Bermuda, but all are rarely seen except the Sargassumfish, which is common and may be shaken out of almost any large patch of fresh, drifting sargassum weed.

Family ANTENNARIIDÆ
Common Sargassumfish; also Mousefish; Toadfish; and Devilfish
Histrio gibba (Mitchill)

Field Characters.—Strange, small, frog-like fish, living among floating sargassum weed; body oval, thick; mouth almost vertical; on the head a long, fleshy tentacle with a bulbous tip, covered with slender, thread-like filaments; the dorsal fin with 3 spines and 12 rays; colour variegated,

spotted yellow, black and white like the seaweed. Reaches
a length of fifteen inches but rarely seen over two.

Distribution.—Bermuda and the West Indies, north to
Key West and the Tortugas. Tropical Atlantic wherever
sargassum weed abounds. In Bermuda found even in the
sounds under floating weed.

Sargassumfish or Mousefish
Histrio pictus (Cuvier and Valenciennes)

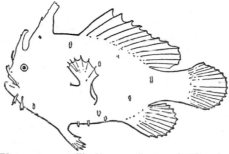

Field Characters.—Similar to those of *Histrio gibba* but
with the fleshy dorsal tentacle with a bifurcated tip, and the
dorsal fin with 3 spines and 14 rays. Reaches a length of
six inches.

Distribution.—Bermuda and the West Indies, north
rarely to Massachusetts; tropical Atlantic in general. The
only Bermuda record is an uncertain one made in 1876.

Brown Mousefish
Histrio jagua Nichols

Field Characters.—Differs from the other two species of
this genus in having a spiral-grooved, pointed bulb on the

tip of the first dorsal spine, and in the colour which is dark chocolate brown with an irregular scattering of white spots. The largest known is four and a half inches in length.

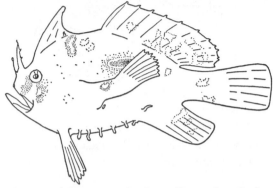

Distribution.—Known only from Bermuda. It is a rare fish, to be looked for in seaweed.

Star-Eyed Frogfish
Antennarius radiosus   Garman

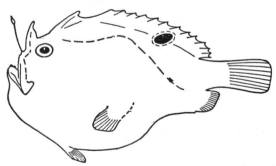

Field Characters.—Strange, small, froglike fishes, with first dorsal spine scarcely longer than the second, and topped with a bulb covered with finger-like protuberances. Colour reddish or yellowish, darker on the nape and dorsal fin, with numerous spots of black; black lines radiating from eye; a large, white-edged, black spot on the base of the dorsal fin. Grows to at least three inches.

Distribution.—Bermuda, Key West and Havana. One Bermuda specimen was taken many years ago by F. Goodwin Gosling.

Black Frogfish
Antennarius nuttingii Garman

Field Characters.—Small, strange, froglike fishes, with the tip of the first dorsal spine bifid, the spine itself short, little longer than the second. Colour uniform black, inside of mouth black. Grows to a length of three inches.

Distribution.—Bermuda, Haiti and Bahamas. Rare in Bermuda.

Reddish Frogfish
Antennarius scaber (Cuvier)

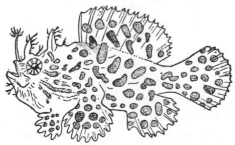

Field Characters.—Small, froglike fishes, with the first dorsal spine as long as the second, and with a bifid bait; the body anteriorly with many dermal flaps; brownish to very dark reddish, sides and fins with dark spots, sometimes forming radiating lines from the eyes; the spots large and more or less round on the fins and frequently with large ocellations; mouth spotted with black within. Grows to four and a half inches.

Distribution.—Bermuda, West Indies and Panama. Occasionally taken in Bermuda.

Yellow Frogfish
Antennarius verrucosus Bean

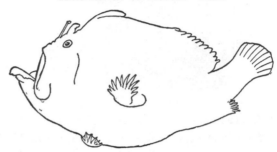

Field Characters.—Small froglike fishes with very small pelvic fins; first dorsal spine shorter than second, and with a terminal bulb set at right angles to the stem; general colour pale yellowish white, with irregular dots and lines of brownish; soft dorsal with four small, rounded, ocellated, dark spots, all smaller than the eye; a dusky blotch on lower portion of soft dorsal; isolated spots and bars on anal and caudal fins; a dusky spot under pectorals. Grows to four inches.

Distribution.—Known only from Bermuda.

White-Spotted Frogfish
Antennarius principis (Cuvier and Valenciennes)

Field Characters.—Small froglike fishes with the first dorsal spine about twice as long as the second, and ending in a small, slender lobe; ground colour black, a small white spot above the pectorals and pelvics. Grows to about three inches.

Distribution.—Bermuda, West Indies and Brazil. Rare in Bermuda.

Green Frogfish
Antennarius stellifer Barbour

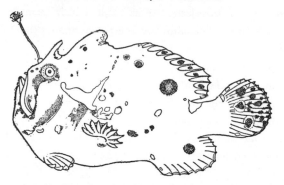

Field Characters.—Small, froglike fishes with the first dorsal spine extremely long and slender, the tip being a tiny sphere from which project numerous delicate filaments; greenish, with many ocellated, blackish spots, especially on the fins; bait, posterior surface of second dorsal ray and under surface of pectoral and pelvic fins dirty white; an irregular white spot on the side of the body; a white saddle on the caudal peduncle. Grows at least to a length of two inches.

Distribution.—Known only from Bermuda.

FISH INTRODUCED BY MAN

Thirteen species of fish belonging to nine families come under the head of being intentionally introduced by man into Bermuda. This number includes the Streaked Grunt (*Hæmulon macrostomum*), specimens of which were introduced fairly recently. This species had previously been reported from Bermuda and it is consequently treated in the main portion of this volume. These are in addition to some, such as the Goldfish and minnows of various species, that are kept for ornament in fresh water pools, or as real aids in the reduction and extermination of mosquito larvæ. The twelve species are inhabitants of salt water and have been brought to the island with reference to future commercial and sporting importance. We have little definite data as to the success of this latter effort, although it seems certain that a few are at least holding their own among the strange elements of their new environment.

These twelve fish are included in the keys for identification but their artificial introduction to the Bermuda fauna automatically excludes them from the general list of the shore fishes of the Island. These fish have been introduced to Bermuda waters by Mr. Louis L. Mowbray, Dr. Charles H. Townsend and Mr. Vincent Astor.

Family PLEURONECTIDÆ
Winter Flounder
Pseudopleuronectes americanus   (Walbaum)

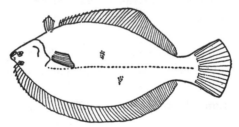

Field Characters.—Small to medium sized fishes with both eyes on the right side of the body. Variable in colour, depending upon the environment; sometimes olive green above with reddish brown spots which may be absent, irregularly placed and of various sizes; white below; fins reddish brown with darker blotches; dorsal and anal greyish. Grows to 21 inches.

Diagnosis.—Dorsal 62 to 69; anal 46 to 53; depth 1.75 to 2.55; head 3.4 to 4; eye 3 to 4.9; snout 4.6 to 5.2; maxillary of right side 3.45 to 4.45; gill-rakers short, about 8; scales 77 to 83.

Distribution.—Northern Labrador to Georgia. Recently introduced into Bermuda.

Family SERRANIDÆ
Common Sea Bass
Centropristes striatus   (Linnaeus)

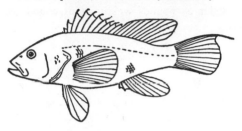

Field Characters.—Small to medium sized, compressed, rather robust fishes; no supplemental bone on the maxillary; caudal fin somewhat double concave, and with one upper ray lengthened in larger specimens; lower jaw projecting; short dermal flaps on the dorsal spines. Dusky brown or black, more or less mottled, and with paler longitudinal streaks along the rows of scales; dorsal fin with several series of elongate whitish spots forming oblique light stripes; other fins dusky mottled; young with a black longitudinal band which later breaks up, forming dark cross shades; a large blackish spot on the last dorsal spines. Grows to 18 inches.

Diagnosis.—Dorsal X, 11; anal III, 7; depth 2.4 to 2.95; head 2.6 to 2.7; eye 3 to 4.9; snout 3.35 to 4.35; interorbital 6.65 to 9.75; maxillary 2.3 to 2.45; gill-rakers 17 or 18; scales 50 to 60.

Distribution.—Massachusetts to northern Florida, rarely north to Maine. Recently introduced into Bermuda.

Family LUTIANIDÆ
Mutton-Fish
Lutianus analis   (Cuvier and Valenciennes)
Field Characters.—Large, elongate, compressed snappers with rather deep head and long snout. Greenish brown above, yellowish green below with a tinge of red on chest and abdomen. Blue lines on head. A small jet black spot,

smaller than the eye, on the lateral line under the anterior rays of the soft dorsal fin, this spot more conspicuous in the young. Fins all reddish, the caudal with a black margin. Grows to about 25 pounds weight, a 21-pound fish measuring 27 inches.

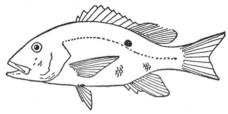

Diagnosis.—Dorsal X, 14, rarely 13; anal III, 8; depth 2.5 to 2.9; head 2.65 to 2.85; eye 3.7 to 5.1; snout 2.2 to 2.9; maxillary 2.3 to 2.7; gill-rakers 7 or 8, exclusive of rudiments; scales 55 to 60.

Distribution.—West Indies, Florida to Brazil, occasionally drifting young find their way to as far north as Massachusetts. This is not a native Bermudian species but was introduced.

Dog Snapper
Lutianus jocu (Bloch and Schneider)

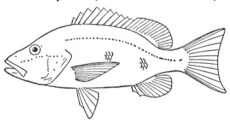

Field Characters.—Medium sized snappers with long pointed snout; scales moderate, the series above the lateral line very oblique, directed strongly upward and backward, those below the lateral line horizontal. Dark brown above, reddish below; bases of scales rusty on upper part of the side, becoming red on lower parts of side, forming more or less distinct lines along the rows of scales; side of head with a blue stripe below the eye, usually broken up into elongate spots in the adult; a broad, whitish bar from eye to angle of mouth, very indistinct or wanting in the young; fins all red, the dorsal and caudal darker red than the others. No black lateral spot. Grows to two feet.

Diagnosis.—Dorsal X, 13 to 14, rarely 15; anal III, 8; depth 2.35 to 2.7; head 2.5 to 2.75; eye 3.45 to 4.8; snout 2.25 to 2.85; maxillary 2.45 to 2.7; gill-rakers 7 to 8; scales in 42 to 46 rows.

Distribution.—Bermuda, West Indies, Florida to Brazil, young occasionally borne northward to Massachusetts in the Gulf Stream. Introduced into Bermuda.

Family HÆMULIDÆ
Grey Grunt
Hæmulon plumieri (Lacépède)

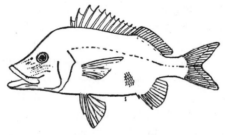

Field Characters.—Medium sized, rather deep, large-mouthed grunts with large scales above the lateral line. Variable in colour, bluish grey, the body sometimes heavily blotched with darker, bases of scales above bright bronze tinged with olive; head bronze with many stripes of clear blue not extending onto the body; body with brown or brassy spotting. Inside of mouth bright orange or red. Grows to about 18 inches, with a maximum weight of 4 pounds.

Diagnosis.—Dorsal XII, 15 or 16; anal III, 8 or 9; depth 2.4 to 2.7; head 2.5 to 2.8; eye 3.9 to 5.2; snout 1.9 to 2.3; maxillary 1.9 to 2; gill-rakers 14 or 15 on the lower limb of the first arch; scales 49 to 53.

Distribution.—Bermuda, West Indies, Cape Hatteras to Brazil. Introduced to Bermuda in 1924, although there is a record in 1891 of one having been sent to New York from Bermuda. This record may be an error.

Pork-Fish
Anisotremus virginicus (Linnaeus)

Field Characters.—Medium sized, deep, small-mouthed grunts with about 7 to 10 horizontal golden lines on a silvery-blue background. A wide black band from the nape through the eye to the angle of the mouth; another from origin of dorsal to or across the base of the pectoral fins. Fins yellow mottled with black, except the pectorals which are golden. Grows to about a foot in length.

Diagnosis.—Dorsal XII, 16 or 17; anal III, 9 or 10; depth 1.9 to 2.1; head 2.8 to 3.2; eye 3 to 4.1; snout 2.65 to 3.1; maxillary 3.3 to 3.7; gill-rakers 13 to 15 on lower limb of the first gill-arch, very short; scales 56 to 63.

Distribution.—Bermuda, West Indies, Florida to Brazil. Introduced in Bermuda.

Family SPARIDÆ
Scup
Stenotomus chrysops Linnaeus

Field Characters.—Medium sized, compressed, rather deep fish; teeth on sides of jaw blunt molars; front teeth narrow, compressed; dorsal spines rather high and slender, the second one more than half the length of the head. Bluish silvery above, plain silver below; young with about 6 dark cross-bars; fins mostly plain, translucent; soft dorsal and sometimes the anal with brownish spots, these spots most distinct in smaller specimens; axil of pectoral fins with a dusky spot. Grows to a weight of four pounds.

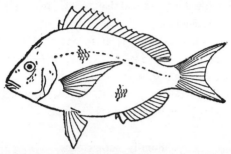

Diagnosis.—Dorsal XII or XIII, 12; anal III, 11 or 12; depth 1.95 to 2.25; head 2.95 to 3.4; eye 2.5 to 3.9; snout 2.3 to 2.55; interorbital 3.1 to 4; maxillary 2.8 to 3.25; scales 49 or 50.

Distribution.—East Coast of the United States, common from South Carolina to Cape Cod, casual in the Gulf of Maine. Recently introduced into Bermuda.

Family EPHIPPIDÆ
Spadefish
Chætodipterus faber Broussonet

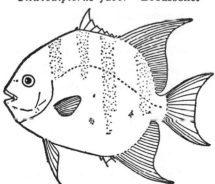

Field Characters.—Moderate sized, compressed, deep fishes with small but rough scales; spinous dorsal somewhat separate from the soft dorsal; dorsal and anal fins with scales; mouth very small, teeth in brush-like bands, slender, closely set and movable. Young with elongate filament on the third dorsal spine. Pearly grey, more or less uniform, the young with dark vertical bands. Grows to 3 feet and a weight of 20 pounds.

Diagnosis.—Dorsal VIII-I, 21 to 23; anal III, 17 to 19; depth 1.15 to 1.4; head 2.7 to 3.5; eye 3 to 4.2; snout 2.2 to 2.6; maxillary 3.1 to 3.35; scales 53 to 60.

Distribution.—Bermuda, West Indies, Massachusetts to Rio de Janeiro. Introduced to Bermuda.

Family SCIÆNIDÆ
Northern Kingfish
Menticirrhus saxatilis (Bloch and Schneider)

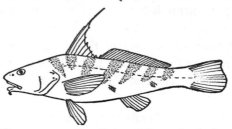

Field Characters.—Small to medium sized elongate fish; snout projecting beyond the mouth; a single small barbel at the chin; spinous dorsal fin rather high anteriorly; dusky above, silvery beneath, sides with oblique bars running upward and backward; a horizontal stripe extending to end of lower lobe of the caudal; pectoral and spinous dorsal fin mostly black; other fins plain to dusky. Grows to about 17 inches.

Diagnosis.—Dorsal X-I, 24 to 26; anal I, 8 or 9; depth 3.65 to 4.3; head 3 to 4.1; eye 2.8 to 4.6; snout 2.9 to 3.5; interorbital 3.5 to 4.5; gill-rakers very short, 6 or less on the lower limb of the first arch; scales 91 to 96.

Distribution.—Cape Cod to Florida, rarely to Maine; recently introduced into Bermuda.

Family CHÆTODONTIDÆ
West Indian Angelfish
Pomacanthus arcuatus (Linnaeus)

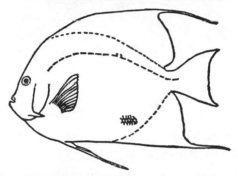

Field Characters.—Small to medium sized, deep, compressed, but robustly built fishes with dorsal and anal fins completely covered with scales, the two fins falcate and produced; mouth small, teeth brush-like and setiform; eight or nine dorsal spines. Greyish or brown, mottled, the young with 4 vertical white cross-bands. Grows to two feet.

Diagnosis.—Dorsal VIII or IX, 32 or 33; anal III, 23 to 25; depth 1.3 to 1.4; head 3.3 to 3.85; gill-rakers short; scales about 80.

Distribution.—Bermuda, West Indies, south to Brazil, north to New Jersey. Introduced into Bermuda.

French Angelfish
Pomacanthus paru (Bloch)

Field Characters.—Small to medium sized, deep, compressed but robustly built fishes with dorsal and anal fins completely covered with scales, the former containing ten spines; mouth small. Black or rich brown, the pectoral fin with an orange or yellow bar at its base. Young with 6 light cross bands. Grows to slightly more than a foot.

Diagnosis.—Dorsal X, 29 to 33; anal III, 22 to 24; depth 1.25 to 1.45; head 3.1 to 3.6; eye 2.45 to 3.6; snout 2.35 to 2.8; gill-rakers very short; scales about 90.

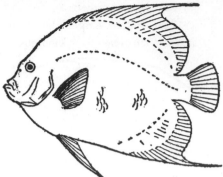

Distribution.—Bermuda, West Indies, Florida to Brazil. Introduced into Bermuda.

Family LABRIDÆ
Tautog; Blackfish
Tautoga onitis Linnaeus

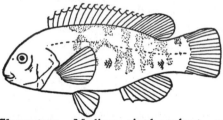

Field Characters.—Medium sized, robust, compressed, **blunt-**headed fishes with stout conical teeth, two or three in front of each jaw larger than the others; caudal peduncle very deep. Colour variable, grey, green or blackish with sides irregularly mottled or blotched with darker,—larger fish are often almost plain. Grows to 3 feet, but large specimens are rare.

Diagnosis.—Dorsal XVI or XVII, 10; anal III, 7 or 8; depth 2.55 to 2.95; head 3.25 to 3.55; snout 2.25 to 3.25; eye 3 to 6; interorbital 3.85 to 5.1; maxillary 3 to 3.55; gill-rakers short, about 9 on the lower limb of the first gill-arch; scales 69 to 73.

Distribution.—Atlantic coast from Bay of Fundy to South Carolina. Recently introduced into Bermuda.

KEYS TO THE SHORE FISHES KNOWN
FROM BERMUDA

To facilitate the identification of Bermuda fish the following keys are included. Colour has been used wherever possible, but because of considerable variation in some species, its use has been limited. The keys are made for Bermuda fishes only, and in other localities they may not work successfully.

In these keys it will be noticed that there are alternatives under each number. To identify a fish start at the first number of the first key and determine which of the alternatives best fits the specimen at hand. Then go to the number or group indicated at the end of the proper alternative and continue the process until you arrive at a species name. When a species name is reached the fish ought to be compared with the illustration and the diagnosis and field characters to determine whether it is actually that species or some form not hitherto recorded from Bermuda.

Certain names and formulas are used to describe fishes. The following notes and accompanying diagram illustrate and explain most of the characters used in identification.

Unlike birds and mammals which attain a definite size when they become adult, fishes continue to grow during practically all of their lifetime. For that reason the use of absolute measurements such as length, size of head, etc., are of little value for identification. Instead, all dimensions are stated in terms of proportion. Thus "Depth 4.2, Head 5.3" indicates that the depth of the fish will go four and two-tenths times into the length of the fish, while the head will be found to be five and three-tenths times in the length. For ease in calculation, the depth of the body and the length of the head are compared to the body length exclusive of the caudal fin (standard length), while diameter of the eye, length of maxillary and smaller measurements are compared to the length of the head.

Measurements of fishes are taken in a straight line, as with a pair of compasses, and not over a curve of the body. LENGTH always means "standard length," and is measured from the snout to the base of the caudal fin. The

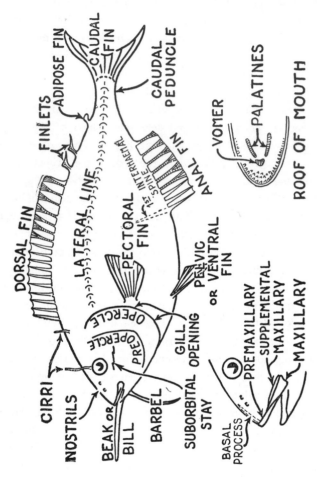

TOTAL LENGTH includes the caudal fin. DEPTH is the great- est vertical distance from the upper to the lower contour of the body excluding the fins. TRUNK is the portion of the body between the head and the anal opening,—the por- tion of the body posterior to the anal opening being considered as the TAIL. The SWIM-BLADDER is a hollow gas-filled bladder inside the abdomen on its upper aspect. The length of the HEAD is measured from the tip of the snout to the most posterior part of the opercle or, when the opercle is not evident, to the gill slit. EYE diameter is the horizontal diameter of the eye socket, unless otherwise stated. The INTERORBITAL space is the least distance from eye to eye, measured across the top of the head. The MAXILLARY is measured from the tip of the snout to the posterior edge of the maxillary bone. The SNOUT is measured from its tip to the front of the eye.

The PECTORAL and the PELVIC or VENTRAL FINS are paired, while the others, the DORSAL, ANAL and CAUDAL FINS, are found on the mid-line of the body. Considerable variation exists as to shape, size and position of these fins, and one or more may be completely lacking. Thus the dorsal may be single and continuous, or divided into two or three fins, while the pelvics may be absent or reduced to a pair of small filaments situated near the chin. The ADIPOSE FIN, found on the Bermuda Lizard- and Snakefish, is small, tab-like, placed on the posterior dorsal surface, and contains neither spines nor rays.

The supporting elements of the fins are usually fairly constant in number, and their number is of importance in classification. These elements are of two types—spines, which are rigid, solid, and more or less sharp-pointed, and rays, which are segmented, flexible and often branched at the tips. In some fishes the distinction between spines and rays is not especially well marked, but in the great majority there is no difficulty in determining which is which. The portion of the dorsal fin containing rays is often called the soft dorsal. In descriptions and in our formulas, the spines are denoted by Roman numerals and the rays by Arabic. If the fin is in two parts, a dash separates the numbers; if the spinous and soft dorsal fins are continuous and connected by a membrane, the numbers are separated by a comma. Thus "Dorsal XII-24" means that there are two separate dorsal fins, the first of 12 spines and the second of 24 rays; if the diagnosis reads XII, 24, it means that the dorsal contains 12 spines and 24 rays, the two fins connected and continuous. Finlets following the fin are also denoted by Roman letters; thus the following formula denoted three finlets following the rest of the fin; "Dorsal XII, 24-III."

The OPERCLE is the posterior, outer, flap-like bone of the head which covers the lateral opening to the gills. Anterior to it is the PREOPERCLE, the posterior edge of which is often slightly free from the side of the head and sometimes armed with teeth or spines. The SHOULDER-GIRDLE, in those Bermuda fish where it is of importance in classification, is immediately beneath the posterior edge of the opercle.

GILL-RAKERS are bony excrescences found regularly placed on the gill arches of some fishes. Each arch will be found to have a sharp angle, and only those gill-rakers on the lower half of the arch below the angle, on one side, are counted in the diagnoses given in this paper and in the following keys. The ISTHMUS is the portion of the body extending forward on the ventral side, just between the gill-covers. The GILL-MEMBRANES are membranes attached to the lower part of the opercles or gill covers,—the membranes of the two sides are occasionally joined together and attached to the isthmus. These membranes are supported by the BRANCHIOSTEGAL RAYS.

The NICTITATING MEMBRANE is a membrane which can be drawn up over the eye from beneath the outer skin; it is found in some of the sharks.

In sharks a SPIRACLE is present in some species, usually somewhere back of the eye,—it is a small hole leading downward into the mouth cavity. The CAUDAL-PITS are pit-like depressions at the base of the caudal fin above and below. LABIAL-FOLDS are small ridge-like folds surrounding the posterior portion of the mouth.

KEY TO THE MAJOR GROUPS OF
BERMUDA FISHES

1.—A well developed head and conspicuous eyes.... **2**
Very small, elongate, worm-like animals without
distinct head or paired eyes....*Lancelets*, p. 21
2.—More than one gill-opening on each side of the
body .... *Sharks and Rays*, p. 273
A single gill opening on each side of the body.... **3**
3.—Body armed with bony keeled shields, the skin
between the shields covered with minute plates;
a long overhanging snout furnished with a pair
of barbels which are far in advance of the
mouth .... *Sturgeon*, p. 31
Without the above combination of characters...... **4**
4.—A long tubular snout with the small jaws and
mouth at its tip............................. **39**
No long tubular snout......................... **5**
5.—A sucking disk on top of the head.............
Sharksuckers, p. 311
No sucking disk on top of the head............. **6**
6.—A sucking-disk on ventral surface of body, the
pelvic fins forming some part or all of it...... **62**
No sucking-disk on the ventral surface of the body **7**
7.—One or both jaws prolonged into a long beak...... **40**
Jaws not prolonged into a long beak.............. **8**
8.—Pectoral fins large, forming "wings".............. **43**
Pectoral fins not forming "wings"............... **9**
9.—Frog-like fishes with the pectoral fins at the end
of long arms .... *Frogfishes*, p. 315
Pectoral fin not at the end of a long arm........ **10**
10.—Fishes which lie flat on one side, with both eyes
on the upper side.............*Flounders*, p. 282
Fishes with eyes on the opposite sides of the body **11**
11.—Fishes with the teeth fused into a beak-like structure **44**

Teeth not fused into a beak-like structure........ 12
12.—Pelvic fins absent 46
Pelvic fins present 13
13.—Pelvic fins placed abdominally, well behind the base
of the pectoral fins 49
Pelvic fins thoracic, arising close to the base of
the pectoral fins 14
14.—Pelvic fins with definitely 1 spine and 5 rays...... 15
Pelvic fins with either more or less than 5 rays,
with or without a spine 54
15.—Pelvic fin bases very close together; no lateral line;
gill-membranes joined to the isthmus, 2 dorsal
fins, the spinous fin least developed...........
Gobies (in part), p. 310
Without the above combination of characters.... 16
16.—Gill openings a small aperture above the pectoral
fin; small, depressed, naked fish, with conspicuous
lateral lines meeting on the nape. Dragonets, p. 311
Gill-openings not restricted to a small aperture
above the pectoral fins 17
17.—A horizontal bony stay across the cheek below the
eye, armed with short spines; usually somewhat
grotesque fishes with dermal flaps and with bony
ridges and spines above the eyes.............
Scorpionfishes, p. 302
No short spines below the eye................... 18
18.—Some or all of the dorsal or anal spines disconnected from each other 57
Dorsal and anal spines, if present, connected by
membrane with each other................... 19
19.—Dorsal and anal fins followed by 2 or more finlets 61
Dorsal and anal fins followed by a single finlet
or without finlets 20
20.—Pelvic fins broad, very large and black; small fishes
growing to six or eight inches, with conspicuous

black vertical bands; usually found in company of Portuguese Man-of-War ....
Man-of-War Fish, p. 100

Without the above combination of characters......   21

21.—A strong movable spine on the side of the caudal peduncle .... *Doctorfish*, p. 302

No movable spine on the side of the caudal peduncle   22

22.—One or two barbels on the lower jaw............   63

No barbels on the lower jaw   23

23.—A single nostril on each side of the head, nearly round; small, short, deep compressed fishes, with gill-membranes free from the isthmus..........
Demoiselles, p. 303

Two nostrils on each side of the head............   24

24.—Small brown or grey fish with conspicuous striped and banded pattern; spinous dorsal fin with a short base, the spines crowded together at their base, the spines quite long; lateral line extending to the tip of the middle rays of the caudal fin
Ribbonfish, p. 300

Without the above combination of characters....   25

25.—Usually brilliantly coloured fishes with small mouths and, for the most part, conspicuous forward-directed pointed teeth; gill-openings small; gill filaments present on the anterior side of the 4th gill-arch only, not on the posterior side....
Wrasses, Slipperydicks, Bermuda Bluefish, p. 304

Gill filaments present on both the anterior and posterior sides of the fourth gill arch...........   26

26.—Teeth brush-like, very slender and movable.......   27

Teeth when present, not brush-like..............   28

27.—Upper edge of the spinous and soft dorsal fins a continuous line, the posterior spines and the anterior rays of about equal length...............
Butterfly- and Angelfish, p. 300

Upper edge of the spinous dorsal and soft dorsal

fins deeply notched, the posterior spines considerably shorter than the anterior rays. *Spadefish,* p. 259

28.—Upper jaw extremely protractile, the mouth capable of being extruded considerably beyond the bones of the head; bright silvery fishes..............
Bermuda Shad, p. 299

Mouth moderately or not at all protractile........ 29

29.—Anal fin base much longer than the soft dorsal fin base; body much compressed, deep forward....
Pempherids, p. 294

Anal fin not much if any longer than base of soft dorsal or much shorter 30

30.—Dorsal fin beginning on the head. *Dolphins,* p. 289

Dorsal fin not beginning on the head............. 31

31.—Dorsal spines very weak, about 6 in number, difficult to differentiate from the rays; elongate, conical-headed fishes with fairly large, curved, conical teeth .... *Whiteys,* p. 172

Dorsal spines stronger, more than 6 in number (except 2 to 4 in the Soapfishes)........... 32

32.—Anal spines two,—three in rare Black-finned Scombrops (*Parasphyrænops atrimanus*); dorsal fins separated .... *Cardinalfish,* p. 289

Anal spines three or absent................... 33

33.—Posterior portion of the upper jaw bone not, or only partly, slipping under the bone beneath the eye (preorbital); opercle with one to three flat spines 34

Posterior portion of the upper jaw bone slipping under the preorbital bone; no spines on the opercle 36

34.—No teeth on the vomer; soft dorsal and anal fins large, similar to the caudal in shape.........
Triple-tails, p. 143

Vomer and palatines with teeth................ 35

35.—Anal fin nearly as long as the soft dorsal and
similar to it; large-eyed scarlet fish..........
Big-eyes, p. 294

Anal fin base shorter than soft dorsal fin base....
Rockfish, etc., p. 290

36.—Teeth on the anterior part of the jaws incisor-
like; scales covering the low soft dorsal and
anal fins; mouth very small; snout blunt......
Chubs, p. 162

Without the above combination of characters.... 37

37.—Vomer with teeth, sometimes very small; teeth in
jaws usually unequal, some of them more or less
canine-like .... *Snappers,* p. 295

No teeth on the vomer........................ 38

38.—Molar teeth on the sides of the jaws; preopercle
not serrate .... *Porgies,* p. 298

Teeth on the sides of the jaws not molar-like,
pointed but with no marked canines; preopercle
usually serrate .... *Grunts,* p. 296

39.—Small spines present in front of the dorsal fin,
or if not present, with the tail fin produced into
a long filament; adults from twelve inches to four
feet in length .... *Trumpetfish,* p. 285

No spines in front of the dorsal fin; tail fin short,
never produced into a long filament...........
Pipefish and Seahorses, p. 284

40.—Both jaws with equally elongate beaks............ 41

One jaw much longer than the other.............. 42

41.—A spinous dorsal fin....*Mackerels,* in part, p. 286

No spinous dorsal fin .... *Gars,* p. 280

42.—Lower jaw longer than the upper. *Halfbeaks,* p. 280

Upper jaw longer than the lower. *Swordfish,* p. 287

43.—Dorsal fin of soft rays only, body not mailed....
Flyingfish, p. 281

Dorsal fin with spines and rays; head heavily
armoured .... *Flying Gurnard,* p. 184

44.—Pelvic fins present .... *Parrotfish,* p. 307

Pelvic fins absent **45**

45.—Two dorsal fins, the anterior of spines.........

Triggerfish, p. 313

A single dorsal fin .... *Puffers,* etc., p. 315

46.—Body enclosed in a hard bony box, only the fins
and caudal peduncle freely movable...........

Trunkfish, p. 314

Body not enclosed in a bony box............... **47**

47.—Body elongate, more or less eel-like............. **48**

Body not eel-like; a spinous dorsal fin.........

Bermuda Catfish, p. 287

48.—Anus at the throat, living in sea-puddings........

Pearlfish, p. 232

Anus not at the throat...............*Eels,* p. 276

49.—A small fleshy fin on the posterior part of the back.

Lizardfish, p. 280

No fleshy adipose fin........................... **50**

50.—Dorsal fin single, of rays only.................. **51**

Two separate dorsal fins **52**

51.—No scales on the head above.................

Herring-like fish, p. 275

Scales on the upper surface of the head.........

Minnows, p. 57

52.—Lateral line present .... *Barracudas,* p. 286

Lateral line absent **53**

53.—Anal fin with a single weak spine. *Silversides,* p. 285

Anal fin with two or three stiff spines.........

Mullets, p. 285

54.—Pelvic fins with more than 5 rays.............

Squirrelfish, p. 283

Pelvic fins with less than 5 rays.................. **55**

55.—No spines in the dorsal fin.......*Brotulids,* p. 312

Spines present in the dorsal fin................. **56**

56.—Finlets following the dorsal and anal fins........

Tapiocafish, p. 287

No finlets following the dorsal fin. *Blennies,* p. 311

57.—Body very elongate, more or less spindle-shaped; head depressed; dorsal fin with eight or nine free spines .... *Cubby-yew,* p. 113

Not as above 58

58.—Anal fin preceded by one or two free spines, not joined to the remainder of the fin and often buried in the skin 59

Anal fin not preceded by separate free spines; mouth exceedingly protractile; body elongate, little compressed .... *Bogas,* p. 163

59.—A single free anal spine. *Mackerels,* in part, p. 286

Two free anal spines 60

60.—Preopercular margin serrate .... *Blue-fish,* p. 112

Preopercular margin smooth ....

Jacks, Bonitos, p. 287

61.—Two dorsal and two anal finlets following the fins.

Tapiocafish, p. 287

More than two dorsal and anal finlets............

Mackerels, p. 286

62. Sucking disk on the ventral surface formed by the altered pelvic fins which are changed into six pairs of fleshy knobs in the centre of a disk which is surrounded by a roughly circular flap of skin .... *Lump-suckers,* p. 185

Sucking disk formed simply by the joined pelvic fins,—cup-like in form.... *Gobies,* in part, p. 310

63.—A single short barbel on the lower jaw..........

Kingfish and Ribbonfish, in part, p. 300

Two barbels on the lower jaw....*Goatfish,* p. 300

Key to Bermuda Sharks and Rays

1.—Body rounded (sharks) 2

Body flattened (rays, sawfish) 12

2.—A fleshy lower eyelid ......:................. 4

No eyelid 3

3.—Mouth with two long barbels; no keels on base of
tail ....

Nurse Shark (*Ginglymostoma cirratum*), p. 23

Barbels absent; wide transverse keels on the side
of the tail base ....

Mackerel Shark (*Isurus tigris*), p. 23

4.—Head hammer-shaped ....

Hammer-head Shark (*Sphyrna zygæna*), p. 29

Head not hammer-shaped 5

5.—Teeth rounded, pavement-like 6

Teeth compressed, pointed 7

6.—Origin of the 1st dorsal fin above the posterior
border of the pectoral fins.....................

Dogfish or Nurse Shark (*Cynias canis*), p. 24

Origin of the 1st dorsal fin in advance of the
posterior border of the pectoral fin..........

Smooth Hound (*Mustelus mustelus*), p. 24

7.—A small aperture (spiracle) behind the eye........

Tiger Shark (*Galeocerdo arcticus*), p. 25

No aperture behind the eye 8

8.—First dorsal fin nearer the pelvics than to the
pectoral fins ....

Great Blue Shark (*Prionace glauca*), p. 26

First dorsal fin nearer the pectorals than to the
pelvics 9

9.—Teeth of the upper jaw nearly triangular, with a
shallow indentation on some of the posterior
margins 11

Teeth of the upper jaw with a deep notch on the
posterior margins 10

10.—Pectoral fin very large, three times as long as
broad ....

Dusky Ground Shark

(*Carcharias obscurus*), p. 28

Pectoral fin shorter, not three times as long as
broad ....

Scythe-finned Shark

(Carcharias falciformis), p. 27

11.—Denticles of skin rounded, with their central keels larger and longer than the others; 28 teeth in the outer row of each jaw.........................

Puppy-shark *(Carcharias platyodon)*, p. 26

Denticles elliptical, with five nearly equal, parallel keels; 30 to 31 teeth in the outer row of each jaw .... oo

Grey Requiem Shark

(Carcharias commersonii), p. 28

12.—A long flattened upper jaw studded with large teeth .... Sawfish *(Pristis pectinatus)*, p. 30

No elongate jaw; body flat and angular.......... 13

13.—Black above with many round white spots........

Whip-ray *(Stoasodon narinari)*, p. 30

Black above, unspotted ....

Devilfish *(Manta birostris)*, p. 31

Key to Bermuda Herring-like Fishes

1.—A bony plate between the arms of the lower jaw..   2

No bony plate   3

2.—Scales very large, lateral line decurved; last ray of the dorsal fin elongate ....

Tarpon *(Tarpon atlanticus)*, p. 33

Scales small; lateral line straight; last dorsal ray not elongate. Ten-pounder *(Elops saurus)*, p. 33

3.—Lateral line present ....

Grubber *(Albula vulpes)*, p. 34

Lateral line absent   4

4.—Mouth large, the long snout overhanging the mouth. Hog-mouth Fry *(Anchoviella chœrostoma)*, p. 38

Mouth moderate, at the tip of the snout   5

5.—Belly with sharp serrations   6

Belly rounded, without serrations ....

Green Fry, Dwarf or Round Herring
(*Jenkinsia lamprotænia*), p. 37

6.—Last dorsal fin ray elongate ....

Bermuda Herring (*Opisthonema oglinum*), p. 37

Last dorsal ray not longer than the others........ 7

7.—Last two anal rays larger than the preceding ones, forming a pseudo-finlet ....

Anchovy, False Sardine
(*Sardinella anchovia*), p. 35

Last two anal rays not larger than the others.... 9

9.—10 to 12 sharp ventral scutes behind the ventral fins, scales easily lost ....

Pilchard (*Harengula sardina*), p. 35

12 to 14 sharp ventral scutes behind the ventral fins, scales not easily lost ....

Hard-Scaled Pilchard
(*Harengula macrophthalmus*), p. 36

Key to Bermuda Eels

1.—Tip of tail ending in a hard point, the dorsal and anal fins, when present, not extending around the tail tip 2

Tip of tail not ending in a hard point, the dorsal and anal fins extending around the tip of the tail,—except in one case where the fins are absent and the body has dark broad chocolate bands 6

2.—No fins on the body anywhere...................

Finless Snake Eel
(*Sphagebranchus ophioneus*), p. 42

Fins present 3

3.—Teeth blunt, mostly molar 4

Teeth small, more or less sharp, not molar........ 5

4.—Dark spots on body on a pale background........

Dark-spotted Snake Eel
(*Myrichthys oculatus*), p. 43

Pale spots on body on a dark background........

Yellow-spotted Snake Eel

(*Myrichthys acuminatus*), p. 43

5.—Pectoral fins rudimentary, present as a minute dermal flap ....

Gosling's Eel (*Quassiremus goslingi*), p. 44

Pectoral fins long, well developed ....

Spotted Sand Eel (*Ophichthus ophis*), p. 44

6.—Pectoral fins present 7

Pectoral fins absent 13

7.—Skin covered with rudimentary scales which are embedded and placed at right angles to each other; mouth terminal, the lower jaw somewhat projecting ....

Common Eel (*Anguilla rostrata*), p. 39

Scales absent 8

8.—Posterior nostril situated in the upper lip.......... 9

Posterior nostril situated above the lip on the side of the head 12

9.—Body short, much compressed; dorsal and anal fins well developed, highest posteriorly..........

Short-bodied Worm Eel

(*Chilorhinus suensonii*), p. 41

Body very elongate, worm-like; dorsal and anal fins low 10

10.—Origin of the dorsal fin nearer vent than tip of snout 11

Origin of dorsal fin approximately midway between tip of snout and the vent ....

Broad-snouted Worm Eel

(*Myrophis platyrhynchus*), p. 41

11.—Snout short, 5½ to 6 times in the length of the head; pectoral fins short, about 7 to 8 in the head..Worm Eel (*Myrophis punctatus*), p. 40

Snout longer, 4½ or less in the head; pectoral fins well developed, about 4½ in the head......

Long-snouted Worm Eel

(*Myrophis dolichorhynchus*), p. 40

12.—Body excessively elongate, worm-like.............

Golden Eel (*Aphthalmichthys mayeri*), p. 45

Body not excessively elongate ....

Bermuda Conger Eel

(*Conger harringtonensis*), p. 46

13.—Dorsal and anal fins well developed..............   14

Dorsal and anal fins rudimentary, confined to the
end of the tail or altogether wanting............

Banded Creeping Eel

(*Channomuræna vittata*), p. 54

14.—Posterior nostril an oblong slit..................   15

Posterior nostril circular, with or without a short
tube   16

15.—Brown or grey, with darker marblings and mottlings ....

Mottled Conger Moray

(*Enchelycore nigricans*), p. 46

Uniform brown ....

Brown Conger Moray

(*Enchelycore brunneus*), p. 47

16.—Teeth molar-like, not sharp ....

Chained Moray (*Echidna catenata*), p. 54

Teeth all, or nearly all, acute, none of them being
molar-like   17

17.—Posterior nostril, as well as anterior, in a short but
conspicuous tube   18

Posterior nostril without a tube, its margin sometimes slightly raised   19

18.—Chocolate brown, covered with small pale, white or
yellow spots, which become slightly larger on the
tail....Conger Moray (*Muræna miliaris*), p. 52

Golden yellow with numerous small darker spots

and reticulations; a few odd-sized and shaped
dark spots on the body and fins................

Golden Moray (*Murœna aurea*), p. 53

19.—Teeth entire, with no serrations anywhere........ 20

Teeth serrate, more or less, especially noticeable on
the bases of the posterior edges of the larger
teeth; dorsal fin with large dark spots on its
edge, these sometimes obsolete, usually running
together to form a dark band.................

Spotted Moray (*Gymnothorax ocellatus*), p. 52

20.—Body with conspicuous marblings, markings or spots
darker or lighter than the ground colour........ 21

Essentially plain-coloured eels; dark brown, green
or blackish 24

21.—Upper lip and lower jaw white.................

White-jawed Moray Eel

(*Gymnothorax albimentis*), p. 50

Upper lip and lower jaw not entirely white........ 22

22.—Teeth in jaws biserial. Brownish black with numerous, irregular pale spots, the largest about
the size of the eye, the smallest mere dots......

Speckled Moray

(*Gymnothorax sanctœ-helenœ*), p. 48

Teeth in jaws uniserial......................... 23

23.—Dark markings forming reticulations, usually dark
lilac in colour, covering the back and sides, some
of them enclosing irregular polygons...........

Reticulated Moray Eel

(*Gymnothorax polygonius*), p. 49

Dark markings in the form of irregular or rounded
spots, sometimes more or less confluent........

Common Spotted Moray

(*Gymnothorax moringa*), p. 50

24.—Upper lip and lower jaw white.................

White-jawed Moray Eel

(*Gymnothorax albimentis*), p. 50

Upper lip and lower jaw not entirely white........ 25
25.—Colour uniformly brilliant green to brown or black-
    ish. Green Moray (*Gymnothorax funebris*), p. 51
    Colour brownish with a black band along the top
    of the dorsal fin.............................
    Dusky-mouthed Moray Eel
                    (*Gymnothorax vicinus*), p. 48

Key to Bermuda Lizard- and Snakefish

1.—Head long, flattened, triangular; snout depressed,
    longer than eye............................... 2
    Head compressed; snout short, not depressed,
    shorter than eye's diameter...................
        Snakefish (*Trachinocephalus myops*), p. 57
2.—Scales larger, 48 to 52 in the lateral line..........
        Lizardfish (*Synodus intermedius*), p. 55
    Scales smaller, 58 to 63 in the lateral line........
    Lizardfish, Galliwasp (*Synodus foetens*), p. 56

Key to Bermuda Gars, Needlefish and Halfbeaks

1.—Lower jaw much longer than the upper............ 2
    Both jaws about equally elongate............... 4
2.—Pelvic fins inserted much nearer base of caudal fin
    than gill-opening; upper lobe of caudal fin
    orange...Gar (*Hemiramphus brasiliensis*), p. 62
    Pelvic fins further forward, usually midway be-
    tween base of caudal and gill-opening.......... 3
3.—Gill rakers 19 to 21.
        Scissors (*Hyporhamphus unifasciatus*), p. 63
    Gill rakers about 29.
        Pajarito (*Hyporhamphus hildebrandi*), p. 63
4.—Small finlets present behind the dorsal and anal
    fins .... Needlefish (*Scomberesox saurus*), p. 61
    No finlets behind dorsal or anal fins............. 5
5.—Body strongly compressed, the width less than half
    the depth ...... Snook (*Ablennes hians*), p. 61

Body moderately compressed, width of body about
two-thirds the depth 6

6.—Dorsal and anal fins with 13 to 19 rays each.... 7

Dorsal and anal with 20 to 24 rays each.......... 8

7.—Anal fin with 13 to 14 rays; tips of dorsal, anal
and caudal fins brick red....................

Red-finned Needlefish (*Strongylura notata*), p. 59

Anal fin with 16 to 19 rays; fins not tipped with red.

Slender Needlefish (*Strongylura ardeola*), p. 59

8.—Beak short and strong, 1½ to 1⅝ times the rest
of the head; 350 scales in the lateral line....

Hound (*Tylosurus raphidoma*), p. 60

Beak longer, about twice rest of head; 380 scales
in the lateral line ....

Hound-fish (*Tylosurus acus*), p. 60

Key to Bermuda Flyingfish

1.— Pelvic fins small, inserted nearer tip of snout than
to base of tail............................... 2

Pelvic fins large, inserted nearer base of tail than
tip of snout................................. 3

2.—Anal fin originating behind origin of dorsal fin.
Two-winged Flyingfish

(*Halocypselus evolans*), p. 64

Anal fin originating in front of dorsal.............
Two-winged Flyingfish

(*Halocypselus obtusirostris*), p. 65

3.—Anal fin long, its base equal to or a little less
than that of the dorsal, with 11 to 13 rays...... 4

Anal fin shorter, its base one-half to two-thirds
that of the dorsal, with 9 or 10, rarely 11 rays 7

4.—Second ray of the pectoral fin simple as well as the
first 5

Second ray of the pectoral fin branched at its tip,
first ray simple 6

5.—Second pectoral ray about as long as first........
    Butterflyingfish (*Exonautes exsiliens*), p. 65
Second pectoral ray half again as long as the first.
    Black-winged Flyingfish
                        (*Exonautes rondeletii*), p. 66

6.—3rd and 4th pectoral rays longest; pectoral fins
    nearly uniform brownish......................
    Brown-winged Flyingfish
                        (*Exonautes rufipinnis*), p. 66
    6th and 7th pectoral rays longest; tips of pectorals
    and pelvics bright orange, the base of each fin
    with a dark spot............................
    Nonsuch Flyingfish (*Exonautes nonsuchæ*), p. 67

7.—Each jaw tooth with a cusp on each side,—tricuspid.
    Atlantic Flyingfish (*Cypselurus heterurus*), p. 67
    No cusps on the jaw teeth.....................   8

8.—Short, dark membranous flaps on the lower jaw.
    Double-bearded Flyingfish
                        (*Cypselurus furcatus*), p. 68
    No membranous flaps on the lower jaw..........   9

9.—Sides and belly without distinct rows of pale spots.
    Dark-winged Flyingfish
                        (*Cypselurus bahiensis*), p. 69
    Sides and belly with distinct rows of pale spots.
    Spotted Flyingfish (*Cypselurus lineatus*), p. 69

Key to Bermuda Flounders

1.—Lateral line with a prominent arch anteriorly......   2
    Lateral line without an arch anteriorly, almost
    straight   3

2.—Anterior profile of head convex.................
    Eyed Platefish (*Platophrys ocellatus*), p. 70
    Anterior profile of head strongly concave, the
    projecting snout leaving a marked angle above it.
                        Platefish (*Platophrys lunatus*), p. 71

3.—Pelvic fins similar in position and shape; eyes and

colour on the right side of the body, the eye-
less side being pale or white...................
Winter Flounder

(*Pseudopleuronectes americanus*), p. 254
Pelvic fins dissimilar in shape and position, the fin
of the eyed side being longer and extending along
the edge of the abdomen; eyes and colour on
the left side................................. **4**

4.—Scales small, 60 to 78 in the lateral line; body
with ring-like ocelli ....
Small-scaled Flounder

(*Syacium micrurum*), p. 72
Scales larger, 50 to 57, no ring-like spots or ocelli.
Large-scaled Flounder

(*Syacium papillosum*), p. 72

Key to Bermuda Squirrelfish

1.—No prominent enlarged spine on lower angle of
the preopercle; eyes with forward as well as
sidewise vision ....
Goggle-eyed Squirrelfish

(*Plectrypops retrospinis*), p. 77
A large spine at lower angle of preopercle........ **2**
2.—13 to 16 gill-rakers on lower limb of 1st gill arch **3**
8 to 10 gill-rakers on lower limb of 1st gill arch **4**
3.—Depth 4 to 4.2; soft dorsal and anal fins low, not
produced ....
Bermuda Squirrelfish (*Holocentrus meeki*), p. 73
Depth 2.8 to 3.4; soft dorsal and anal fins high,
considerably produced ....
Common Squirrelfish

(*Holocentrus ascensionis*), p. 74
4.—Depth less than length of head; a black spot on
the anterior portion of the spinous dorsal......
West Indian Squirrelfish

(*Holocentrus tortugæ*), p. 75

Depth equal to or greater than length of head;
dorsal fin with a dusky or dark red area in front
of each spine on the membrane, the remainder
of the membrane transparent...................
Black-barred Squirrelfish
    (*Holocentrus vexillarius*), p. 76

Key to Bermuda Sea Horses and Pipefish

1.—Body robust; head at right angles to body........
    Sea Horse (*Hippocampus punctulatus*), p. 78
    Body elongate; head in line or almost in line
    with rest of body..............................   2
2.—Tail prehensile ....
    Prehensile-tailed Pipefish
        (*Amphelikturus dendriticus*), p. 79
    Tail not prehensile   3
3.—Ridge on middle of side of body continuous with
    ridge on lower side of tail....................   4
    Ridge on middle of side of body ending beneath
    dorsal fin, not continuous with lower ridge on
    caudal portion of body.........................   5
4.—Body with about 22 bright yellow and 22 darker
    brown rings ....
    Harlequin Pipefish
        (*Corythoichthys ensenadæ*), p. 80
    Orange to blackish brown; body and tail with ir-
    regular vertical bars, every third or fourth one
    more conspicuous than the others, so that there
    are about three pale areas on the trunk and
    seven on the tail ....
        Jones's Pipefish (*Micrognathus jonesi*), p. 79
5.—Snout short (3.1 in head length), upturned........
    Bermuda Pipefish
        (*Corythoichthys bermudensis*), p. 80
    Snout longer, 1.6 to 2.1 in head length............   6
6.—20 to 23 body segments ....

Louisiana Pipefish (*Syngnathus louisianæ*), p. 81

16 to 18 body segments 7

7.—18 to 26 rays in the dorsal fin 8

28 or more dorsal fin rays..................... 9

8.—26 segments in the tail ....

Little Pipefish (*Syngnathus pipulus*), p. 81

31 to 34 segments in the tail....................

Duckfish (*Syngnathus elucens*), p. 82

9.—29 to 33 tail segments; dorsal fin with dark mottlings and bars; a brown band extending down the snout ....

Ocean Pipefish (*Syngnathus pelagicus*), p. 82

35 to 39 tail segments; dorsal fin without pattern; snout mottled ....

Mackay's Pipefish (*Syngnathus mackayi*), p. 83

Key to Bermuda Trumpetfish

1.—Spiny finlets present in front of dorsal fin; tail not ending in a long filament ....

Trumpetfish (*Aulostomus maculatus*), p. 83

No spiny finlets in front of dorsal fin; tail ending in a long filament ....

Cornetfish (*Fistularia tabacaria*), p. 84

Key to Bermuda Silversides

1.—Anus considerably in advance of the origin of the anal fin ....

Blue-fry, Rush-fry

(*Atherina harringtonensis*), p. 85

Anus immediately in front of the anal fin origin.

Whitebait (*Menidia notata*), p. 85

Key to Bermuda Mullets

1.—Soft dorsal and anal fins almost scaleless; dark longitudinal stripes along the sides ....

Striped Mullet (*Mugil brasiliensis*), p. 86

Soft dorsal and anal fins closely scaled; no dark
stripes along the sides 2

2.—Scales 35 to 43 in a lateral series.................

Mullet (*Mugil curema*), p. 87

Scales 29 to 33 in a lateral series ....

Fan-tail Mullet (*Mugil trichodon*), p. 88

Key to Bermuda Barracudas

1.—Scales large, 75 to 85 in the lateral line........

Great Barracuda (*Sphyræna barracuda*), p. 89

Scales smaller, 123 to 150 in the lateral line...... 2

2.—Origin of spinous dorsal before the origin of the
pelvics; 150 scales in the lateral line...........

European Barracuda (*Sphyræna sphyræna*), p. 90

Spinous dorsal origin directly over the origin of the
pelvics; 123 to 125 scales in the lateral line.... 3

3.—Eye smaller, 5.3 to 5.7 in head; interorbital area
rather strongly convex ....

Northern Sennet (*Sphyræna borealis*), p. 89

Eye larger, 4.8 to 5 in head; interorbital area flat-
tish. Southern Sennet (*Sphyræna picudilla*), p. 90

Key to Bermuda Mackerels

1.—Dorsal fin with about 25 spines ....

Wahoo, Kingfish (*Acanthocybium petus*), p. 92

Dorsal fin with considerably less than 25 spines.. 2

2.—10 to 12 gill rakers on lower limb of first arch;
elongate rather slim fishes ....

Spanish Mackerel

(*Scomberomorus maculatus*), p. 91

23 or more gill rakers on the first gill arch.... 3

3.—Scales present anteriorly on a corselet, posteriorly
along the lateral line only 4

Body covered with small scales 5

4.—15 or 16 dorsal spines ....

Mackerel (*Euthynnus alletteratus*), p. 94

9 or 10 dorsal spines ....
Frigate Mackerel (*Auxis rochei*), p. 95
5.—A single median keel on the side of the caudal
peduncle. Giant Tunny (*Thunnus thynnus*), p. 93
Two small lateral keels on the caudal peduncle, no
median one ....
Chub Mackerel (*Pneumatophorus grex*), p. 93

Key to Bermuda Tapioca and Catfish

1.—Pelvic fins with 1 spine and 5 rays; skin with bony
tubercles. Tapiocafish (*Ruvettus pretiosus*), p. 96
Pelvic fins of 1 spine only (minute rays present
in the young) ; scales very smooth ....
Bermuda Catfish
(*Promethichthys prometheus*), p. 96

Key to Bermuda Spearfish and Swordfish

1.—Body scaly; pelvic fins present ....
Bermuda Spearfish (*Makaira bermudæ*), p. 98
Body scaleless; pelvic fins wanting ....
Swordfish (*Xiphias gladius*), p. 97

Key to Bermuda Jacks, Gwellys, Amber-Fish, Bonitos, etc.

1.—Lateral line armed with scutes, at least posteriorly   2
No scutes on the lateral line.....................   9
2.—Soft dorsal and anal fins followed by a single finlet   3
No finlet behind the dorsal and anal fins..........   4
3.—36 to 50 lateral line scutes ....
Robin (*Decapterus punctatus*), p. 101
20 to 30 lateral line scutes ....
Ocean Robin (*Decapterus macarellus*), p. 102
4.—A deep furrow on the shoulder girdle near its junction with the isthmus, a fleshy projection above
the furrow. (Lift up gill-cover to see this.)..

Goggle-eyed Jack, Goggler
    (*Trachurops crumenophthalmus*), p. 103
Shoulder girdle normal, not as above.............   5
5.—Arch of the lateral line long and low, much longer
    than the straight part; lips thick, papillose......
            Gwelly (*Caranx guara*), p. 103
Lateral line arch moderate or high, usually shorter
    than the straight portion, never noticeably longer   6
6.—13 to 18 gill rakers on the lower limb of the first
    arch   7
24 to 32 gill-rakers on the lower limb of the first
    arch   8
7.—Dorsal fin with 26 to 28 soft rays; anal fin with
    22 to 24 soft rays ....
        Yellow Jack (*Caranx bartholamæi*), p. 104
Dorsal fin with 20 to 22 soft rays; anal fin with
    17 or 18 rays.......Jack (*Caranx latus*), p. 105
8.—Dorsal fin with 27 to 28 soft rays; 30 to 32 gill-
    rakers on the lower limb of the 1st gill arch.
      Skip-jack, Never-bite (*Caranx ruber*), p. 105
Dorsal fin with 22 to 25 soft rays; 24 or 25 gill-
    rakers on lower limb of the first arch..........
        Hardtail (*Caranx crysos*), p. 106
9.—Base of soft dorsal fin about equal in length to
    that of the anal fin   10
Base of soft dorsal fin considerably longer than
    that of the anal fin   13
10.—Body markedly compressed, its outlines everywhere
    sharp   11
Body less compressed, the abdomen never with a
    sharp ridge   12
11.—Dorsal and ventral outlines convex, the ventral out-
    line considerably more so than the dorsal; 26
    to 28 anal rays ....
      Bumper (*Chloroscombrus chrysurus*), p. 107

Profiles not convex, anterior profile oblique, nearly
vertical; 18 to 20 anal rays ....
Lookdown, Moonfish (*Argyreiosus vomer*), p. 107
12.—Depth of body 2 to 2.2 in length; head 3.66 to 4.
Gaff-topsail Pampano
(*Trachinotus palometa*), p. 108
Depth of body about 2.6 in length; head 3........
Alewife (*Trachinotus goodei*), p. 109
13.—Spinous dorsal with 3 or 4 spines, very low; membrane of spinous dorsal disappearing with age.
Pilotfish (*Naucrates ductor*), p. 109
Spinous dorsal with 6 to 8 slender spines; membrane of fin present at all ages................ 14
14.—Anterior part of the soft dorsal fin elevated, but
not produced into a high fin.................. 15
Anterior part of the soft dorsal fin high, falcate.
Bonito (*Zonichthys falcatus*), p. 111
15.—Dorsal rays 36 to 38 ....
Amberfish, Crevalle (*Seriola zonata*), p. 110
Dorsal rays 30 to 34 ....
Horse-eyed Bonito (*Seriola dumerili*), p. 111

Key to Bermuda Dolphins

1.—Dorsal fin 55 to 65; anal fin 26 to 30..........
Common Dolphin (*Coryphæna hippurus*), p. 99
Dorsal fin 51 to 55; anal fin 24 to 26............
Little Dolphin (*Coryphæna equisetis*), p. 100

Key to Bermuda Cardinalfish

1.—3 anal spines; body elongate ....
Black-finned Scombrops
(*Parasphyrænops atrimanus*), p. 117
2 anal spines; body short, robust................. 2
2.—Pelvic fins short, the tips extending to base of the
anal fin 3

Pelvic fins long, the tips extending to the 4th to
7th anal ray ....
Conchfish (*Astrapogon stellatus*), p. 117

3.—Bronzy or coppery, not scarlet; no spot on body at
base of soft dorsal fin ....
Pigmented Cardinalfish
(*Apogon pigmentarius*), p. 114

Scarlet   4

4.—A narrow vertical black band from base of soft
dorsal fin toward the ventral outline; a similar
band on the caudal peduncle....................
Two-lined Cardinalfish (*Apogon binotata*), p. 115

A roundish black blotch beneath soft dorsal......   5

5.—A black saddle on the caudal peduncle. Scales
27 to 29 ....
Saddle-tailed Cardinalfish
(*Apogon sellicauda*), p. 115

A lateral spot, not a saddle, on the caudal peduncle,
disappearing with age. Scales 23 to 25.........
Spotted Cardinalfish (*Apogon maculatus*), p. 116

Key to Bermuda Rockfish, Groupers, Hinds, etc.

1.—A small, slightly movable bone under the skin
(supplemental maxillary) along the upper posterior edge of the upper jaw bone................   2
No movable bone on the upper jaw bone..........   22

2.—Dorsal fin with 2 or 3 spines only...............   3
Dorsal fin with at least 9 spines.................   4

3.—Two dorsal spines; opercle with 3 strong spines.
Two-spined Soapfish
(*Rypticus bistrispinus*), p. 132
Three dorsal spines; opercle with 2 spines only.
Three-spined Soapfish
(*Rypticus saponaceus*), p. 133

4.—Dorsal fin with 9 spines........................   5
Dorsal fin normally with 10 or 11 spines..........   6

5.—Dorsal fin with 14 rays; anal with 8 rays.........

Graysby (*Petrometopon cruentatus*), p. 119

Dorsal fin with 15 to 17 rays; anal with 9 rays.

Coney (*Cephalopholis fulvus*), p. 119

6.—Anal fin with 7 to 9 rays 7

Anal fin with 11 or 12 soft rays................. 16

7.—A small but strong, forward-pointing spine on the
lower limb of the preopercle, near its angle,
sometimes hidden in the skin ....

Red Nigger Hamlet (*Alphestes afer*), p. 126

Lower limb of preopercle without a forward-pointing spine 8

8.—Scales of the lateral line with 4 to 6 strong radiating ridges; dorsal spines very low.............

Spotted Jew-Fish (*Promicrops itaiara*), p. 126

Scales not as above 9

9.—Top of head very broad and flat above, space between eyes little concave ....

Black Jew-Fish (*Garrupa nigrita*), p. 125

Top of head narrow; space between eyes concave.. 10

10.—Teeth rather small with few, if any, canines;
body rather deep; scales small, embedded; brown,
mottled with darker and covered with whitish
blotches ....

Mutton Hamlet (*Dermatolepis inermis*), p. 124

Teeth fairly strong, canines present 11

11.—Posterior nostril 2½ to 3 times the diameter of
the anterior; brownish, with about 8 darker
cross-bands ....

Black Grouper (*Epinephelus mystacinus*), p. 120

Nostrils equal in size or nearly so; not as above... 12

12.—Second dorsal spine about as high as 3rd or 4th;
caudal fin lunate ....

Red Grouper (*Epinephelus morio*), p. 121

Second dorsal spine lower than the 3rd or 4th;
caudal fin more or less rounded............... 13

13.—Posterior upper jaw bone scaleless; body and head
and base of fins covered with red or orange spots.
Rock-Hind (*Epinephelus adscensionis*), p. 122
Posterior upper jaw bone more or less scaly...... 14
14.—Body, head and fins reddish brown, profusely covered with small, pearly white spots.............
John Paw (*Epinephelus drummond-hayi*), p. 124
No white spots 15
15.—Body covered with small orange or brown spots;
soft dorsal and anal fins broadly edged with
blue-black.
Red Hind (*Epinephelus guttatus*), p. 122
No orange or brown spots; fins not edged with
blue-black; caudal peduncle with a large black
blotch above; small black spots about the eye.
Hamlet (*Epinephelus striatus*), p. 123
16.—Nostrils small, nearly or quite equal in size, separated from each other 17
Posterior nostril decidedly larger than the anterior,
with a cross septum within, the nostrils close
together 20
17.—Angle of the preopercle more or less sharp, the
teeth somewhat enlarged; 12 or more gill rakers
on the lower limb of the first arch............ 18
Angle of the preopercle not sharp, the teeth
scarcely enlarged; 8 or 9 gill rakers developed
on the first arch, plus a few rudiments........ 19
18.—Gill-rakers about 12 ....
Velvet Rockfish (*Trisotropis microlepis*), p. 127
Gill-rakers 14 or more ....
Harlequin Rockfish
(*Trisotropis dimidiatus*), p. 128
19.—Pectoral fins tipped with yellow or orange yellow.
Yellow-finned Grouper
(*Trisotropis venenosa*), p. 129
Pectoral fins not tipped with yellow. Colour vari-

able, usually dark, sides of head and body with
rivulations of dark bluish or greyish around
roundish dark bronze spots ....
Rockfish (*Trisotropis bonaci*), p. 129

20.—Gill rakers elongate, 16 to 20 on the lower limb
of the first arch ....
Salmon Rockfish (*Mycteroperca falcata*), p. 130
5 to 12 gill rakers on the lower limb of the first
gill-arch 21

21.—10 to 12 gill-rakers on 1st gill arch; grey reticulations about brown or blood-red spots ....
Princess Rockfish (*Mycteroperca bowersi*), p. 131
5 to 7 gill rakers on 1st arch, plus 1 or 2 rudiments;
pale, oblique, narrow cross-bands on the upper
sides ....
Gag, Rag-tailed Rockfish
(*Mycteroperca tigris*), p. 131

22.—Lateral line continuous from head to caudal fin
base, parallel with the back 23
Lateral line broken below the centre of the soft
dorsal fin, beginning again lower down on the
centre of the side of the caudal peduncle......
Fairy Basslet (*Gramma hemicrysos*), p. 139

23.—Gill-rakers long, 25 to 29 in number 24
Gill-rakers short, 10 to 18 in number 26

24.—Soft dorsal fin with 19 or 20 soft rays; colour pur-
plish and reddish ....
Barber (*Paranthias furcifer*), p. 134
Soft dorsal fin with about 15 rays................ 25

25.—54 scales in the lateral line; depth 3.4 in length.
Small-scaled Anthias (*Anthias tenuis*), p. 137
35 to 38 scales in the lateral line; depth 2.6 in the
length..Bermuda Anthias (*Anthias louisi*), p. 138

26.—Gill-rakers 17 to 18; dorsal spines with dermal
flaps; caudal fin with a lengthened tip on its

upper angle ....

Sea-bass (*Centropristes striatus*), p. 255

Gill-rakers 10 to 13 in number 27

27.—Soft dorsal rays 10 to 12; depth of body 3 or
more in the length 28

Soft dorsal rays usually 14 or 15; depth less than
3 in the length ....

Butter Hamlet (*Hypoplectrus unicolor*), p. 134

28.—Margin of the preopercle finely serrate, the serræ
not arranged in clusters 29

Margin of the preopercle with one or two clusters
of strong diverging spines; dark horizontal
stripes along the sides........................

Aguavina (*Diplectrum radiale*), p. 135

29.—A vertical, shining white bar on the lower sides,
extending upward from just before the vent......

Tattler (*Prionodes phœbe*), p. 136

No white bar; colour yellow and white with conspicuous black spots, lines and bars............

Harlequin Serranid (*Prionodes tigrinus*), p. 137

Key to Bermuda Big-Eyes and Pempherids

1.—Colour bright red or pinkish; dorsal fin fairly long   2

Colour silvery; dorsal fin very short; anal fin very
long ....

Glassy Pempherid (*Pempheris mulleri*), p. 142

2.--Scales larger, 35 to 50 in a lateral series; body
deep, its depth more than half its length; soft
dorsal and anal fin each with 9 to 11 soft rays.

Short Big-Eye (*Pseudopriacanthus altus*), p. 141

Scales smaller, 80 to 100 in a lateral series; body
elongate, its depth not half the length; soft dorsal and anal fins each with 12 to 15 rays........   3

3.—Pelvic fins about as long as head; 22 to 23 gill-
rakers on the lower limb of the first arch......

Big-Eye (*Priacanthus cruentatus*), p. 140

Pelvic fins much shorter than the head; 16 to 18
gill-rakers on the lower limb of the first arch.
Blear-Eye (*Priacanthus arenatus*), p. 140

Key to Bermuda Snappers

1.—Space between eyes wide and flat; posterior dorsal
spines much shorter than the rays; eye very
large; crimson, becoming silvery below..........
Blear-eyed Snapper (*Etelis oculatus*), p. 144
Space between eyes not wide and flat; posterior
dorsal spines not markedly shorter than the rays   2

2.—Gill-rakers 17 to 20 on lower limb of 1st arch....   3
Gill-rakers less than 12 on the lower limb of the
1st arch   4

3.—Colour crimson; iris deep salmon red...........
Chub-headed Snapper
(*Rhomboplites aurorubens*), p. 145
Colour green, purplish and yellow, never red; a
wide yellow stripe along the side.............
Yellow-tail (*Ocyurus chrysurus*), p. 145

4.—Vomerine patch of teeth more or less triangular
in shape, without a median backwardly projecting patch..Mutton-fish (*Lutianus analis*), p. 255
Vomerine patch of teeth more or less anchor-
shaped, with a distinct median backward projection   5

5.—Dorsal normally with 12 soft rays ....
Silk-snapper (*Lutianus synagris*), p. 146
Dorsal normally with 14 rays   6

6.—Iris bright lemon yellow becoming orange-red in
large fish   7
Iris not yellow   8

7.—Pectoral fins reaching the vertical through the origin of the anal fin; pelvic fins reaching to or
past the vent ....

Day Snapper; Long-fin Red Snapper
(Lutianus vivanus), p. 147

Pectoral fins extending to vertical of the vent only; pelvic fin not reaching the vent by a space equal to about half the eye........................

Bermuda Silk Snapper
(Lutianus hastingsi), p. 148

8.—Colour crimson; base of pectoral fin with a jet black patch ....

Black-fin Snapper (Lutianus buccanella), p. 148

Not crimson in colour   9

9.—A broad white bar from eye to angle of mouth; about 7 or 8 rows of scales from lateral line to base of 1st dorsal spine ....

Dog Snapper (Lutianus jocu), p. 256

No white bar from eye to angle of mouth; 5 or 6, rarely 7 rows of scales from lateral line to 1st dorsal spine   10

10.—Caudal fin not edged with black; sides usually greenish or greyish with 8 to 9 vertical pale bars; fins pale yellow to green, the pelvics usually orange ....

Schoolmaster (Lutianus apodus), p. 149

Caudal fin edged with black; usually grey, sometimes with an oblique dark band on head; sometimes reddish or brown, the scales with rusty centres forming lines along the sides; fins reddish....Grey Snapper (Lutianus griseus), p. 150

Key to Bermuda Grunts

1.—Soft dorsal and anal fins covered with scales (except in the very young)   2

Soft dorsal and anal fins without scales, or with a few on the membranes only   11

2.—Dorsal spines normally 13; body somewhat elongate   3

Dorsal spines normally 12, occasionally 11 or 13;
body deeper 4

3.—65 to 72 lateral line scales ....

White Grunt (*Bathystoma striatum*), p. 151

50 to 60 lateral line scales; depth 3.1 to 3.7 in
length ....

White Grunt (*Bathystoma aurolineatum*), p. 151

4.—Scales below the lateral line notably enlarged,
very deep; yellow stripes on sides, parallel with
lateral line above it, oblique below it..........

Yellow Grunt (*Hæmulon flavolineatum*), p. 152

Scales below lateral line not especially enlarged;
colour not as above........................... 5

5.—About 4 rows of scales between the lateral line
and the origin of the dorsal fin; head bronze with
many narrow stripes of clear blue not extending
upon the body................................

Grey Grunt (*Hæmulon plumierii*), p. 257

5 or more rows of scales between the lateral line
and the origin of the dorsal fin.............. 6

6.—16 to 18 gill-rakers on lower limb of the 1st gill-
arch 7

11 to 14 gill-rakers on lower limb of 1st arch...... 8

7.—Head and body with horizontal blue stripes, well
defined on snout and cheeks ....

Blue-striped Grunt (*Hæmulon sciurus*), p. 154

No stripes on cheeks; upper part of sides with 4
or 5 horizontal dark stripes ....

Streaked Grunt (*Hæmulon macrostomum*), p. 156

8.—Posterior margin of upper jaw bone reaching
nearly or quite to middle of eye; sides with about
10 golden stripes, and usually with a dark band
along the dorsal fin to the caudal ....

Comical Grunt (*Hæmulon melanurum*), p. 153

Posterior margin of upper jaw bone reaching to
or slightly past the anterior margin of the eye.. 9

9.—Sides with horizontal bronze stripes ....
Black-tailed Grunt

(*Hæmulon carbonarium*), p. 154
Sides with dark or pearly grey stripes following
the rows of scales 10

10.—Scales of sides with dark spots which coalesce to
form continuous undulating stripes ....
Black Grunt (*Hæmulon bonariense*), p. 157
Stripes on sides not conspicuous, usually with two
or three horizontal dark stripes...............
Margate Fish (*Hæmulon album*), p. 155

11.—No conspicuous black vertical bands; yellow or
brownish stripes on the sides ....
Sailor's Choice

(*Orthopristis chrysopterus*), p. 157
A wide black band from nape through eye to angle
of mouth, another band from origin of dorsal
to and across base of pectoral fin; horizontal
golden stripes on a silvery blue background;
second anal spine notably enlarged ....
Pork-fish (*Anisotremus virginicus*), p. 258

Key to Bermuda Porgies and Breams

1.—Front teeth conical or pointed, not compressed or
incisor-like 3
Front teeth narrow or broad, but compressed and
incisor-like * 3

2.—A blue stripe below the eye extending forward and
downward; a shorter similar stripe above the
eye; no violet bar on base of pectoral fin; depth
usually slightly less, 2.2 to 2.5 in the length..
Blue-bone Porgy (*Calamus bajanado*), p. 159
A deep violet streak below the eye not extending
forward on the snout, nor backward on the oper-

* If the incisor teeth are conspicuously matched, see *Lagodon rhomboides*, p. 160.

cles; base of the pectoral fin above with a violet
bar; depth usually greater, 1.9 to 2.3 in the
length ....
Sheepshead Porgy (*Calamus calamus*), p. 159
3.—62 to 65 scales in the lateral line; a large black
spot on the caudal peduncle ....
Bream (*Diplodus argenteus*), p. 161
49 to 50 scales in the lateral line; no black spot
on the caudal peduncle ....
Scup (*Stenotomus chrysops*), p. 258

Key to Bermuda Shad

1.—2 anal spines ....
Long Bone Shad (*Ulœma lefroyi*), p. 167
3 anal spines 2
2.—Posterior end of swim-bladder bifurcated, the bi-
furcations extending on either side of the bone
supporting the anal fin spines ....
Shad (*Xystœma cinereum*), p. 164
Posterior end of swim-bladder not bifurcated, its
tip fastened into a cavity in the bone supporting
the anal spine 3
3.—Bone supporting the anal spines with a large and
deep cone-shaped funnel on its anterior side into
which the tip of the air bladder descends........ 4
Bone supporting the anal spine with its funnel reduced to a small depression or groove at the
lower end of the bone, into which the air-bladder
is fastened 5
4.—A small oval scaleless spot on the anterior upper
surface of the head ....
Shad (*Eucinostomus gula*), p. 165
Naked space on snout continued backward in a narrow groove on the mid-line of the head, no
naked oval spot ....
Shad (*Eucinostomus californiensis*), p. 165

5.—3rd anal spine markedly smaller in diameter than
the second...Shad (*Eucinostomus havana*), p. 166
3rd anal spine considerably heavier and greater in
diameter than the second ....
Mowbray's Shad
(*Eucinostomus mowbrayi*), p. 167

Key to Bermuda Goatfish

1.—Teeth absent on the upper jaw; no spine on the
opercle ....
Northern Goatfish (*Mullus auratus*), p. 168
Teeth present on both jaws; opercle with one spine　2
2.—30 to 32 rows of scales in a lateral series; several
large dark blotches along the sides.............
Spotted Goatfish (*Upeneus maculatus*), p. 169
39 or 40 rows of scales in a lateral series; a yellow
lateral band ....
Yellow Goatfish (*Upeneus martinicus*), p. 170

Key to Bermuda Ribbonfish and Kingfish

1.—A single short barbel on the chin ....
Kingfish (*Menticirrhus saxatilis*), p. 260
No barbels on the chin ....　2
2.—More than 50 soft rays in the dorsal fin..........
Lance-shaped Ribbonfish
(*Equetus lanceolatus*), p. 170
37 to 41 rays in the dorsal fin ....
Cluck (*Pareques acuminatus*), p. 171

Key to Bermuda Angel- and Butterflyfish

1.—No spines on the preopercle....................　2
A strong spine at the lower angle of the preopercle　5
2.—Rows of scales below the middle of the sides extending downward and backward, forming an
angle with the rows above the middle of the sides　3

Rows of scales below middle of body extending upward and backward, the lowermost rows more or less horizontal 4

3.—12 dorsal spines; body with dark vertical bands..
Banded Butterflyfish (*Chætodon striatus*), p. 173

13 dorsal spines; a band on head downward from dorsal fin; an ocellus below soft dorsal (very young with an additional ocellus on the anterior part of the soft dorsal) ....
Four-eyed Butterflyfish
(*Chætodon capistratus*), p. 174

4.—A large black spot on the base of the soft dorsal fin; occasionally extending downward as a narrow band ....
Two-spotted Butterflyfish
(*Chætodon ocellatus*), p. 175

A wide dark band between the soft dorsal and anal fins ....
Least Butterflyfish (*Chætodon sedentarius*), p. 176

5.—8 to 11 dorsal spines............................ 6

About 14 dorsal spines 7

6.—Base of pectoral with a conspicuous yellow spot; 10 dorsal spines ....
French Angelfish (*Pomacanthus paru*), p. 261

No yellow spot at the base of the pectoral fin; 8 or 9 dorsal spines ....
West Indian Angelfish
(*Pomacanthus arcuatus*), p. 261

7.—Head, anterior third of body, and tail rich orange or yellow; rest of body black ....
Black Angel (*Holacanthus tricolor*), p. 177

Yellows, green and blue, with long trailing fins....
Angelfish (*Angelichthys bermudensis*), p. 177

Key to Bermuda Doctorfish

1.—25 to 27 soft rays in the dorsal fin.............. 2

  21 to 23 soft rays in the dorsal fin.............. 3

2.—Colour blue, blackish or brown, or pale, never
  yellow ....

  Blue Doctorfish (*Acanthurus cœruleus*), p. 179

  Colour bright yellow ....

  Yellow Doctorfish (*Acanthurus helioides*), p. 179

3.—Caudal fin deeply concave, the upper lobe
  lengthened in the adult, and with a broad white
  posterior margin; dorsal fin with about eight
  horizontal dark lines. No vertical bars on the
  side in the young.............................

  Ocean Tang (*Acanthurus bahianus*), p. 180

  Caudal fin only moderately concave, the upper lobe
  not produced and not much longer than the lower,
  the fin with a very narrow white margin or none;
  dorsal fin dark, almost black; young with narrow
  vertical bars ....

  Doctorfish (*Acanthurus hepatus*), p. 181

Key to Bermuda Scorpionfish

1.—Pectoral fin with some of its upper and middle rays
  branched 2

  None of the pectoral fin-rays branched...........

  Small-scaled Scorpionfish

                    (*Pontinus microlepis*), p. 184

2.—A distinct pit below the anterior margin of the
  eye; posterior base of pectoral fin usually black
  with small white or pale blue spots; eye 3.6 to
  5.5 in head ....

              Prickly Hind (*Scorpæna plumieri*), p. 182

  No distinct pit below anterior margin of eye...... 3

3.—Tentacles above eye small; eye large, 2.5 to 2.9 in
  head ....

Agassiz's Scorpionfish

$\qquad$ (*Scorpæna agassizi*), p. 182

Tentacle above eye very large, wide and fringed; eye smaller, 3 to 3.85 ....

$\qquad$ Lionfish (*Scorpæna grandicornis*), p. 183

Key to Bermuda Demoiselles, Sergeant-Majors, etc.

1.—Teeth on the jaws small, in bands, the outer ones enlarged 2

Teeth in the jaws in one or two series only, compressed, more or less incisor-like 4

2.—12 dorsal spines; upper and lower margins of caudal fin black 3

13 or 14 dorsal spines; upper and lower margins of the caudal fin not black ....

$\qquad$ Bermuda Chromis (*Heliases bermudæ*), p. 188

3.—Base of the anal fin shorter than the longest anal ray; no black axillary spot; colour blue and black. Blue Chromis (*Demoisellea cyanea*), p. 187

Base of anal fin longer than longest anal ray; a black axillary spot, conspicuous; colour light brown and black ....

$\qquad$ Brown Chromis (*Demoisellea marginatus*), p. 187

4.—Teeth not movable; no deep notch on the lower edge of the bone between the nostril and the upper jaw bone 5

Teeth movable; a deep notch on the lower edge of the bone between the nostril and the upper jaw.. 9

5.—Green and yellow with conspicuous black vertical bars ....

$\qquad$ Sergeant-Major (*Abudefduf marginatus*), p. 191

Not as above 6

6.—Body averaging deeper, the depth 2 or less in the length; general colour bright yellow to greenish yellow or dark green with narrow vertical darker

stripes on the sides; a large black spot bordered
with blue on the posterior base of the spinous
dorsal; a black spot on the upper side of the caudal peduncle; a very small spot at the base of
the upper pectoral rays ....
Yellow Demoiselle
(*Eupomacentrus chrysus*), p. 189
Averaging less deep, without the above series of
characters 7
7.—Bluish, upper surface of body and anterior part of
the dorsal fin scarlet ....
Scarlet-backed Demoiselle
(*Eupomacentrus rubridorsalis*), p. 189
Upper part of body not scarlet 8
8.—Lower posterior half of the body dark, like the
anterior part ....
Demoiselle (*Eupomacentrus fuscus*), p. 190
Lower posterior half of the body unlike the anterior half, being usually more or less bright yellow; caudal fin bright yellow; usually a blue
spot at base of last anal ray; region below lateral
line with many blue spots; blue spots and lines
present on the head ....
Yellow-belly (*Eupomacentrus leucostictus*), p. 191
9.—Brownish or black, sometimes with very small
bluish spots on the head and dorsal surfaces....
Yellow-tailed Demoiselle
(*Stegastes chrysurus*), p. 192
Sides with conspicuous blue-white spots, each about
the size of a scale ....
Turquoise-spotted Demoiselle
(*Stegastes niveatus*), p. 193

Key to Bermuda Wrasses, Hogfish, etc.

1.—11 to 16 dorsal spines 2
8 or 9 dorsal spines 5

2.—15 to 16 dorsal spines; teeth in two series in each
    jaw; sombrely coloured ....
                    Tautog (*Tautoga onitis*), p. 262
    11 to 14 dorsal spines; teeth in a single series in
    each jaw; usually brightly coloured   3
3.—Anterior teeth small and bluntish, not canine-like.
    Purple-tailed Wrasse (*Clepticus parræ*), p. 194
    Anterior canine teeth strong   4
4.—Anterior dorsal spines longer than the rest, some-
    times produced into long streamers ....
            Hogfish (*Lachnolaimus maximus*), p. 195
    Anterior dorsal spines not longer than the rest.
          Spanish Hogfish (*Bodianus rufus*), p. 195
5.—Lateral line complete and continuous..............   6
    Lateral line interrupted posteriorly, beginning again
    on the caudal peduncle at the level of the axis
    of the body   14
6.—9 dorsal spines, a canine tooth developed on the
    side of the jaw posteriorly   7
    8 dorsal spines; no canine tooth posteriorly........
    Blue-head; King Slippery Dick
                (*Thalassoma bifasciatum*), p. 201
7.—Caudal fin biconcave; a broken yellow or greenish
    stripe along the sides; a yellow or green stripe
    from snout to eye, bifurcating on the opercles;
    a turquoise-green spot on the sides below the
    lateral line and just above the middle of the
    pectoral fin ....
        Deep-water Wrasse (*Iridio bathyphilus*), p. 196
    Caudal fin not biconcave; colour not as above....   8
8.—Small block dots on the scales of the nape; a series
    of pronounced, short, narrow black or dark blue
    lines radiating from the eye upward and back-
    ward. Variegated Wrasse (*Iridio garnoti*), p. 197
    No small black dots on the nape.................   9

9.—One or two dark horizontal bands on the sides.... 10

No dark bands on the sides........................ 12

10.—About 8 rows of scales on the nape before the dorsal fin. A black spot at the base of the pectoral; an elongate black blotch on the spinous dorsal followed by a dusky streak ....

Nichols' Wrasse (*Iridio similis*), p. 197

4 to 6 rows of scales on the nape before the dorsal fin 11

11.—Two horizontal bands on the sides, the lowermost extending from the base of the pectoral fin to above the anal fin,—or if only a single band present then with a black spot in the soft dorsal fin, not on the spinous portion of the fin; 4 forward projecting teeth in the lower jaw........

Slippery-dick (*Iridio bivittata*), p. 198

Lowermost horizontal band absent; 3 conspicuous brown cross bands on top of head, two between the eyes and one just in back of the eyes; a conspicuous blue-black spot on the spinous dorsal between the 5th and 7th or 8th spines; 2 or 3 narrow bluish streaks across the cheeks; 2 canine teeth only anteriorly in the lower jaw ....

Band-headed Wrasse (*Iridio maculipinna*), p. 199

12.—4 canine teeth anteriorly in the lower jaw........ 13

2 canine teeth anteriorly in lower jaw; three conspicuous brown cross bands on top of head,—two between the eyes and one back of the eyes......

Band-headed Wrasse (*Iridio maculipinna*), p. 199

13.—Body deeper, the depth 2.6 to 3.1 in the length; usually two oblique red or orange, blue-bordered, bands near the base of the pectoral fins; outer rays of the pelvic fin produced, more than twice as long as the inner ....

Pudding-wife (*Iridio radiatus*), p. 200

Body more elongate, the depth about 4 in the

length; outer rays of the pelvic fins not elongate or produced; no oblique red or orange bands
near pectoral; tips of caudal fin dusky; a violet
or black spot on the opercle ....
Slippery-dick (*Iridio bivittatus*), p. 198

14.—Body with irregular vertical dark crossbands. No
black lateral spot ....
Razor-fish (*Xyrichthys rosipes*), p. 202

Body without dark cross bands. A small black
lateral spot ....
Splendid Razorfish (*Xyrichthys splendens*), p. 202

Key to Bermuda Parrotfish

1.—Lower teeth included within the upper when jaw is
closed 2

Upper teeth included within the lower 11

2.—Teeth pale, pinkish or white 3

Teeth blue or green 10

3.—Projecting canine teeth present on outer posterior
aspect of the upper jaw 4

No canine teeth on posterior upper jaw.......... 8

4.—Cheeks, counting the scales on the preopercle downward from the eye, with 2 or 3 rows of scales.. 5

Cheeks with 3½ or 4 rows of scales............ 7

5.—3 or 4 posterior canine teeth; no longitudinal band
of colour on side of head..(*Scarus trispinosus*)*

1 or 2 posterior canine teeth; a longitudinal band
of colour on the head, either from the snout to
eye, or from eye backward 6

6.—Outer rays of the caudal fin deep green, rest of fin
bright greenish-blue, the membrane between the
inner rays orange; orange of the dorsal fin with

* This problematical species has been reported from Bermuda. It is known from dried skins and its status is exceedingly questionable.

a blue line, that of the anal with a line of bluish
spots ....
Dotted-fin Parrotfish (*Scarus punctulatus*), p. 209
Outer rays of the caudal fin orange, the fin some-
times with a very narrow black margin, re-
mainder of fin bluish; no spots or lines in the
orange of the dorsal or anal fin................
Painted-tail Parrotfish
(*Scarus tæniopterus*), p. 210
7.—Brown, with a broad whitish band on sides......
White-banded Parrotfish
(*Scarus gnathodus*), p. 211
Bright blues and greens, fins brightly coloured....
Bluefish (*Scarus vetula*), p. 210
8.—Bright blue, young more or less shaded with reddish brown. Blue Parrot (*Scarus cæruleus*), p. 212
Brown, red, yellow, usually with longitudinal light
and dark bands   9
9.—Conspicuous black or white longitudinal lines on the
anterior belly; last scale on middle of sides longer
than wide, much longer than the scale preceding it....Mud Belly (*Scarus croicensis*), p. 213
No longitudinal bands on the belly; last scale on
middle of side obtuse, not much longer than the
scale that precedes it........................
Mud Belly (*Scarus acutus*), p. 212
10.—Olive green or reddish brown; green markings on
head ....
Rainbow Parrotfish
(*Pseudoscarus guacamaia*), p. 214
Deep blackish purple tending toward black......
Wine-coloured Parrotfish
(*Pseudoscarus plumbeus*), p. 214
11.—Teeth fully coalesced into a beak-like structure, a
median suture evident externally..............   12
Anterior teeth not fully coalesced into a beak-like

structure, the anterior teeth enlarged, more or less canine-like ....
Many-toothed Parrotfish
(*Cryptotomus roseus*), p. 204

12.—Upper jaw with posterior lateral canine teeth.... 13
Upper jaw without posterior lateral canine teeth.. 16

13.—General colour dark red or brown; scales along back with dark edges; margin of opercles black.
Red Parrotfish (*Sparisoma abildgaardi*), p. 204
Paler; scales along back without dark edges; margin of opercles not black 14

14.—2 to 4 posterior canines on each side; caudal fin rounded or truncate ....
Mud-belly (*Sparisoma radians*), p. 205
1 to 2 posterior canines on each side; caudal fin lunate or forked 15

15.—A golden yellow spot on and below the 5th scale of the lateral line; outer angles of tail tipped with black ....
Red-banded Parrotfish
(*Sparisoma aurofrenatum*), p. 206
No yellow spot on and below the 5th scale of the lateral line; outer angle of tail not tipped with black; tail with crescents of orange and blue on its posterior margin ....
Dark Green Parrotfish (*Sparisoma viride*), p. 206

16.—No black spot at base of upper pectoral rays; body robust, not much compressed ....
Stocky Parrotfish (*Sparisoma flavescens*), p. 207
A very evident black spot at base of upper pectoral rays; body considerably compressed 17

17.—Caudal fin reddish brown with irregular bars and spots, most prominent on the upper and lower borders ....
Grey Parrotfish (*Sparisoma squalidum*), p. 208

Caudal fin clear peach red, its outer and posterior
margins bluish ....
Red-tailed Parrotfish
                        (*Sparisoma brachiale*), p. 208

Key to Bermuda Gobies

1.—Bases of pelvic fins close together, but not united
    and forming a sucking-disk   2
    Pelvic fins united, forming a sucking-disk........   3
2.—Head somewhat flattened with small embedded
    scales; no dermal keel on the nape..............
                    Sleeper (*Eleotris pisonis*), p. 215
    Head compressed, scaleless; a low dermal keel on
    the nape ....
        Bronze-headed Goby (*Eviota personata*), p. 216
3.—Scales present   4
    Scales absent ....
            Naked Goby (*Gobiosoma longum*), p. 221
4.—Upper rays of pectoral fin free, silky and thread-
    like ....
    Sheep's Head Molly Miller
                    (*Bathygobius soporator*), p. 217
    Upper rays of the pectoral like the others, not free   5
5.—Nape with a fleshy longitudinal crest   6
    Nape without a crest   7
6.—Colour dark; crest rather high and thin; snout
    short, about 4 to 4½ in the head..............
    Crested Goby (*Lophogobius cyprinoides*), p. 217
    Colour pale, with darker spots and blotches on the
    body; crest low, not thin and membranous......
    Translucent Crested Goby
                    (*Lophogobius glaucofrænum*), p. 218
7.—Cheeks and opercles with scales.................
    Thompson's Goby (*Gnatholepis thompsoni*), p. 219
    No scales on the cheeks or opercles.............   8

8.—Anal fin with 9 or 10 rays, the fin with an equal or
smaller number of rays than the soft dorsal;
12 to 14 conspicuous broad reddish bars, between
which on the pale spaces, are narrow dark hair
lines ....
Mowbray's Goby (*Rhinogobius mowbrayi*), p. 219
Anal fin with 11 to 13 rays, the fin usually with
one more ray than the soft dorsal; without the
above pattern   9
9.—Nape fully scaled, no narrow naked region........
Spot-tailed Goby
                    (*Gobionellus stigmaturus*), p. 220
Nape without scales ....
Darting Goby (*Gobionellus boleosoma*), p. 220

Key to Bermuda Shark-suckers

1.—20 to 28 laminæ in the sucking disk ....
Suckfish (*Echeneis naucrates*), p. 222
13 to 18 laminæ in the sucking disk..............
Off-Shore Remora (*Remora remora*), p. 223

Key to Bermuda Dragonets

1.—4 to 5 anal rays ....
Bermuda Dragonet
                    (*Callionymus bermudarum*), p. 223
9 anal rays ....
West Indian Dragonet
                    (*Callionymus boekei*), p. 224

Key to Bermuda Blennies

1.—Scales present   2
Scales absent   4
2.—Dorsal fin entirely of spines or with one soft ray
posteriorly ....
Fajardo Blenny (*Auchenopterus fajardo*), p. 225
Dorsal fin with about 12 soft rays posteriorly.....   3

3.—Pelvic fins reaching almost to vent; a black spot on the opercle and one on the anterior part of the soft dorsal fin.............................

Molly Miller (*Labrisomus nuchipinnis*), p. 226

Pelvic fins reaching scarcely more than half way to the vent; no spot on opercle or spinous dorsal fin ....

Short-finned Molly Miller

(*Labrisomus lentiginosus*), p. 227

4.—Teeth implanted on the skin of the lips, freely movable ....

Soft-toothed Tide-pool Blenny

(*Salariichthys textilis*), p. 227

Teeth firmly fixed on the jaws.................   5

5.—10 to 12 spines in the dorsal fin................   6

About 22 spines in the dorsal fin.................

Mark's Blenny (*Emblemaria markii*), p. 229

6.—A fringe of tentacles on the nape; gill-openings free below ....

Scaleless Molly Miller

(*Blennius cristatus*), p. 228

No fringe of tentacles on the nape; gill-openings restricted to the sides, not open below..........

Bermuda Blenny

(*Hypleurochilus bermudensis*), p. 228

Key to Bermuda Brotulids

1.—Barbels present on the snout and lower jaw.......

Brotula (*Brotula barbata*), p. 230

No barbels on snout or lower jaw   2

2.—Body brownish, striped and blotched; about 110 scales in a lateral series......................

Verrill's Brotulid (*Ogilbia verrilli*), p. 231

Body uniform brownish; about 87 to 90 scales in a lateral series ....

West Indian Brotulid (*Ogilbia cayorum*), p. 231

Key to Bermuda Triggerfish and Filefish

1.—A single dorsal spine, followed occasionally by a rudiment 2

Three dorsal spines 9

2.—Bone (pubic) supporting the ventral flap with a small spine or barb at its lower end............ 3

Bone supporting the ventral flap without a spine at its end 7

3.—Dorsal spine not barbed, its edge merely rough.... 4

Dorsal spine armed with small but strong barbs.... 5

4.—Pelvic spine movable; dark chocolate brown, body covered with small dull orange spots with a dark centre ....

Orange-spotted Filefish

(*Cantherines pullus*), p. 237

Pelvic spine not movable; brownish or greenish with lighter and darker patches; a saddle-like patch of colour on the back..................

False Filefish (*Cantherines amphioxys*), p. 238

5.—Elongate, the depth, measured at the vertical of the origin of the soft dorsal fin, averaging 2.7 to 3 ....

Tucker's Filefish (*Monacanthus tuckeri*), p. 238

Deeper, the depth averaging from 1.7 to 2.5...... 6

6.—Adults with the ventral flap greatly developed, extending far beyond the pelvic spine; 2 or 3 pairs of recurved spines on the sides of the caudal peduncle ....

Common Filefish (*Monacanthus ciliatus*), p. 240

Adults with the ventral flap never reaching beyond the pelvic spine; no recurved spines on the caudal peduncle at any age ....

Leather fish (*Monacanthus hispidus*), p. 239

7.—35 to 38 dorsal rays ....

Orange Filefish (*Alutera schœpfi*), p. 240

45 to 48 dorsal rays 8

8.—Head and body with irregular blue spots and lines, besides small, round black spots; caudal fin elongate, with rounded angles ....

Scrawled Filefish (*Alutera scripta*), p. 241

Head and body bluish grey, lighter below with blackish marks; caudal fin short, rounded with fairly acute angles ....

Unicorn Filefish (*Alutera monoceros*), p. 241

9.—Enlarged bony plates behind the gill-opening...... 10

No enlarged plates behind the gill-opening........ 12

10.—Head with prominent stripes and bars; 26 to 28 anal rays ....:........

Queen Triggerfish (*Balistes vetula*), p. 233

No stripes or bars; 23 to 26 anal rays.......... 11

11.—Body with conspicuous dark blue spots ....

Ocean Turbot (*Balistes forcipatus*), p. 234

No conspicuous blue spots ....

Turbot (*Balistes capriscus*), p. 234

12.—Cheek with 3 to 5 narrow, parallel grooves........
Red-tailed Triggerfish

(*Xanthichthys ringens*), p. 236

No grooves on the cheek 13

13.—Anal fin with 24 or 25 rays....................

Ocean Triggerfish (*Canthidermis sobaco*), p. 235

Anal fin with 19 to 21 rays ....

Ocean Turbot (*Canthidermis maculatus*), p. 236

Key to Bermuda Cowfish and Trunkfish

1.—No projecting spines on carapace ....

Smooth Trunkfish (*Lactophrys triqueter*), p. 242

Projecting spines present, one pointing backward on each side of the ventral ridge being always present 2

2.—No spines in front of and above eye.............
Cuckold, Common Trunkfish

(*Lactophrys trigonus*), p. 243

A large spine projecting forward on each side in
front of eye 3
3.—Caudal fin truncate, its outer rays sometimes pro-
duced ....
Cowfish, Buffalo Cow
(*Lactophrys quadricornis*), p. 243
Caudal fin rounded; colour dark ....
Bermuda Cowfish (*Lactophrys saxatilis*), p. 244

Key to Bermuda Puffers and Porcupinefish

1.—Body covered with strong, sharp spines........... 2
Body smooth or slightly prickly 3
2.—Spines slender, stiff, movable ....
Porcupinefish (*Diodon hystrix*), p. 247
Spines short, stiff, not movable ....
Sea Porcupine (*Chilomycterus atinga*), p. 247
3.—12 to 13 anal rays ....
Jugfish (*Lagocephalus pachycephalus*), p. 245
6 to 9 anal rays 4
4.—Nostrils without a tube, single ....
Sharp-nosed Puffer
(*Canthigaster rostratus*), p. 246
Nostrils with a tube, double; a series of round
black spots along the middle of the sides......
Southern Puffer (*Sphæroides spengleri*), p. 245

Key to Bermuda Frogfish

1.—Pelvic fins long, reaching nearly to anal fin........ 2
Pelvic fins short, scarcely reaching to pectoral fin 4
2.—Variegated, yellow, black and white 3
Dark chocolate brown, with a few scattered white
spots..Brown Mousefish (*Histrio jagua*), p. 249
3.—12 rays in soft dorsal fin; "bait" * on 1st dorsal

* The first dorsal spine in these fishes is small, quite unlike the remaining spines and rays. It is often found
pressed close to the side of the second dorsal spine.

spine spherical with small filaments............

Common Sargassumfish (*Histrio gibba*), p. 248

14 rays in soft dorsal fin; "bait" on 1st dorsal spine bifurcated ....

Sargassumfish (*Histrio picta*), p. 249

4.—Bulbous "bait" * on tip of 1st dorsal spine bifid or with finger-like protuberances 5

Bulbous "bait" on tip of 1st dorsal spine more or less spherical, sometimes covered with small filaments or papillæ ...., 7

5.—1st dorsal spine "bait" with finger-like protuberances; sides with dark streaks and reticulations; a large ocellus under middle of soft dorsal fin..

Star-eyed Frogfish (*Antennarius radiosus*), p. 250

Not as above 6

6.—Uniform black, inside of mouth black, sometimes with white spots ....

Black Frogfish (*Antennarius nuttingi*), p. 251

Reddish or brownish with darker spots, those about the eye radiating ....

Reddish Frogfish (*Antennarius scaber*), p. 251

7.—1st dorsal spine not extending beyond the tip of the 2nd, terminating in a horizontal oblong bulb set at an acute angle to the stem; colour pale with dark spots ....

Yellow Frogfish (*Antennarius verrucosus*), p. 252

1st dorsal spine extending beyond the tip of the 2nd 8

8.—Black with a small white spot above the pectoral fin; tips of pectoral and ventral fins white....

White-spotted Frogfish

(*Antennarius principis*), p. 252

Green or brownish with ocellated dark spots and irregular whitish spots on the sides ....

Green Frogfish (*Antennarius stellifer*), p. 253

BIBLIOGRAPHY OF BERMUDA SHORE FISH

ANONYMOUS

1929 (Introduction of West Indian species of Fish to Bermuda.) Bushnells Handbook, 20th edition, p. 109.

—— Catalogue Bermuda Fishes. 16 pp. (List of fishes able to be supplied to institutions by the Bermuda Aquarium.)

AREY, L. B.

1915 Orientation of Amphioxus during Locomotion. Journ. Experimental Zool., Vol. 19, No. 1, pp. 37-44.

BARBOUR, T. H.

1905 Notes on Bermudian Fishes. Bull. Mus. Comp. Zool., Vol. XLVI, No. 7, pp. 109-134.

BEAN, T. H.

1898 Notes upon Fishes Received at the New York Aquarium, with descriptions of a new species of Snapper from Bermuda. Bull. Am. Mus. Nat. Hist., X, pp. 45-51.

1906 Descriptions of New Bermudian Fishes. Proc. Biol. Soc. Wash., XIX, pp. 29-33.

1906 A Catalogue of the Fishes of Bermuda, with notes on a Collection made in 1905 for the Field Museum. Field Columbian Museum, 1906, Publ. 108, Zool. Ser., Vol. VII, No. 2, pp. 21-89.

1912 Descriptions of New Fishes of Bermuda, Proc. Biol. Soc. Wash., XXV, pp. 121-126.

BEEBE, W.

1930 The Bermuda Oceanographic Expedition. Bull. New York Zool. Soc., Vol. XXXIII, No. 2, p. 35.

1931 Notes on the Gill-finned Goby. Zoologica, Vol. XII, No. 5, p. 55.

1932 Note on a Hand-book of Bermuda Shore Fish. Royal Gazette, Hamilton, Bermuda, Feb. 13, 1932.

1932 Nonsuch: Land of Water. Harcourt, Brace and Co.

1932 The World of Bermuda Fish. Bull. New York Zool. Soc., Vol. XXXV, No. 2, p. 36.

BEEBE, W., and TEE-VAN, J.

1928 The Fishes of Port-au-Prince Bay, Haiti, with a Summary of the Known Species of Marine Fishes of the Island of Haiti and Santo Domingo. Zoologica, Vol. X, No. 1, pp. 1-279.

1932 New Bermuda Fish, including Six New Species and Forty-three Species hitherto unrecorded from Bermuda. Zoologica, Vol. XIII, No. 5, pp. 109-120.

1933 Nomenclatural Notes on the Shore Fishes of Bermuda. Zoologica, Vol. XIII, No. 7.

BREDER, C. M., JR.

1927 Fishes, Bingham Oceanog. Coll., Vol. I, No. 1, pp. 1-90.

1929 Field Book of Marine Fishes of the Atlantic Coast from Labrador to Texas. Putnam, xxxviii-332 pages.

BRISTOL, C. L.

(Numerous newspaper and magazine articles on fishes brought to the New York Aquarium by Professor Bristol are recorded in Coles' "Bermuda in Periodical Literature," 1907.)

1903 Bermuda Fish; How they are brought to the New York Aquarium. Bull. N. Y. Zool. Soc., 1903, No. 9, pp. 77-91.

1903 On the Color Patterns of Certain Bermuda Fishes. Science, 1903, n. s., XVII, p. 492.

BRISTOL, C. L., and CARPENTER, F. W.

1900 On the Occurrence of Amphioxus in Bermuda. Science, n. s., XI, p. 170.

COLE, G. W.

1907 Bermuda in Periodical Literature, with Occasional References to Other Works. xii-276.

(This volume contains records of many small, mainly newspaper, accounts of Bermuda shore fish, which have not been recorded in the present bibliography.)

CROZIER, W. J.

1916 On a Barnacle, *Conchoderma virgatum,* attached to a Fish, *Diodon hystrix.* Amer. Nat., Vol. L, No. 598.

1917 Studies on Amphioxus by E. L. Mark and W. J. Crozier. I. The photo receptors of Amphioxus. Anat. Rec., Vol. XI, No. 6.

1919 On the resistance of *Fundulus* to concentrated Sea Water. Anat. Rec., Vol. LIII, No. 625, pp. 180-185.

1921 Notes on some problems of adaptation. IV. The photic sensitivity of *Ogilbia.* Biol. Bull., Vol. XLI, No. 2, pp. 98-101.

EVERMANN, B. W., and MARSH, M. C.

1902 The Fishes of Porto Rico. Bull. U. S. Fish. Comm. for 1900 (1902), pp. 49-350.

FOWLER, H. W.

1906 Some New and Little Known Percoid Fishes. Proc. Acad. Nat. Sci. Phila., Vol. 58, pp. 510-528.

1907 Notes on Lancelets and Lampreys. Proc. Acad. Nat. Sci. Phila., 1907, p. 461.

1915 Cold-blooded Vertebrates from Florida, the West Indies, Costa Rica and Eastern Brazil. Proc. Acad. Nat. Sci. Phila., Vol. 67, pp. 244-269.

1919 Notes on Tropical American Fishes. Proc. Acad. Nat. Sci. Phila., Vol. 71, pp. 128-155.

1930 Notes on Percoid and Related Fishes. Proc. Acad. Nat. Sci. Phila., Vol. 81, 1929 (1930), pp. 633-657.

GARMAN, S.

1900 Additions to the Ichthyological Fauna of the Bermudas, from the Collections of the Yale Expedition of 1898.   Trans. Conn. Acad. Sci., Vol. 10, pp. 510-512.

1913   The Plagiostoma.   Mem. Mus. Comp. Zool., Cambridge, Vol. XXXVI, pp. 1-528.

GILL, T.

1878   Catalogue of the Fishes of the East Coast of North America.   Misc. Coll. Smiths. Inst., Vol. 14, p. 283.

GODET, T. L.

1860   Bermuda; its History, Geology, Climate, Products, Agriculture, Commerce and Government.   London, pp. 77 to 80.

GOODE, G. B.

1874   Descriptions of two new species of fishes from the Bermuda Islands.   Amer. Journ. Sci., Vol. VIII, pp. 123-125.   Ann. Mag. Nat. Hist., (3) 14, pp. 379-381.   Amer. Sportsman, 4, pp. 307-308.

1876   Bermuda and Its Fish Markets.   Forest and Stream, Vol. 6, pp. 83-84.

1876   Catalogue of the Fishes of the Bermudas, based chiefly upon the Collections of the United States National Museum.   Bull. U. S. Nat. Mus., 5, pp. 1-82.

1877   A preliminary Catalogue of the Reptiles, Fishes and Leptocardians of the Bermudas, with descriptions of four species of fish believed to be new.   Amer. Journ. Sci. and Arts., Ser. 3, Vol. 14, pp. 289-298.

1877   Provisional Catalogue of the Fishes of Bermuda. Hamilton, Bermuda, 1877, pp. 1-8.   Bermuda Almanac, 1878-81, pp. 116-122.

1879   On two fishes from the Bermudas, mistakenly described as new by Doctor Günther.   Proc. U. S. Nat. Mus., I, pp. 462-463; Amer. Journ. Sci., 17, p. 340.

GOODE, G. B., and BEAN, T. H.

1878   On a new Serranoid Fish, *Epinephilus drummondhayi,* from the Bermudas and Florida.   Proc. U. S.

Nat. Mus., I, pp. 173-175. Smith. Misc. Coll., 19, art. 1.

GUDGER, E. W.

1929 On the Morphology, Coloration and Behavior of Seventy Teleostean Fishes of Tortugas, Florida. Carn. Inst. of Washington, Publ. No. 391, pp. 149-204.

GUDGER, E. W., and MOWBRAY, L. L.

1927 The Oil-fish (*Ruvettus pretiosus*) at Bermuda. Science, New York, 65, pp. 145-146.

GÜNTHER, A.

1874 Descriptions of New Species of Fishes in the British Museum, Ann. Mag. Nat. Hist., (4) 14, pp. 453-455.

1879 Report on the Shore Fishes; Voyage of Challenger, Vol. I, pt. 6, pp. 1-82.

1879 On two new species of fish from the Bermudas. Ann. Mag. Nat. Hist., (5) 3, pp. 150-151.

1879 Note on two Bermuda Fish recently described as new. Ann. Mag. Nat. Hist., (5) 3, pp. 389-390.

HILDEBRAND, S. F., and GINSBURGH, I.

1927 Descriptions of Two New Species of Fishes from Key West, Florida, with Notes on Nine Other Species Collected in the Same Locality. Bull. U. S. Bur. Fish., XLII, 1926, pp. 207-215.

HILDEBRAND, S. F., and SCHROEDER, W. C.

1928 Fishes of Chesapeake Bay, Bull. U. S. Bur. Fish., XLIII, 1927 (1928), Part 1, pp. 1-366.

HOLLISTER, G.

1930 Fish Magic. Bull. N. Y. Zool. Soc., Vol. XXXIII, No. 2, p. 72.

HUBBS, C. L.

1922 A List of the Lancelets of the World with Diagnoses of five new species of *Branchiostoma*. Occ. Pap. Mus. Zool., Univ. of Michigan, No. 105.

Hurdis, J. L.

1897 Rough Notes relating to the Natural History of the Bermudas. London, pp. vi-408.

Jones, J. M.

1872 A pelagic floating fish-nest. Nature, Vol. V, p. 462.

1874 A new fish *Lefroyia bermudensis.* Zoologist, (2), IX, pp. 3837-3838.

1876 The Visitor's Guide to Bermuda, with a sketch of its Natural History. London, New York, Montreal, pp. xii-156.

1879 The Gulf Weed (*Sargassum bacciferum*), a means of migration for fishes and marine invertebrates. Nature, 19, p. 363.

Jones, J. M.; Wedderburn, J. W., and Hurdis, J. L.

1859 The Naturalist in Bermuda, a Sketch of the Geology, Zoology and Botany of that Remarkable Group of Islands. London, Reeves and Turner. xii-200 pp.

Jordan, D. S.

1923 A Classification of Fishes, Including Families and Genera as Far as Known. Stanford Univ. Publ., Biological Sciences, Vol. III, No. 2.

Jordan, H.

1917 Rheotropism of *Epinephilus striatus.* Proc. Nat. Acad. Sci., III, No. 3, pp. 157-159.

1917 Rheotropic Responses of Epinephelus striatus Bloch. Amer. Journ. Phys., XLIII, No. 3, pp. 438-454.

1917 Integumentary photosensitivity in a marine fish, *Epinephelus striatus.* Amer. Journ. Phys., XLIV, No. 3, pp. 259-274.

1919 Concerning Reissner's fiber in teleosts. Journ. Comp. Neurol., XXX, No. 2, pp. 217-227.

Jordan, D. S., and Evermann, B. W.

1896-1900 The Fishes of North and Middle America; A

Descriptive Catalogue of the Species of Fish-Like Vertebrates found in the Waters of North America, north of the Isthmus of Panama. Part I, 1896; Part II, 1898; Part III, 1898; Part IV, 1900. Bull. U. S. Nat. Mus. 47.

JORDAN, D. S.; EVERMANN, B. W., and CLARK, H. W.
1930 Check List of the Fishes and Fish-like Vertebrates of North and Middle America north of the northern boundary of Venezuela and Colombia. Rep. U. S. Com. Fisheries, 1928, pp. 1-670.

JORDAN, D. S., and THOMPSON, J. C.
1905 The Fish Fauna of the Tortugas Archipelago. Bull. U. S. Bur. Fish., XXIV, 1904 (1905), pp. 229-256.

KUTCHIN, H. L.
1913 Studies on the peripheral nervous system of Amphioxus. Proc. Am. Acad. Arts and Sciences, XLIX, No. 10.

LEFROY, J. H.
1877 Memorials of the Discovery and Early Settlement of the Bermudas or Somers Islands. London, 2 vols.

LINTON, E.
1907 Notes on Parasites of Bermuda Fishes. Proc. U. S. Nat. Mus., XXXIII, No. 1560, pp. 85-126.

MARK, E. L.
1904 *Asymmetron lucayanum* at Bermuda. Science, n.s., Vol. 20, p. 179.

MEEK, S. E., and HILDEBRAND, S. F.
1923-1928 The Marine Fishes of Panama. Field Mus. of Nat. Hist., Publ. 215; Zoological Series, Vol. XV, Part I, 1923, pp. 1-330; Part II, 1925, pp. 331-707; Part III, 1928, pp. 708-1045.

MELLEN, I. M.
1919 Prehensile-tailed Pipe-fishes. Bull. N. Y. Zool. Soc., 22, pp. 133-135.

METZELAAR, J.
   1919 Over Tropisch Atlantische Visschen, Amsterdam, pp. 1-316.

MOWBRAY, L. L.
   1916 Some Habits of the Four-eye Fish. Bull. New York Zool. Society, 19, pp. 1339-1341.
   1922 *Corythoichthys ensenadæ* from Bermuda. Copeia, No. 104, p. 19.
   1922 Habit Note on Snipe Eel. Copeia, 108, p. 49.
   1931 Fauna Bermudensis. Number 1 (8 pp.). (No pagination.)

NICHOLS, J. T.
   1919 On *Caranx guara* from Bermuda. Copeia, 76, p. 98.
   1920 A Contribution to the Ichthyology of Bermuda. Proc. Biol. Soc. Wash., 33, pp. 59-64.
   1922 *Tekla,* a new genus of blennies, and other notes. Copeia, 110, p. 67.
   1929 The Fishes of Porto Rico and the Virgin Islands. Sci. Surv. of Porto Rico and the Virgin Islands, Vol. X, parts 2 and 3, pp. 161 to 295, 297 to 399.

NICHOLS, J. T., and BREDER, C. M., JR.
   1928 An Annotated List of the Synentognathi, with Remarks on their Development and Relationships. Zoologica, VIII, No. 7, pp. 423-444.

NICHOLS, J. T., and MOWBRAY, L. L.
   1917 Certain Marine Tropical Fishes as Food. Copeia, 48, pp. 77-84.

PARKER, G. H.
   1908 The sensory reactions of Amphioxus. Proc. Amer. Acad. Arts and Sciences, XLIII, No. 16, pp. 415-455.

PARR, A. E.
   1930 Teleostean Shore and Shallow-Water Fishes from the Bahamas and Turks Island. Bull. Bingham Ocean. Coll., Vol. III, Art. 4, 148 pages.

REGAN, C. T.

  1917 A Revision of the Clupeoid Fishes of the Genera
        Sardinella, Harengula, etc. Ann. Mag. Nat. Hist.,
        (8), XIX, pp. 377-395.

SCHMIDT, J.

  —— On the distribution of the freshwater eels (An-
        guilla) throughout the world. I. The Atlantic.
        Medd. f. Komm. f. Havund., Kjobenhavn, Ger.
        Fiskeri, Bd. III, No. 7, pp. 1-45.

SCHUFELDT, R. W.

  1917 On the osteology of the fishes of Bermuda.
        Aquarium Bull., Brooklyn Aquarium Soc., 1917.

SILVESTER, C. F.

  1918 Fishes new to the Fauna of Porto Rico, with de-
        scriptions of eight new species. Papers Dept.
        Mar. Biol., Carnegie Inst., Washington, Vol. XII,
        No. 2.

TEE-VAN, J.

  1928 (See Beebe, W., 1928.)

  1930 How Bermuda Acquired its Shore Fishes. Bull.
        N Y Zool. Soc., Vol. XXXIII, No. 2, p. 67.

  1932 (See Beebe W., 1932.)

  1932 Color Changes in the Blue-head Wrasse. Bull.
        N. Y. Zool. Soc., Vol. XXXV, No. 2, p. 43.

  1933 (See Beebe, W., 1933.)

TOWNSEND, C. H.

        (Numerous small articles by Dr. Townsend not
        recorded here and relating directly and indirectly
        to Bermuda fish are in the Bull. and Reports of
        the N. Y. Zool. Soc.)

  1891 Official Guide and Catalogue, New York Aquarium.
        (Also other editions.)

  1905 Ann. Report New York Aquarium. N. Y. Zool.
        Soc. Ann. Report.

  1929 Records of Changes in Color among Fishes. Zoo-
        logica, IX, No. 9, pp. 321-378.

TOWNSEND, C. H., and BARBOUR, T.

1906 Description of a new species of Sea-horse from Bermuda. Bull. N. Y. Zool. Soc., 1906, 23, p. 304.

VERRILL, A. E.

1901 A Remarkable Instance of Death of Fishes at Bermuda in 1901. Amer. Journ. Sci., 4 ser., 12, p. 88.

1902 The Bermuda Islands. An account of the scenery, climate, productions, physiology, natural history and geology, with sketches of their discovery and early history, and the changes in their flora and fauna due to man. New Haven, x-548 pp.

1903 Additions to the fauna of the Bermudas from the Yale Expeditions of 1901, with notes on other species. Trans. Conn. Acad. Sci., Vol. II, pp. 55-57.

INDEX

A

Ablennes hians, 61
Abudefduf marginatus, 191
Acanthocybiidae, Family, 92
Acanthocybium petus, 92
Acanthuridae, Family, 179
Acanthurus bahianus, 180
  caeruleus, 179
  heliodes, 179
  hepatus, 181
Acipenseridae, Family, 32
Acipenser sturio, 32
Aetobatidae, Family, 30
Aguavina, 135
Albula vulpes, 34
Albulidae, Family, 34
Alewife, 108, 109
Alphestes afer, 126
Alutera monoceros, 241
  schoepfi, 240
  scripta, 241
Amber-Fish, 110
Amphelikturus dendriticus, 79
Amphioxus, Bermuda, 21
Anchoviella choerostoma, 38
Anchovy, 35
Angel, Black, 177
Angelfish, 173, 177
  French, 261
  West Indian, 261
Angelichthys bermudensis, 177
Anglers, 248
Anguilla rostrata, 39
Anguillidae, Family, 39
Anisotremus virginicus, 258
Antennariidae, Family, 248
Antennarius nuttingi, 251
  principis, 252
  radiosus, 250
  scaber, 251
  stellifer, 253
  verrucosus, 252

Anthias, Bermuda, 138
  Small-Scaled, 137
Anthias louisi, 138
  tenuis, 137
Aphthalmichthys mayeri, **45**
Apogon binotatus, 115
  maculatus, 116
  pigmentarius, 114
  sellicauda, 115
Apogonidae, Family, 114
Argyreiosus vomer, 107
Astrapogon stellatus, 117
Asymmetron lucayanum, 21
Atherina harringtonensis, 85
Atherinidae, Family, 85
Auchenopterus fajardo, 225
Aulostomidae, Family, 83
Aulostomus maculatus, 83
Auxis rochei, 95

B

Balistes capriscus, **234**
  forcipatus, 234
  vetula, 233
Balistidae, Family, 233
Banana Fish, 34
Barbel, 264
Barber, 134
Barracuda, European, 90
  Great, 89
Barracudas, 88
Bass, Common Sea, 255
Basslet, Blue and Gold
  Fairy, 139
Bathygobius soporator, 217
Bathystoma aurolineatum, 151
  striatum, 151
Beak, 264
Beau Gregory, 191
Beauty, Rock, 177
Belonidae, Family, 59
Big-Eye, 140
  Short, 141

327

A CATALOGUE OF SELECTED DOVER BOOKS
IN ALL FIELDS OF INTEREST

A CATALOGUE OF SELECTED DOVER BOOKS
IN ALL FIELDS OF INTEREST

WHAT IS SCIENCE?, *N. Campbell*
The role of experiment and measurement, the function of mathematics, the nature of scientific laws, the difference between laws and theories, the limitations of science, and many similarly provocative topics are treated clearly and without technicalities by an eminent scientist. "Still an excellent introduction to scientific philosophy," H. Margenau in *Physics Today*. "A first-rate primer . . . deserves a wide audience," *Scientific American*. 192pp. 5⅜ x 8.
60043-2 Paperbound $1.25

THE NATURE OF LIGHT AND COLOUR IN THE OPEN AIR, *M. Minnaert*
Why are shadows sometimes blue, sometimes green, or other colors depending on the light and surroundings? What causes mirages? Why do multiple suns and moons appear in the sky? Professor Minnaert explains these unusual phenomena and hundreds of others in simple, easy-to-understand terms based on optical laws and the properties of light and color. No mathematics is required but artists, scientists, students, and everyone fascinated by these "tricks" of nature will find thousands of useful and amazing pieces of information. Hundreds of observational experiments are suggested which require no special equipment. 200 illustrations; 42 photos. xvi + 362pp. 5⅜ x 8.
20196-1 Paperbound $2.75

THE STRANGE STORY OF THE QUANTUM, AN ACCOUNT FOR THE GENERAL READER OF THE GROWTH OF IDEAS UNDERLYING OUR PRESENT ATOMIC KNOWLEDGE, *B. Hoffmann*
Presents lucidly and expertly, with barest amount of mathematics, the problems and theories which led to modern quantum physics. Dr. Hoffmann begins with the closing years of the 19th century, when certain trifling discrepancies were noticed, and with illuminating analogies and examples takes you through the brilliant concepts of Planck, Einstein, Pauli, Broglie, Bohr, Schroedinger, Heisenberg, Dirac, Sommerfeld, Feynman, etc. This edition includes a new, long postscript carrying the story through 1958. "Of the books attempting an account of the history and contents of our modern atomic physics which have come to my attention, this is the best," H. Margenau, Yale University, in *American Journal of Physics*. 32 tables and line illustrations. Index. 275pp. 5⅜ x 8.
20518-5 Paperbound $2.00

GREAT IDEAS OF MODERN MATHEMATICS: THEIR NATURE AND USE, *Jagjit Singh*
Reader with only high school math will understand main mathematical ideas of modern physics, astronomy, genetics, psychology, evolution, etc. better than many who use them as tools, but comprehend little of their basic structure. Author uses his wide knowledge of non-mathematical fields in brilliant exposition of differential equations, matrices, group theory, logic, statistics, problems of mathematical foundations, imaginary numbers, vectors, etc. Original publication. 2 appendixes. 2 indexes. 65 ills. 322pp. 5⅜ x 8.
20587-8 Paperbound $2.50

THE MUSIC OF THE SPHERES: THE MATERIAL UNIVERSE — FROM ATOM TO QUASAR, SIMPLY EXPLAINED, *Guy Murchie*
Vast compendium of fact, modern concept and theory, observed and calculated data, historical background guides intelligent layman through the material universe. Brilliant exposition of earth's construction, explanations for moon's craters, atmospheric components of Venus and Mars (with data from recent fly-by's), sun spots, sequences of star birth and death, neighboring galaxies, contributions of Galileo, Tycho Brahe, Kepler, etc.; and (Vol. 2) construction of the atom (describing newly discovered sigma and xi subatomic particles), theories of sound, color and light, space and time, including relativity theory, quantum theory, wave theory, probability theory, work of Newton, Maxwell, Faraday, Einstein, de Broglie, etc. "Best presentation yet offered to the intelligent general reader," *Saturday Review*. Revised (1967). Index. 319 illustrations by the author. Total of xx + 644pp. 5⅜ x 8½.
21809-0, 21810-4 Two volume set, paperbound $5.00

FOUR LECTURES ON RELATIVITY AND SPACE, *Charles Proteus Steinmetz*
Lecture series, given by great mathematician and electrical engineer, generally considered one of the best popular-level expositions of special and general relativity theories and related questions. Steinmetz translates complex mathematical reasoning into language accessible to laymen through analogy, example and comparison. Among topics covered are relativity of motion, location, time; of mass; acceleration; 4-dimensional time-space; geometry of the gravitational field; curvature and bending of space; non-Euclidean geometry. Index. 40 illustrations. x + 142pp. 5⅜ x 8½.   61771-8 Paperbound $1.50

HOW TO KNOW THE WILD FLOWERS, *Mrs. William Starr Dana*
Classic nature book that has introduced thousands to wonders of American wild flowers. Color-season principle of organization is easy to use, even by those with no botanical training, and the genial, refreshing discussions of history, folklore, uses of over 1,000 native and escape flowers, foliage plants are informative as well as fun to read. Over 170 full-page plates, collected from several editions, may be colored in to make permanent records of finds. Revised to conform with 1950 edition of Gray's Manual of Botany. xlii + 438pp. 5⅜ x 8½.   20332-8 Paperbound $2.50

MANUAL OF THE TREES OF NORTH AMERICA, *Charles Sprague Sargent*
Still unsurpassed as most comprehensive, reliable study of North American tree characteristics, precise locations and distribution. By dean of American dendrologists. Every tree native to U.S., Canada, Alaska; 185 genera, 717 species, described in detail—leaves, flowers, fruit, winterbuds, bark, wood, growth habits, etc. plus discussion of varieties and local variants, immaturity variations. Over 100 keys, including unusual 11-page analytical key to genera, aid in identification. 783 clear illustrations of flowers, fruit, leaves. An unmatched permanent reference work for all nature lovers. Second enlarged (1926) edition. Synopsis of families. Analytical key to genera. Glossary of technical terms. Index. 783 illustrations, 1 map. Total of 982pp. 5⅜ x 8.
20277-1, 20278-X Two volume set, paperbound $6.00

It's Fun to Make Things From Scrap Materials,
Evelyn Glantz Hershoff
What use are empty spools, tin cans, bottle tops? What can be made from rubber bands, clothes pins, paper clips, and buttons? This book provides simply worded instructions and large diagrams showing you how to make cookie cutters, toy trucks, paper turkeys, Halloween masks, telephone sets, aprons, linoleum block- and spatter prints — in all 399 projects! Many are easy enough for young children to figure out for themselves; some challenging enough to entertain adults; all are remarkably ingenious ways to make things from materials that cost pennies or less! Formerly "Scrap Fun for Everyone." Index. 214 illustrations. 373pp. 5⅜ x 8½.   21251-3 Paperbound $2.00

Symbolic Logic and The Game of Logic, *Lewis Carroll*
"Symbolic Logic" is not concerned with modern symbolic logic, but is instead a collection of over 380 problems posed with charm and imagination, using the syllogism and a fascinating diagrammatic method of drawing conclusions. In "The Game of Logic" Carroll's whimsical imagination devises a logical game played with 2 diagrams and counters (included) to manipulate hundreds of tricky syllogisms. The final section, "Hit or Miss" is a lagniappe of 101 additional puzzles in the delightful Carroll manner. Until this reprint edition, both of these books were rarities costing up to $15 each. Symbolic Logic: Index. xxxi + 199pp. The Game of Logic: 96pp. 2 vols. bound as one. 5⅜ x 8.
20492-8 Paperbound $2.50

Mathematical Puzzles of Sam Loyd, Part i
selected and edited by M. Gardner
Choice puzzles by the greatest American puzzle creator and innovator. Selected from his famous collection, "Cyclopedia of Puzzles," they retain the unique style and historical flavor of the originals. There are posers based on arithmetic, algebra, probability, game theory, route tracing, topology, counter and sliding block, operations research, geometrical dissection. Includes the famous "14-15" puzzle which was a national craze, and his "Horse of a Different Color" which sold millions of copies. 117 of his most ingenious puzzles in all. 120 line drawings and diagrams. Solutions. Selected references. xx + 167pp. 5⅜ x 8.
20498-7 Paperbound $1.35

String Figures and How to Make Them, *Caroline Furness Jayne*
107 string figures plus variations selected from the best primitive and modern examples developed by Navajo, Apache, pygmies of Africa, Eskimo, in Europe, Australia, China, etc. The most readily understandable, easy-to-follow book in English on perennially popular recreation. Crystal-clear exposition; step-by-step diagrams. Everyone from kindergarten children to adults looking for unusual diversion will be endlessly amused. Index. Bibliography. Introduction by A. C. Haddon. 17 full-page plates, 960 illustrations. xxiii + 401pp. 5⅜ x 8½.
20152-X Paperbound $2.50

Paper Folding for Beginners, *W. D. Murray and F. J. Rigney*
A delightful introduction to the varied and entertaining Japanese art of origami (paper folding), with a full, crystal-clear text that anticipates every difficulty; over 275 clearly labeled diagrams of all important stages in creation. You get results at each stage, since complex figures are logically developed from simpler ones. 43 different pieces are explained: sailboats, frogs, roosters, etc. 6 photographic plates. 279 diagrams. 95pp. 5⅜ x 8⅜.
20713-7 Paperbound $1.00

PRINCIPLES OF ART HISTORY,
H. Wölfflin
Analyzing such terms as "baroque," "classic," "neoclassic," "primitive,"
"picturesque," and 164 different works by artists like Botticelli, van Cleve,
Dürer, Hobbema, Holbein, Hals, Rembrandt, Titian, Brueghel, Vermeer, and
many others, the author establishes the classifications of art history and style
on a firm, concrete basis. This classic of art criticism shows what really
occurred between the 14th-century primitives and the sophistication of the
18th century in terms of basic attitudes and philosophies. "A remarkable
lesson in the art of seeing," *Sat. Rev. of Literature*. Translated from the 7th
German edition. 150 illustrations. 254pp. 6⅛ x 9¼. 20276-3 Paperbound $2.50

PRIMITIVE ART,
Franz Boas
This authoritative and exhaustive work by a great American anthropologist
covers the entire gamut of primitive art. Pottery, leatherwork, metal work,
stone work, wood, basketry, are treated in detail. Theories of primitive art,
historical depth in art history, technical virtuosity, unconscious levels of pat-
terning, symbolism, styles, literature, music, dance, etc. A must book for the
interested layman, the anthropologist, artist, handicrafter (hundreds of unusual motifs), and the historian. Over 900 illustrations (50 ceramic vessels,
12 totem poles, etc.). 376pp. 5⅜ x 8. 20025-6 Paperbound $2.50

THE GENTLEMAN AND CABINET MAKER'S DIRECTOR,
Thomas Chippendale
A reprint of the 1762 catalogue of furniture designs that went on to influence
generations of English and Colonial and Early Republic American furniture
makers. The 200 plates, most of them full-page sized, show Chippendale's
designs for French (Louis XV), Gothic, and Chinese-manner chairs, sofas,
canopy and dome beds, cornices, chamber organs, cabinets, shaving tables,
commodes, picture frames, frets, candle stands, chimney pieces, decorations, etc.
The drawings are all elegant and highly detailed; many include construction
diagrams and elevations. A supplement of 24 photographs shows surviving
pieces of original and Chippendale-style pieces of furniture. Brief biography
of Chippendale by N. I. Bienenstock, editor of *Furniture World*. Reproduced
from the 1762 edition. 200 plates, plus 19 photographic plates. vi + 249pp.
9⅛ x 12¼. 21601-2 Paperbound $4.00

AMERICAN ANTIQUE FURNITURE: A BOOK FOR AMATEURS,
Edgar G. Miller, Jr.
Standard introduction and practical guide to identification of valuable
American antique furniture. 2115 illustrations, mostly photographs taken by
the author in 148 private homes, are arranged in chronological order in extensive chapters on chairs, sofas, chests, desks, bedsteads, mirrors, tables, clocks,
and other articles. Focus is on furniture accessible to the collector, including
simpler pieces and a larger than usual coverage of Empire style. Introductory
chapters identify structural elements, characteristics of various styles, how to
avoid fakes, etc. "We are frequently asked to name some book on American
furniture that will meet the requirements of the novice collector, the beginning dealer, and . . . the general public. . . . We believe Mr. Miller's two
volumes more completely satisfy this specification than any other work,"
Antiques. Appendix. Index. Total of vi + 1106pp. 7⅞ x 10¾.
21599-7, 21600-4 Two volume set, paperbound $10.00

THE BAD CHILD'S BOOK OF BEASTS, MORE BEASTS FOR WORSE CHILDREN, and A MORAL ALPHABET, *H. Belloc*
Hardly and anthology of humorous verse has appeared in the last 50 years without at least a couple of these famous nonsense verses. But one must see the entire volumes — with all the delightful original illustrations by Sir Basil Blackwood — to appreciate fully Belloc's charming and witty verses that play so subacidly on the platitudes of life and morals that beset his day — and ours. A great humor classic. Three books in one. Total of 157pp. 5⅜ x 8.
20749-8 Paperbound $1.25

THE DEVIL'S DICTIONARY, *Ambrose Bierce*
Sardonic and irreverent barbs puncturing the pomposities and absurdities of American politics, business, religion, literature, and arts, by the country's greatest satirist in the classic tradition. Epigrammatic as Shaw, piercing as Swift, American as Mark Twain, Will Rogers, and Fred Allen, Bierce will always remain the favorite of a small coterie of enthusiasts, and of writers and speakers whom he supplies with "some of the most gorgeous witticisms of the English language" (H. L. Mencken). Over 1000 entries in alphabetical order. 144pp. 5⅜ x 8.
20487-1 Paperbound $1.25

THE COMPLETE NONSENSE OF EDWARD LEAR.
This is the only complete edition of this master of gentle madness available at a popular price. *A Book of Nonsense, Nonsense Songs, More Nonsense Songs and Stories* in their entirety with all the old favorites that have delighted children and adults for years. The Dong With A Luminous Nose, The Jumblies, The Owl and the Pussycat, and hundreds of other bits of wonderful nonsense. 214 limericks, 3 sets of Nonsense Botany, 5 Nonsense Alphabets, 546 drawings by Lear himself, and much more. 320pp. 5⅜ x 8. 20167-8 Paperbound $1.75

THE WIT AND HUMOR OF OSCAR WILDE, *ed. by Alvin Redman*
Wilde at his most brilliant, in 1000 epigrams exposing weaknesses and hypocrisies of "civilized" society. Divided into 49 categories—sin, wealth, women, America, etc.—to aid writers, speakers. Includes excerpts from his trials, books, plays, criticism. Formerly "The Epigrams of Oscar Wilde." Introduction by Vyvyan Holland, Wilde's only living son. Introductory essay by editor. 260pp. 5⅜ x 8.
20602-5 Paperbound $1.50

A CHILD'S PRIMER OF NATURAL HISTORY, *Oliver Herford*
Scarcely an anthology of whimsy and humor has appeared in the last 50 years without a contribution from Oliver Herford. Yet the works from which these examples are drawn have been almost impossible to obtain! Here at last are Herford's improbable definitions of a menagerie of familiar and weird animals, each verse illustrated by the author's own drawings. 24 drawings in 2 colors; 24 additional drawings. vii + 95pp. 6½ x 6. 21647-0 Paperbound $1.00

THE BROWNIES: THEIR BOOK, *Palmer Cox*
The book that made the Brownies a household word. Generations of readers have enjoyed the antics, predicaments and adventures of these jovial sprites, who emerge from the forest at night to play or to come to the aid of a deserving human. Delightful illustrations by the author decorate nearly every page. 24 short verse tales with 266 illustrations. 155pp. 6⅝ x 9¼.
21265-3 Paperbound $1.50

THE PRINCIPLES OF PSYCHOLOGY,
William James
The full long-course, unabridged, of one of the great classics of Western literature and science. Wonderfully lucid descriptions of human mental activity, the stream of thought, consciousness, time perception, memory, imagination, emotions, reason, abnormal phenomena, and similar topics. Original contributions are integrated with the work of such men as Berkeley, Binet, Mills, Darwin, Hume, Kant, Royce, Schopenhauer, Spinoza, Locke, Descartes, Galton, Wundt, Lotze, Herbart, Fechner, and scores of others. All contrasting interpretations of mental phenomena are examined in detail—introspective analysis, philosophical interpretation, and experimental research. "A classic," *Journal of Consulting Psychology.* "The main lines are as valid as ever," *Psychoanalytical Quarterly.* "Standard reading . . . a classic of interpretation," *Psychiatric Quarterly.* 94 illustrations. 1408pp. 5⅜ x 8.
20381-6, 20382-4 Two volume set, paperbound $6.00

VISUAL ILLUSIONS: THEIR CAUSES, CHARACTERISTICS AND APPLICATIONS,
M. Luckiesh
"Seeing is deceiving," asserts the author of this introduction to virtually every type of optical illusion known. The text both describes and explains the principles involved in color illusions, figure-ground, distance illusions, etc. 100 photographs, drawings and diagrams prove how easy it is to fool the sense: circles that aren't round, parallel lines that seem to bend, stationary figures that seem to move as you stare at them — illustration after illustration strains our credulity at what we see. Fascinating book from many points of view, from applications for artists, in camouflage, etc. to the psychology of vision. New introduction by William Ittleson, Dept. of Psychology, Queens College. Index. Bibliography. xxi + 252pp. 5⅜ x 8½.
21530-X Paperbound $1.75

FADS AND FALLACIES IN THE NAME OF SCIENCE,
Martin Gardner
This is the standard account of various cults, quack systems, and delusions which have masqueraded as science: hollow earth fanatics, Reich and orgone sex energy, dianetics, Atlantis, multiple moons, Forteanism, flying saucers, medical fallacies like iridiagnosis, zone therapy, etc. A new chapter has been added on Bridey Murphy, psionics, and other recent manifestations in this field. This is a fair, reasoned appraisal of eccentric theory which provides excellent inoculation against cleverly masked nonsense. "Should be read by everyone, scientist and non-scientist alike," R. T. Birge, Prof. Emeritus of Physics, Univ. of California; Former President, American Physical Society. Index. x + 365pp. 5⅜ x 8.
20394-8 Paperbound $2.00

ILLUSIONS AND DELUSIONS OF THE SUPERNATURAL AND THE OCCULT,
D. H. Rawcliffe
Holds up to rational examination hundreds of persistent delusions including crystal gazing, automatic writing, table turning, mediumistic trances, mental healing, stigmata, lycanthropy, live burial, the Indian Rope Trick, spiritualism, dowsing, telepathy, clairvoyance, ghosts, ESP, etc. The author explains and exposes the mental and physical deceptions involved, making this not only an exposé of supernatural phenomena, but a valuable exposition of characteristic types of abnormal psychology. Originally titled "The Psychology of the Occult." 14 illustrations. Index. 551pp. 5⅜ x 8. 20503-7 Paperbound $3.50

FAIRY TALE COLLECTIONS, *edited by Andrew Lang*
Andrew Lang's fairy tale collections make up the richest shelf-full of traditional children's stories anywhere available. Lang supervised the translation of stories from all over the world—familiar European tales collected by Grimm, animal stories from Negro Africa, myths of primitive Australia, stories from Russia, Hungary, Iceland, Japan, and many other countries. Lang's selection of translations are unusually high; many authorities consider that the most familiar tales find their best versions in these volumes. All collections are richly decorated and illustrated by H. J. Ford and other artists.

THE BLUE FAIRY BOOK. 37 stories. 138 illustrations. ix + 390pp. 5⅜ x 8½.
21437-0 Paperbound $1.95

THE GREEN FAIRY BOOK. 42 stories. 100 illustrations. xiii + 366pp. 5⅜ x 8½.
21439-7 Paperbound $2.00

THE BROWN FAIRY BOOK. 32 stories. 50 illustrations, 8 in color. xii + 350pp. 5⅜ x 8½.
21438-9 Paperbound $1.95

THE BEST TALES OF HOFFMANN, *edited by E. F. Bleiler*
10 stories by E. T. A. Hoffmann, one of the greatest of all writers of fantasy. The tales include "The Golden Flower Pot," "Automata," "A New Year's Eve Adventure," "Nutcracker and the King of Mice," "Sand-Man," and others. Vigorous characterizations of highly eccentric personalities, remarkably imaginative situations, and intensely fast pacing has made these tales popular all over the world for 150 years. Editor's introduction. 7 drawings by Hoffmann. xxxiii + 419pp. 5⅜ x 8½.
21793-0 Paperbound $2.25

GHOST AND HORROR STORIES OF AMBROSE BIERCE,
edited by E. F. Bleiler
Morbid, eerie, horrifying tales of possessed poets, shabby aristocrats, revived corpses, and haunted malefactors. Widely acknowledged as the best of their kind between Poe and the moderns, reflecting their author's inner torment and bitter view of life. Includes "Damned Thing," "The Middle Toe of the Right Foot," "The Eyes of the Panther," "Visions of the Night," "Moxon's Master," and over a dozen others. Editor's introduction. xxii + 199pp. 5⅜ x 8½.
20767-6 Paperbound $1.50

THREE GOTHIC NOVELS, *edited by E. F. Bleiler*
Originators of the still popular Gothic novel form, influential in ushering in early 19th-century Romanticism. Horace Walpole's *Castle of Otranto*, William Beckford's *Vathek*, John Polidori's *The Vampyre*, and a *Fragment* by Lord Byron are enjoyable as exciting reading or as documents in the history of English literature. Editor's introduction. xi + 291pp. 5⅜ x 8½.
21232-7 Paperbound $2.00

BEST GHOST STORIES OF LEFANU, *edited by E. F. Bleiler*
Though admired by such critics as V. S. Pritchett, Charles Dickens and Henry James, ghost stories by the Irish novelist Joseph Sheridan LeFanu have never become as widely known as his detective fiction. About half of the 16 stories in this collection have never before been available in America. Collection includes "Carmilla" (perhaps the best vampire story ever written), "The Haunted Baronet," "The Fortunes of Sir Robert Ardagh," and the classic "Green Tea." Editor's introduction. 7 contemporary illustrations. Portrait of LeFanu. xii + 467pp. 5⅜ x 8.
20415-4 Paperbound $2.50

EASY-TO-DO ENTERTAINMENTS AND DIVERSIONS WITH COINS, CARDS,
STRING, PAPER AND MATCHES, *R. M. Abraham*
Over 300 tricks, games and puzzles will provide young readers with absorbing
fun. Sections on card games; paper-folding; tricks with coins, matches and
pieces of string; games for the agile; toy-making from common household
objects; mathematical recreations; and 50 miscellaneous pastimes. Anyone in
charge of groups of youngsters, including hard-pressed parents, and in need of
suggestions on how to keep children sensibly amused and quietly content
will find this book indispensable. Clear, simple text, copious number of delightful line drawings and illustrative diagrams. Originally titled "Winter Nights'
Entertainments." Introduction by Lord Baden Powell. 329 illustrations. v +
186pp. 5⅜ x 8½.   20921-0 Paperbound $1.25

AN INTRODUCTION TO CHESS MOVES AND TACTICS SIMPLY EXPLAINED,
Leonard Barden
Beginner's introduction to the royal game. Names, possible moves of the
pieces, definitions of essential terms, how games are won, etc. explained in
30-odd pages. With this background you'll be able to sit right down and play.
Balance of book teaches strategy — openings, middle game, typical endgame
play, and suggestions for improving your game. A sample game is fully
analyzed. True middle-level introduction, teaching you all the essentials without oversimplifying or losing you in a maze of detail. 58 figures. 102pp.
5⅜ x 8½.   21210-6 Paperbound $1.25

LASKER'S MANUAL OF CHESS, *Dr. Emanuel Lasker*
Probably the greatest chess player of modern times, Dr. Emanuel Lasker held
the world championship 28 years, independent of passing schools or fashions.
This unmatched study of the game, chiefly for intermediate to skilled players,
analyzes basic methods, combinations, position play, the aesthetics of chess,
dozens of different openings, etc., with constant reference to great modern
games. Contains a brilliant exposition of Steinitz's important theories. Introduction by Fred Reinfeld. Tables of Lasker's tournament record. 3 indices.
308 diagrams. 1 photograph. xxx + 349pp. 5⅜ x 8. 20640-8 Paperbound $2.50

COMBINATIONS: THE HEART OF CHESS, *Irving Chernev*
Step-by-step from simple combinations to complex, this book, by a well-
known chess writer, shows you the intricacies of pins, counter-pins, knight
forks, and smothered mates. Other chapters show alternate lines of play to
those taken in actual championship games; boomerang combinations; classic
examples of brilliant combination play by Nimzovich, Rubinstein, Tarrasch,
Botvinnik, Alekhine and Capablanca. Index. 356 diagrams. ix + 245pp.
5⅜ x 8½.   21744-2 Paperbound $2.00

HOW TO SOLVE CHESS PROBLEMS, *K. S. Howard*
Full of practical suggestions for the fan or the beginner — who knows only the
moves of the chessmen. Contains preliminary section and 58 two-move, 46
three-move, and 8 four-move problems composed by 27 outstanding American
problem creators in the last 30 years. Explanation of all terms and exhaustive
index. "Just what is wanted for the student," Brian Harley. 112 problems,
solutions. vi + 171pp. 5⅜ x 8.   20748-X Paperbound $1.50

SOCIAL THOUGHT FROM LORE TO SCIENCE,
H. E. Barnes and H. Becker
An immense survey of sociological thought and ways of viewing, studying, planning, and reforming society from earliest times to the present. Includes thought on society of preliterate peoples, ancient non-Western cultures, and every great movement in Europe, America, and modern Japan. Analyzes hundreds of great thinkers: Plato, Augustine, Bodin, Vico, Montesquieu, Herder, Comte, Marx, etc. Weighs the contributions of utopians, sophists, fascists and communists; economists, jurists, philosophers, ecclesiastics, and every 19th and 20th century school of scientific sociology, anthropology, and social psychology throughout the world. Combines topical, chronological, and regional approaches, treating the evolution of social thought as a process rather than as a series of mere topics. "Impressive accuracy, competence, and discrimination . . . easily the best single survey," *Nation.* Thoroughly revised, with new material up to 1960. 2 indexes. Over 2200 bibliographical notes. Three volume set. Total of 1586pp. 5⅜ x 8.
20901-6, 20902-4, 20903-2 Three volume set, paperbound $10.50

A HISTORY OF HISTORICAL WRITING, *Harry Elmer Barnes*
Virtually the only adequate survey of the whole course of historical writing in a single volume. Surveys developments from the beginnings of historiography in the ancient Near East and the Classical World, up through the Cold War. Covers major historians in detail, shows interrelationship with cultural background, makes clear individual contributions, evaluates and estimates importance; also enormously rich upon minor authors and thinkers who are usually passed over. Packed with scholarship and learning, clear, easily written. Indispensable to every student of history. Revised and enlarged up to 1961. Index and bibliography. xv + 442pp. 5⅜ x 8½.
20104-X Paperbound $3.00

JOHANN SEBASTIAN BACH, *Philipp Spitta*
The complete and unabridged text of the definitive study of Bach. Written some 70 years ago, it is still unsurpassed for its coverage of nearly all aspects of Bach's life and work. There could hardly be a finer non-technical introduction to Bach's music than the detailed, lucid analyses which Spitta provides for hundreds of individual pieces. 26 solid pages are devoted to the B minor mass, for example, and 30 pages to the glorious St. Matthew Passion. This monumental set also includes a major analysis of the music of the 18th century: Buxtehude, Pachelbel, etc. "Unchallenged as the last word on one of the supreme geniuses of music," John Barkham, *Saturday Review Syndicate.* Total of 1819pp. Heavy cloth binding. 5⅜ x 8.
22278-0, 22279-9 Two volume set, clothbound $15.00

BEETHOVEN AND HIS NINE SYMPHONIES, *George Grove*
In this modern middle-level classic of musicology Grove not only analyzes all nine of Beethoven's symphonies very thoroughly in terms of their musical structure, but also discusses the circumstances under which they were written, Beethoven's stylistic development, and much other background material. This is an extremely rich book, yet very easily followed; it is highly recommended to anyone seriously interested in music. Over 250 musical passages. Index. viii + 407pp. 5⅜ x 8.
20334-4 Paperbound $2.50

THE TIME STREAM
John Taine
Acknowledged by many as the best SF writer of the 1920's, Taine (under the
name Eric Temple Bell) was also a Professor of Mathematics of considerable
renown. Reprinted here are *The Time Stream,* generally considered Taine's
best, *The Greatest Game,* a biological-fiction novel, and *The Purple Sapphire,*
involving a supercivilization of the past. Taine's stories tie fantastic narratives
to frameworks of original and logical scientific concepts. Speculation is often
profound on such questions as the nature of time, concept of entropy, cyclical
universes, etc. 4 contemporary illustrations. v + 532pp. 5⅜ x 8⅜.
21180-0 Paperbound $3.00

SEVEN SCIENCE FICTION NOVELS,
H. G. Wells
Full unabridged texts of 7 science-fiction novels of the master. Ranging from
biology, physics, chemistry, astronomy, to sociology and other studies, Mr.
Wells extrapolates whole worlds of strange and intriguing character. "One
will have to go far to match this for entertainment, excitement, and sheer
pleasure . . ."*New York Times.* Contents: The Time Machine, The Island of
Dr. Moreau, The First Men in the Moon, The Invisible Man, The War of the
Worlds, The Food of the Gods, In The Days of the Comet. 1015pp. 5⅜ x 8.
20264-X Clothbound $5.00

28 SCIENCE FICTION STORIES OF H. G. WELLS.
Two full, unabridged novels, *Men Like Gods* and *Star Begotten,* plus 26 short
stories by the master science-fiction writer of all time! Stories of space, time,
invention, exploration, futuristic adventure. Partial contents: *The Country of
the Blind, In the Abyss, The Crystal Egg, The Man Who Could Work Miracles,
A Story of Days to Come, The Empire of the Ants, The Magic Shop, The
Valley of the Spiders, A Story of the Stone Age, Under the Knife, Sea Raiders,*
etc. An indispensable collection for the library of anyone interested in science
fiction adventure. 928pp. 5⅜ x 8. 20265-8 Clothbound $5.00

THREE MARTIAN NOVELS,
Edgar Rice Burroughs
Complete, unabridged reprinting, in one volume, of Thuvia, Maid of Mars;
Chessmen of Mars; The Master Mind of Mars. Hours of science-fiction adventure by a modern master storyteller. Reset in large clear type for easy reading.
16 illustrations by J. Allen St. John. vi + 490pp. 5⅜ x 8½.
20039-6.Paperbound $2.50

AN INTELLECTUAL AND CULTURAL HISTORY OF THE WESTERN WORLD,
Harry Elmer Barnes
Monumental 3-volume survey of intellectual development of Europe from
primitive cultures to the present day. Every significant product of human
intellect traced through history: art, literature, mathematics, physical sciences,
medicine, music, technology, social sciences, religions, jurisprudence, education,
etc. Presentation is lucid and specific, analyzing in detail specific discoveries,
theories, literary works, and so on. Revised (1965) by recognized scholars in
specialized fields under the direction of Prof. Barnes. Revised bibliography.
Indexes. 24 illustrations. Total of xxix + 1318pp.
21275-0, 21276-9, 21277-7 Three volume set, paperbound $7.75

Hear Me Talkin' to Ya, *edited by Nat Shapiro and Nat Hentoff*
In their own words, Louis Armstrong, King Oliver, Fletcher Henderson, Bunk
Johnson, Bix Beiderbecke, Billy Holiday, Fats Waller, Jelly Roll Morton,
Duke Ellington, and many others comment on the origins of jazz in New
Orleans and its growth in Chicago's South Side, Kansas City's jam sessions,
Depression Harlem, and the modernism of the West Coast schools. Taken
from taped conversations, letters, magazine articles, other first-hand sources.
Editors' introduction. xvi + 429pp. 5⅜ x 8½.   21726-4 Paperbound $2.50

The Journal of Henry D. Thoreau
A 25-year record by the great American observer and critic, as complete a
record of a great man's inner life as is anywhere available. Thoreau's Journals
served him as raw material for his formal pieces, as a place where he could
develop his ideas, as an outlet for his interests in wild life and plants, in
writing as an art, in classics of literature, Walt Whitman and other contemporaries, in politics, slavery, individual's relation to the State, etc. The
Journals present a portrait of a remarkable man, and are an observant social
history. Unabridged republication of 1906 edition, Bradford Torrey and
Francis H. Allen, editors. Illustrations. Total of 1888pp. 8⅜ x 12¼.
                        20312-3, 20313-1 Two volume set, clothbound $30.00

A Shakespearian Grammar, *E. A. Abbott*
Basic reference to Shakespeare and his contemporaries, explaining through
thousands of quotations from Shakespeare, Jonson, Beaumont and Fletcher,
North's *Plutarch* and other sources the grammatical usage differing from the
modern. First published in 1870 and written by a scholar who spent much of
his life isolating principles of Elizabethan language, the book is unlikely ever
to be superseded. Indexes. xxiv + 511pp. 5⅜ x 8½. 21582-2 Paperbound $3.00

Folk-Lore of Shakespeare, *T. F. Thistelton Dyer*
Classic study, drawing from Shakespeare a large body of references to supernatural beliefs, terminology of falconry and hunting, games and sports, good
luck charms, marriage customs, folk medicines, superstitions about plants,
animals, birds, argot of the underworld, sexual slang of London, proverbs,
drinking customs, weather lore, and much else. From full compilation comes
a mirror of the 17th-century popular mind. Index. ix + 526pp. 5⅜ x 8½.
                        21614-4 Paperbound $3.25

The New Variorum Shakespeare, *edited by H. H. Furness*
By far the richest editions of the plays ever produced in any country or
language. Each volume contains complete text (usually First Folio) of the
play, all variants in Quarto and other Folio texts, editorial changes by every
major editor to Furness's own time (1900), footnotes to obscure references or
language, extensive quotes from literature of Shakespearian criticism, essays
on plot sources (often reprinting sources in full), and much more.

Hamlet, *edited by H. H. Furness*
Total of xxvi + 905pp. 5⅜ x 8½.
                        21004-9, 21005-7 Two volume set, paperbound $5.50
Twelfth Night, *edited by H. H. Furness*
Index. xxii + 434pp. 5⅜ x 8½.   21189-4 Paperbound $2.75

LA BOHEME BY GIACOMO PUCCINI,
translated and introduced by Ellen H. Bleiler
Complete handbook for the operagoer, with everything needed for full enjoy-
ment except the musical score itself. Complete Italian libretto, with new,
modern English line-by-line translation—the only libretto printing all repeats;
biography of Puccini; the librettists; background to the opera, Murger's La
Boheme, etc.; circumstances of composition and performances; plot summary;
and pictorial section of 73 illustrations showing Puccini, famous singers and
performances, etc. Large clear type for easy reading. 124pp. 5⅜ x 8½.
20404-9 Paperbound $1.50

ANTONIO STRADIVARI: HIS LIFE AND WORK (1644-1737),
W. Henry Hill, Arthur F. Hill, and Alfred E. Hill
Still the only book that really delves into life and art of the incomparable
Italian craftsman, maker of the finest musical instruments in the world today.
The authors, expert violin-makers themselves, discuss Stradivari's ancestry, his
construction and finishing techniques, distinguished characteristics of many
of his instruments and their locations. Included, too, is story of introduction
of his instruments into France, England, first revelation of their supreme
merit, and information on his labels, number of instruments made, prices,
mystery of ingredients of his varnish, tone of pre-1684 Stradivari violin and
changes between 1684 and 1690. An extremely interesting, informative account
for all music lovers, from craftsman to concert-goer. Republication of original
(1902) edition. New introduction by Sydney Beck, Head of Rare Book and
Manuscript Collections, Music Division, New York Public Library. Analytical
index by Rembert Wurlitzer. Appendixes. 68 illustrations. 30 full-page plates.
4 in color. xxvi + 315pp. 5⅜ x 8½. 20425-1 Paperbound $3.00

MUSICAL AUTOGRAPHS FROM MONTEVERDI TO HINDEMITH,
Emanuel Winternitz
For beauty, for intrinsic interest, for perspective on the composer's personality,
for subtleties of phrasing, shading, emphasis indicated in the autograph but
suppressed in the printed score, the mss. of musical composition are fascinating
documents which repay close study in many different ways. This 2-volume
work reprints facsimiles of mss. by virtually every major composer, and many
minor figures—196 examples in all. A full text points out what can be learned
from mss., analyzes each sample. Index. Bibliography. 18 figures. 196 plates.
Total of 170pp. of text. 7⅞ x 10¾. 21312-9, 21313-7 Two volume set, paperbound $5.00

J. S. BACH,
Albert Schweitzer
One of the few great full-length studies of Bach's life and work, and the
study upon which Schweitzer's renown as a musicologist rests. On first appearance (1911), revolutionized Bach performance. The only writer on Bach to
be musicologist, performing musician, and student of history, theology and
philosophy, Schweitzer contributes particularly full sections on history of German Protestant church music, theories on motivic pictorial representations
in vocal music, and practical suggestions for performance. Translated by
Ernest Newman. Indexes. 5 illustrations. 650 musical examples. Total of xix
+ 928pp. 5⅜ x 8½. 21631-4, 21632-2 Two volume set, paperbound $5.00

THE METHODS OF ETHICS, *Henry Sidgwick*
Propounding no organized system of its own, study subjects every major methodological approach to ethics to rigorous, objective analysis. Study discusses and relates ethical thought of Plato, Aristotle, Bentham, Clarke, Butler, Hobbes, Hume, Mill, Spencer, Kant, and dozens of others. Sidgwick retains conclusions from each system which follow from ethical premises, rejecting the faulty. Considered by many in the field to be among the most important treatises on ethical philosophy. Appendix. Index. xlvii + 528pp. 5⅜ x 8½.
21608-X Paperbound $3.00

TEUTONIC MYTHOLOGY, *Jakob Grimm*
A milestone in Western culture; the work which established on a modern basis the study of history of religions and comparative religions. 4-volume work assembles and interprets everything available on religious and folkloristic beliefs of Germanic people (including Scandinavians, Anglo-Saxons, etc.). Assembling material from such sources as Tacitus, surviving Old Norse and Icelandic texts, archeological remains, folktales, surviving superstitions, comparative traditions, linguistic analysis, etc. Grimm explores pagan deities, heroes, folklore of nature, religious practices, and every other area of pagan German belief. To this day, the unrivaled, definitive, exhaustive study. Translated by J. S. Stallybrass from 4th (1883) German edition. Indexes. Total of lxxvii + 1887pp. 5⅜ x 8½.
21602-0, 21603-9, 21604-7, 21605-5 Four volume set, paperbound $12.00

THE I CHING, *translated by James Legge*
Called "The Book of Changes" in English, this is one of the Five Classics edited by Confucius, basic and central to Chinese thought. Explains perhaps the most complex system of divination known, founded on the theory that all things happening at any one time have characteristic features which can be isolated and related. Significant in Oriental studies, in history of religions and philosophy, and also to Jungian psychoanalysis and other areas of modern European thought. Index. Appendixes. 6 plates. xxi + 448pp. 5⅜ x 8½.
21062-6 Paperbound $2.75

HISTORY OF ANCIENT PHILOSOPHY, *W. Windelband*
One of the clearest, most accurate comprehensive surveys of Greek and Roman philosophy. Discusses ancient philosophy in general, intellectual life in Greece in the 7th and 6th centuries B.C., Thales, Anaximander, Anaximenes, Heraclitus, the Eleatics, Empedocles, Anaxagoras, Leucippus, the Pythagoreans, the Sophists, Socrates, Democritus (20 pages), Plato (50 pages), Aristotle (70 pages), the Peripatetics, Stoics, Epicureans, Sceptics, Neo-platonists, Christian Apologists, etc. 2nd German edition translated by H. E. Cushman. xv + 393pp. 5⅜ x 8.
20357-3 Paperbound $3.00

THE PALACE OF PLEASURE, *William Painter*
Elizabethan versions of Italian and French novels from *The Decameron*, Cinthio, Straparola, Queen Margaret of Navarre, and other continental sources — the very work that provided Shakespeare and dozens of his contemporaries with many of their plots and sub-plots and, therefore, justly considered one of the most influential books in all English literature. It is also a book that any reader will still enjoy. Total of cviii + 1,224pp.
21691-8, 21692-6, 21693-4 Three volume set, paperbound $8.25

The Wonderful Wizard of Oz, *L. F. Baum*
All the original W. W. Denslow illustrations in full color—as much a part of
"The Wizard" as Tenniel's drawings are of "Alice in Wonderland." "The
Wizard" is still America's best-loved fairy tale, in which, as the author expresses
it, "The wonderment and joy are retained and the heartaches and nightmares
left out." Now today's young readers can enjoy every word and wonderful picture of the original book. New introduction by Martin Gardner, A Baum
bibliography. 23 full-page color plates. viii + 268pp. 5⅜ x 8.
20691-2 Paperbound $1.95

The Marvelous Land of Oz, *L. F. Baum*
This is the equally enchanting sequel to the "Wizard," continuing the adventures of the Scarecrow and the Tin Woodman. The hero this time is a little
boy named Tip, and all the delightful Oz magic is still present. This is the
Oz book with the Animated Saw-Horse, the Woggle-Bug, and Jack Pumpkin-
head. All the original John R. Neill illustrations, 10 in full color. 287pp.
5⅜ x 8.   20692-0 Paperbound $1.75

Alice's Adventures Under Ground, *Lewis Carroll*
The original *Alice in Wonderland*, hand-lettered and illustrated by Carroll
himself, and originally presented as a Christmas gift to a child-friend. Adults
as well as children will enjoy this charming volume, reproduced faithfully
in this Dover edition. While the story is essentially the same, there are slight
changes, and Carroll's spritely drawings present an intriguing alternative to
the famous Tenniel illustrations. One of the most popular books in Dover's
catalogue. Introduction by Martin Gardner. 38 illustrations. 128pp. 5⅜ x 8½.
21482-6 Paperbound $1.00

The Nursery "Alice," *Lewis Carroll*
While most of us consider *Alice in Wonderland* a story for children of all
ages, Carroll himself felt it was beyond younger children. He therefore provided this simplified version, illustrated with the famous Tenniel drawings
enlarged and colored in delicate tints, for children aged "from Nought to
Five." Dover's edition of this now rare classic is a faithful copy of the 1889
printing, including 20 illustrations by Tenniel, and front and back covers
reproduced in full color. Introduction by Martin Gardner. xxiii + 67pp.
6⅛ x 9¼.   21610-1 Paperbound $1.75

The Story of King Arthur and His Knights, *Howard Pyle*
A fast-paced, exciting retelling of the best known Arthurian legends for young
readers by one of America's best story tellers and illustrators. The sword
Excalibur, wooing of Guinevere, Merlin and his downfall, adventures of Sir
Pellias and Gawaine, and others. The pen and ink illustrations are vividly
imagined and wonderfully drawn. 41 illustrations. xviii + 313pp. 6⅛ x 9¼.
21445-1 Paperbound $2.00

Prices subject to change without notice.

Available at your book dealer or write for free catalogue to Dept. Adsci,
Dover Publications, Inc., 180 Varick St., N.Y., N.Y. 10014. Dover publishes more
than 150 books each year on science, elementary and advanced mathematics,
biology, music, art, literary history, social sciences and other areas.